Those Who Do, Can

Those Who Do, Can

TEACHERS WRITING, WRITERS TEACHING

A Sourcebook

Robert L. Root, Jr.
Central Michigan University

Michael Steinberg
Michigan State University

National Council of Teachers of English
1111 W. Kenyon Road, Urbana, Illinois 61801-1096

National Writing Project
University of California, 615 University Hall #1040,
Berkeley, California 94720-1040

Manuscript Editor: Jennifer Wilson

Production Editors: Michael Greer, Jamie Hutchinson

Interior Design: Doug Burnett

Cover Design: Loren Kirkwood

NCTE Stock Number: 18607-3050

It is the policy of NCTE in its journals and other publications to provide a forum for the open discussion of ideas concerning the content and the teaching of English and the language arts. Publicity accorded to any particular point of view does not imply endorsement by the Executive Committee, the Board of Directors, or the membership at large, except in announcements of policy, where such endorsement is clearly specified.

Library of Congress Cataloging-in-Publication Data

Those who do, can: teachers writing, writers teaching /edited by Robert L.
    Root, Michael Steinberg.
        p. cm.
    Includes bibliographical references.
    ISBN 0-8141-1860-7
    1. English language—Rhetoric—Study and teaching. 2. Creative
writing—Study and teaching. 3. English teachers—Training of. 4.
Teachers' writings, American. I. Root, Robert L. II. Steinberg, Michael,
1940– . III. National Council of Teachers of English.
PE1404.T49 1996
808'.042'07—dc20   96–22113
                                                                CIP

To the teachers and writers of Traverse Bay

I find already, in just a few hours' time, that I am constantly drawing parallels between what I am experiencing and feeling and what my students go through. If nothing more came of this week than consciousness-raising, I'd say it was worth it.

> Maryalice Stoneback,
> from a Workshop Log

Most of all is the sense of beginning that I feel. I can write. I have much ground to cover, but it is a start. A part of me has been reconnected. I am ready to be a better writing teacher, and I know where to start.

> Kathie Johnson,
> from a Workshop Log

A Clerk ther was of Oxenford also. . . .
But al that he mighte of his freendes hente,
On bookes and on lernynge he it spente,
And bisily gan for the soules preye
Of hem that yaf hym wherwith to scoleye. . . .
Souninge in moral vertu was his speche,
And gladly wolde he lerne and gladly teche.

> Geoffrey Chaucer,
> Prologue to *The Canterbury Tales*

Contents

Preface

Michael Steinberg
Michigan State University

Teachers don't have to profess writing, but they should experience it, and that experience, as any graduate of National Writing Project training will attest, is life-changing. (194)

—Wendy Bishop

Every June from 1986 to 1992, fifty to one hundred public school English teachers met at a small college campus in Traverse City, on the shoreline of Lake Michigan. For six days and nights we lived in dormitory rooms, ate common meals, went to the beach, attended cookouts and poetry readings, and toured the surrounding area. But mostly, for that entire week, we wrote and talked about our writing.

A typical writing week would go like this: the first four mornings, we'd work in genre-based writing groups, where we'd create and share our own fiction, poetry, and personal essays. Each afternoon, we'd take our works-in-progress to the writing center for additional feedback. On the last day, like kindergartners, each group used scissors, poster board, and crayons to display the week's writing. By mid-morning, the walls were covered with teachers' poems, stories, and plays. Every year, this ritual evoked the same exhilaration and sadness—exhilaration, because the writing was so personal, so powerful; sadness, because this liberating week was ending.

Like all summer writing workshops, the Traverse Bay workshops were a wonderfully playful interlude. As our writing center coordinator, John Dinan, once told a first-night gathering, "Teachers come to the Traverse Bay Workshop not to work, but to escape, to take a break from the world of considerations, as well as from the often pedestrian writing of that world. They come to play for a while—to play with their writing, play with other teacher-writers, and through play to be and become writers." John was right: at times during the writing week, it felt like recess on the playground. And we always left Traverse Bay feeling rejuvenated and promising each other, with the best of intentions, that we'd continue to write and spend more time with our creative selves.

But like all playful activities, at some point reality intervenes. For high school English teachers, reality comes each year around

September. That's when they become busy grading papers, attending committee meetings, and preparing students for state-wide tests. And that's when they're usually forced to put their personal writing on the back burner. But the majority of teachers who attended Traverse Bay workshops claim that their week-long experience as practicing writers has had a positive effect on their classroom teaching. As Maryalice Stoneback put it in one of her log entries, "[E]ven though I have always tried to pass on my zeal for writing to my students, I will approach the new school year better qualified to do so."

In June of 1986, three college writing teachers—Bob Root, John Kelley, and I—began the Traverse Bay Writing Workshops for Teachers. We'd originally thought of this as a week-long workshop to further the notion of teachers as writers and to spotlight teachers' emerging writing. We wanted to bring high school English teachers together for a week in a retreat atmosphere, an environment where, without workaday constraints and distractions, we could write together, share teaching ideas, and build a network of resources.

Our original schedule went something like this: each morning, teachers went to a self-selected narrative writing workshop, which they attended for the entire week. In the afternoon, they attended self-selected pedagogy sessions. Those who enrolled for college credit were required to do a variety of other activities such as keeping learning logs, where they'd reflect on their week-long experiences; responding to suggested readings about writing and teaching in reading logs; developing one-page teaching ideas; submitting a finished piece of writing to a group publication; and attending a final-day, full-group sharing session.

As we felt our way through the first few years of our program, we began to see that many of the teachers responded more positively to the personal and expressive writing sessions than we'd anticipated. So, in our third year, we added fiction writing, playwriting, and poetry. In the fourth year, we developed a writing center where people could drop in at will and share drafts-in-progress with staff members and other workshoppers.

For the seven years of the program's existence, what distinguished it from other summer writing projects was that for the majority of the week, we worked on our own writing—not simply for professional development, not only as it had bearing on our teaching, but mainly for the sheer joy we found in being and becoming a community of writers. For my part, I used to love to walk up and down the halls of the dorm at night, peeking into the rooms, listening to computers humming and typewriters clicking away, and eavesdropping on teachers as they were sharing their day's writing. They seemed so excited and absorbed, chattering away like children, interrupting each other's writing to say "Hey, you gotta listen to this paragraph." After a few years, alums started referring to us as "The Traverse Bay Writing Camp for Teachers."

> *It's possible, I guess, to teach writing without ever having felt like a writer, but shouldn't we insist it be otherwise (194)?*

> Wendy Bishop

The Traverse Bay workshops ceased operating in 1992, largely because there were so many other summer workshops for teachers. When we began in 1986, there were just us and the Martha's Vineyard workshops. Today, in Michigan alone, there are at least a half-dozen National Writing Project sites, as well as the Walloon Institute just down the road from us. So, in 1993, Bob Root and I began talking about gathering together and printing up a "Best of Traverse Bay" anthology. Our intention was to offer the collection to our 700-plus workshop alums. But in re-reading the learning logs, workshop leaders' journals, the annual anthology of teaching ideas, and the genre writing, we discovered that the materials reflected a coherent, practical, and self-motivating teaching and learning philosophy. That's when we decided to write this book.

Those Who Do, Can: Teachers Writing, Writers Teaching is intended to be an inside-out approach to teaching and writing, an approach that teachers can use for personal growth and self-enrichment as well as for application and inspiration in their public school classrooms. As you leaf through the text and appendices, you will discover a variety of methods for teaching and for learning to write. The first section, "Gladly Would They Learn . . .," establishes a principle of organization and a rationale that is reinforced throughout the book. My chapter, for example, explains an inductive, hands-on workshop, specifically designed (like all the other workshops) to give teachers permission to be writers; Bob Root uses a journal-to-essay rationale; Steve Tchudi encourages multi-genre free writing; Gloria Nixon-John uses a reading-to-writing format for poetry; Anne Marie Oomen and Ruth Nathan's poetry workshop stresses literary forms borrowed from Ponsot and Deen's *Beat Not the Poor Desk*; John Smolens's fiction workshop is set up like a creative writing class; Alan Weber utilizes a variety of short prompts and readings to get anecdotal writing started; and Paul Wolbrink has his group work on generating frames as a way of engaging them in their writing.

We've designed the section one chapters as focused dialogues between the workshop leaders and participating teacher-writers. Each chapter begins with a reflective log entry written by one of the work-shoppers. The log entry is followed in turn by the workshop leader's essay detailing how the workshop was run, a list of teaching suggestions for classroom application, a final log entry, and a piece of a teacher's writing that grew out of each workshop.

The book's second section, "The Writing Center: Being and Becoming Writers," offers individualized and group strategies and activities for responding to writing. The third section, " . . . And Gladly Teach," emphasizes the ways writer-teachers approach content and subject matter; and the appendices offer additional ideas for teaching writing, selected samples of teachers' essays, stories, and poems, and a detailed and reflective guide on the nuts and bolts of organizing and administrating a writing workshop for public school English teachers.

However diverse these approaches may seem, all are informed by the idea that meaningful and pleasurable writing results from necessity, from what Steve Tchudi calls "real writing for real purposes" as well as from immersion—that is, from regular practice and feedback throughout the writing process. *Those Who Do, Can,* therefore, is an attempt not simply to show how theory and research can be turned into practice, nor is it directed at replicating our experience at Traverse Bay. It is a point of view and a working model of an *integrated* approach to teaching and writing. As such, it can and should extend beyond the boundaries of a week-long workshop or, for that matter, a public school writing classroom. The teachers who attended our writing workshop know the nuts and bolts of writing, because they have experienced firsthand what it is like to be working writers. It follows that they cannot help but bring their knowledge—and their successes and failures—back into their classrooms. That is, after all, what good teachers and good teaching are all about.

> *To write is to be transformed as a teacher of writing.*
>
>   Janet Emig

As important as good teaching is, that's only part of the payoff. A few cases in point: recently, I received a complimentary copy of *The Teacher as Writer*, a new book edited by Maureen Barbieri and Linda Rief. It happens that I'd written a guest essay for that book (a portion of which appears in this Preface), so naturally, I was pleased to see it. An added surprise was my discovery of an essay/poem by Rich Havinga.

In Traverse Bay's final year, Rich had been a student in Bob Root's "Writing the Outdoors" workshop, and his piece is a re-working of a draft he'd presented in that session. Moreover, Tom Watson, a five-time Traverse Bay participant, informs me that in the last three years he's published a chapbook of essays, a memoir, a poem, and a short story. And he's now enrolled in an MFA program in Creative Writing.

And finally: last month, I received a copy of the first annual *English Journal* issue specifically devoted to teachers' writing. As I eagerly leafed through it, I was elated to see the variety of teachers' short stories, poems, personal essays, and photographs. Then I came across "Suspenders," the first-place essay written by Barbara Rebbeck. Barbara's someone I've known for years as a first-rate teacher and dedicated professional. But she's also a Traverse Bay alum, and it was gratifying to see that she was still writing. I'd like to believe that sometimes when Barbara thinks about all her teaching and professional responsibilities and perhaps hesitates to surrender herself to her writing, she remembers Traverse Bay and gladly gives herself permission.

Northport, Michigan, June 19, 1995

Reference

Bishop, Wendy. "Crossing the Lines: On Creative Composition and Composing Creative Writing." *Colors of a Different Horse: Rethinking Creative Writing Theory and Pedagogy.* Ed. Wendy Bishop and Hans Ostrom. Urbana, IL: NCTE (1994), 181–97.

Introduction

Robert L. Root, Jr.
Central Michigan University

Log Entry

I can sum it up in one word: FREEDOM. The workshops delivered a twofold freedom:

1. Personal freedom to spend more time expressing myself in writing because I am a writer, and
2. Permission to encourage freedom in my students, whether those students be young or old.

Oh, I can certainly talk more knowledgeably about "the process," and I have a whole backpack full of teaching hints and directives. But the truth is that what I received this past week did not come in sessions or in a handout. It came from the staff who conducted the workshop and the people who attended it.

I want to be with writers more and I want to open the doors that I have left closed far too long already. And even though I have always tried to pass on my zeal for writing to my students, I will approach the new school year better qualified to do so.

—**Maryalice Stoneback**

Learning and Teaching

Chaucer's description of the Clerk of Oxenford, which serves as one of the epigraphs for this book, is a haunting one for English teachers. They can easily identify with the portrait of a young scholar so in love with learning that he spends all the resources granted by his friends on books and learning and prays for the souls of those who give him the wherewithal to study. The love of reading and written expression, of learning through books, of sharing learning with others is frequently the force that channels the learner into English Language Arts education. But when undergraduate college ends and the English educator begins to teach elementary and secondary students, often the arc of a career is a trajectory away from the learner's experience, especially when graduate courses serve as training in specializations or in professional applications or when textbooks and curriculum guides direct teachers' preparations. The gap between teacher and learner widens over the years, and as the teacher gains distance from her own experience, she also becomes distanced from that of her students. From time to time teachers need the opportunity to somehow become learners again, to connect again with the experiences that drew them to reading and writing and with the experiences their students are having with the same things.

The balance between the two parts of Chaucer's concluding sentence about the Clerk of Oxenford—"gladly would he learn and gladly teach"—indicates a necessary balance in the lives of teachers, the importance of the simultaneity of learning and teaching, not its sequentiality, and it may suggest the advisability of seeing learning not as the stage to be completed before teaching starts, but rather, as an activity that needs to be engaged in continuously, alongside teaching.

My belief in the relationship between learning and teaching may have been originally inspired by my first reading of Chaucer, but as a teacher I can trace it back to a single event in the late 1970s: the Gull Lake English Festival, a weekend retreat of English teachers assembled by Stephen Tchudi, then at Michigan State University. We were divided into five different groups, each put through a separate learning experience. My group, led by Rhoda Maxwell, started out by freewriting for ten minutes nonstop. We found ourselves responding to the activity as our students do, understanding what they went through, understanding how the freewriting could help free them and ourselves from the inhibitions and anxieties that deadened our language and our ideas. Later we wrote more controlled work for the group, some of us creating poetry, some essays, all self-conscious but wanting to share, eager to let others see our discoveries about ourselves and our writing.

In the evening the five groups joined together to share their writing. One group read myths. Another read "writing for giving," books in progress meant to be given to someone else. Susan Tchudi had written a bestiary for a little boy, an ABC book in which he was the hero; Sheila Fitzgerald had started a picture book for her siblings about the house they grew up in, now about to be torn down; someone else wrote a calendar of messages, inspirational sayings, jokes, and poems for his daughter at college. Our group began to worry that the good poem about kindergarten one of our members had written would not get read; we were supportive of one another, and we wanted our contributions heard and appreciated. In all the sharing, the laughter and delight and understanding and affectionate tears, I realized how we had been freed for sharing and how that freedom had helped us communicate. I thought, suppose we had all been assigned to simply write a report, a five-paragraph theme, on our group meetings—how deadly that would have been.

We had come together like students, had been treated like students, and learned, from the master teachers who had been our group leaders, what students could learn at any age. Suddenly I realized how much I had interpreted Chaucer's line to mean, "Gladly would he learn, and *then* gladly teach," the learning preceding the teaching in time-honored tradition; I knew then that in fact they went hand in hand—the learner wasn't a larval stage one shed like a chrysalis in order to emerge a teaching butterfly. Instead, the learner was a part of the teacher, a guide and companion to help keep learning and teaching intertwined. By connecting with the learner inside himself, the teacher might more readily connect with the learners in his own students.

For English teachers this recursive duality is especially valuable. In the teaching of literature, for example, it matters whether the teacher is herself a reader rather than simply a drill instructor in techniques of exegesis. In the high school where I taught at the start of my career, a veteran English teacher once blurted out, "I don't read literature because I like it—I read it because it's good for me." That approach to reading as obligation, as duty, almost as penance, was markedly discouraging to his students, who rightly saw literature as something imposed on them. More effective was another English teacher whose enthusiasm for books infected his students, sending them to the school library for outside reading he had only mentioned energetically in passing. That teacher's energy and enthusiasm may have been partly generated by youth, by fresh experience in college courses where inclination and obligation match and where people who love to read spend their days reading and talking to other people who love to read. Yet, one of the most discouraging aspects of teaching is the way our responsibilities to our students and our busywork for our administrators drain away energy and enthusiasm, even for things we love to do. How often do we hear fellow English teachers say, "I never read anymore, I just don't have the time"? In contrast, how often do we hear anyone say, "I was just telling my class about this terrific book I'm reading"? Somehow, in meeting all the other obligations our profession imposes, we surrender our obligation to ourselves as readers, without even realizing we've done it. Perhaps we need a summer reading camp for English teachers, where we gather in hammocks and lawn chairs to read the books we never get to read and talk about them with other readers. Perhaps we need to find a way to give ourselves permission to be readers again—gladly would we read and gladly teach reading.

Consider, then, the case with writing, which may be a passion for many teachers but is often harder to make room for than reading, which is an easier bedtime or beach activity. Some thirty years ago, when I was taking "Methods and Materials in Secondary English Teaching," the course devoted twelve weeks to literature and three weeks to grammar; it was only when I was thrust into a classroom that I discovered I would also have to teach writing, and only painful experience showed me that I couldn't teach writing by teaching grammar. Yet, even after a golden age of composition research and the emergence of composition teaching as a significant part of English teacher training, we still find ourselves removed by our responsibilities, as with literature, from regular rediscovery of what writing does for us, even as we are encouraged to tell students what it will do for them. "We urge our students to write expressively, to discover their own voices, and to write about what they know best," Mike Steinberg has observed:

> We tell them that writing is a valuable tool for self-discovery and personal growth. If we want to transform our students' lives, though, we need to pay some attention to transforming our own lives. It is because of our classroom commitments and busy schedules that we owe it to ourselves to find some time, even if it's only a few minutes, to do some of our own writing (11).

In essence, this book is an effort to encourage English teachers to give themselves permission to be writers, for their own sakes as well as for their students' sakes; also, it is an attempt to suggest ways of gladly writing and gladly teaching writing as well.

Process and the Teacher as Writer

It has now been a quarter of a century since Janet Emig's study, *The Composing Processes of Twelfth Graders*, established the importance of research into the processes by which writers arrive at a final product. Her work, along with the London Schools Project study in Great Britain, *The Development of Writing Abilities (11–18)*, legitimated the study of how writing gets written. Prior to this period, the whole of the history of writing instruction may be said to have been concerned with the analysis of writing products and prescriptions for their production. The result was essentially what Maxine Hairston has identified as a "paradigm shift," a fundamental change in the way writing teachers view their subject matter. The product-centered paradigm or model tended (and still tends) to treat writing as the recording or transcription of thoughts; it provided formats for the presentation of knowledge obtained or generated prior to writing—cause and effect, comparison and contrast, thesis and support—and concerned itself extensively with correctness and conformity in grammar, usage, and text conventions of spelling and punctuation. More significantly, it tended to encourage a view of writing as an act where generating ideas, finding language, organizing for both aesthetics and logic, observing standard conventions, and demonstrating both mechanical skill in orthography and sophistication of thought all occurred simultaneously, as if the goal of writing instruction were to bring student writers to the point where their first drafts would also be their final drafts.

The process-centered model, in contrast, tended to treat writing as the discovery and incremental modification of thoughts and language. It provided strategies for focusing on various stages or subprocesses or subskills, generally classified as prewriting, drafting, revising, and editing, and for delaying the concentration on correctness and conformity until the end of the process. Significantly, the process-centered model reduced the attention to the preparation of a presentation text by expanding the attention to the ways writers arrived at a point where their texts were ready to be prepared to present to someone else (probably the teacher, but often other audiences as well). Consequently, the process-centered model promoted a shift in the teacher's view of his or her role, de-emphasizing the evaluative, judgmental role as grader, promoting the cooperative, advisory role as consultant. The emphasis shifted from teacher as purveyor of rules and formats and as assessor to teacher as coach of developing skills and as mentor; it helped teachers see students as apprentices, novices needing to be advised *while* they learned their skills rather than simply to have their products evaluated *after* they had completed them.

Implicit in a model of teaching writing that places the student in the role of apprentice, however, is the placement of the teacher in the corresponding role of journeyman or master, the composition equivalent of a skilled tradesperson. Somehow Johnny Tremain apprenticing himself to Paul Revere comes to mind, and the analogy is both valid and useful. Paul Revere was an experienced and skilled silversmith, one eminently qualified to model for and to instruct an eager apprentice like Johnny because he understood not only what a superb artifact looked like, but also how to create it. If we push that analogy, of course—and we have to push it—it also implies that the writing teacher has to have the composition equivalent of the silver-smith's skills in order to nurture writing apprentices. In other words, the writing teacher needs to be able to come at writing instruction both as a teacher and as a writer.

In the past decade or more, we have seen that happen more and more on first the elementary and then the middle school levels, where whole language techniques have integrated writing into literacy learning in ways that have fostered the willingness of students to see themselves as writers and to use writing to connect with themselves as well as with others. Teachers like Donald Graves, Lucy Calkins, Nancie Atwell, and Linda Rief have disseminated writer-centered approaches to the teaching of writing in elementary and middle school, with highly effective results, but as the students who have benefitted from those approaches reach the threshold of secondary education, they are more likely to find content- or teacher-centered classrooms where writing is most often produced for evaluation on content learning and where both student and teacher have been distanced from writing.

While many researchers have examined the composing processes of a wide range of novice and experienced writers, some teachers have turned their scholarly eye upon their own processes, most notably perhaps Donald Murray, Donald Graves, and Peter Elbow. Their insights into their own writing have helped set the stage for writing pedagogy that adapts the strategies and techniques that help experienced writers overcome problems and accomplish both self-selected and assigned tasks. The literature on "teachers writing, writers teaching" has grown since these teachers' early work. Writing teachers have examined their own writing processes in collections like Tom Waldrep's two-volume anthology *Writers on Writing,* Mimi Schwartz's *Writer's Craft, Teacher's Art,* and Ruth Nathan's *Writers in the Classroom;* approaches to the training of writing teachers through writing at various sites of the National Writing Project and similar programs have been documented in books like Myers and Gray's *Theory and Practice in the Teaching of Composition* and Daniels and Zemelman's *A Writing Project;* NCTE's Committee on Professional Writing Networks for Teachers and Supervisors culminated their work with the publication of *Teacher as Writer,* edited by Karin L. Dahl, which promoted the writing of professional articles on pedagogy by classroom teachers. Concurrently with much of this activity, our group of writer-teachers designed and facilitated a *unique* writing and teaching workshop at Traverse Bay, which gave public school teachers a chance to connect their teaching with their own writing. Writing with the workshop participants, the workshop leaders gave themselves permission to be writers and conferred it upon the teachers in their workshop sessions, who in turn went back to their classrooms determined to grant permission to their own students and make the word "writing" in the term "writing teacher" refer as much to something the teacher herself does as to the subject matter of her teaching. Teachers discovered and experienced approaches to composing processes which helped them to create and share writing that mattered to them. They learned something about themselves as writers and, because they were teachers too, they recognized how strategies that helped them write might help their students as well.

One Teacher Writing

Writers consistently say that before writing does anything for anyone else, it has to do the writer's business. Donald Murray cites many authors whose explanations of why they write are strikingly similar: Edward Albee—"I write to find out what I'm thinking about"; Joan Didion—"I write entirely to find out what I'm thinking, what I'm looking at, what I see and what it means"; Cecelia Holland—"One of the reasons a writer writes, I think, is that his stories reveal so much he never thought he knew"; Wallace Stegner—"We do not write what we know; we write what we want to find out" (*Shoptalk* 4–9). In a recent book on writing, Anne Lamott writes that

> [P]ublication is not all it's cracked up to be. But writing is. Writing has so much to give, so much to teach, so many surprises. That thing you had to force yourself to do—the actual act of writing—turns out to be the best part. It's like discovering that while you thought you needed the tea ceremony for the caffeine, what you really needed was the tea ceremony. The act of writing turns out to be its own reward (xxvi).

Writers need to discover and rediscover that no matter what becomes of the writing, its greatest value lies in what it does for the writer. In the anguish and labor of writing, it is possible for writers to often lose sight of this truth; it may be something our students never discover, an insight that is unlikely to be shared or nurtured by a teacher who hasn't discovered it for herself. But the teacher who sees herself as a writer has something vital to bring to her teaching and to inculcate in her students.

This kind of talk may strike some readers as rather highblown and idealistic, but happily, the workshoppers whose logs and works-in-progress are cited and quoted in and around the following chapters give evidence that such talk is justified. As a case in point, consider the learning log that Catherine Short kept during her week in Mike Steinberg's personal narrative workshop and the work those sessions produced, "The Crossing." Together they give us some insight into not only her composing processes, but also her processes of discovery about the relationship between the teacher-writer and the student-writer. The story itself, which follows, is an account of a pivotal moment in her relationship with a traveling companion; it opens and closes during a train trip through England, the significance of which is revealed in flashbacks to events that preceded it.

The Crossing

Catherine Short

Christine sits rigid in seat number six—on the aisle—with a drug-induced, tight-lipped stare.

"How dare you," she slices the silence.

Her thin perm looks dark and greasy and just touches the shoulders of her dirty black jacket. She wears too many gold flea-market bangle bracelets on both wrists, and a long blue and black fringed scarf drapes around her neck. Its heavy knot hangs low and grazes her hands, which are folded tightly in her lap. Long fingernails dig into her flesh, as she sucks her teeth and shakes her head back and forth in disgust. She is someone I am not allowed to disappoint.

I stuff my bulging green backpack next to her red one, which is already secure in the overhead wirerack.

She scares me.

She is proud of her ability to scare people shitless with just one look—something she calls "The Wrath of Christine." At first I think that it is that wrathful look that I see, but something is different. Christine is scared.

"I could just cuff that goddamned look right off of your face," she says. I take a seat across from her, our knees close, but not touching. "How DARE you?" she says more loudly, her voice throaty and coarse.

The train lurches and whines. She glares at her watch. It reads 7:55.

How dare me? How dare you.

It was 6:30 the same day, and we had just parked our packs under a small round table in the train station pub. "Waiting for trains doesn't HAVE to be boring," Christine sang, doorbell-style. I recognized that tone of voice and tried to guess who Christine planned to sink her barbed hooks into. A tall Scotsman leaned against a small table on the far side of the dark bar. He had the polish of a soldier—his uniform carefully pressed, creases down the legs. A perfect knot held his starched shirt tightly closed. His dark cropped hair framed a light, handsome face and broad, toothy smile.

I sat back to watch the master seductress at work. She stared. He stared. He walked over to our table and sat down.

I imagined myself running around the station in a panic, dragging both backpacks, looking for Christine and the soldier. In my mind, I found her someplace dirty and dark—maybe an alley or between parked cars. I day-dreamed that our train pulled out of Edinburgh without us.

"Americans, right?" he said through a thick accent.

"That's right—'Mitch-i-gan,'" Christine mimicked the British pronunciation. He laughed, sucked in by, drawn to her expert flirting.

Then it happened.

"What's your name?" he asked. Me. Not her.

"Cathy—Catherine," I said.

"David," he said and nodded. "Would you care to walk a bit?"

"I'll be back in a little while . . . OK?" I didn't wait for Christine's response.

David reached for my hand as we walked from one end of the station to the other. He was on his way back to base after a weekend leave. "I fly out of London tomorrow morning," I said. David reached over and placed his hat on my head. We laughed when it fell over my eyes.

We were sitting on a bench next to a closed flower shop when he grabbed me and kissed me long and hard.

When we ran back to the dark little bar less than one hour later, Christine was gone. At the end of platform 15, David and I exchanged addresses and promised to write, and I climbed aboard the very first car. Leaning out of the first window I came to, I waved and smiled one last time. He waved back and yelled, "You're a nice girl, Catherine."

"You bitch," Christine hisses. The *eeek-chug-sssss* of the train throws me back into my chair and I face her again.

I see her only from the waist up. She holds me square—eye to eye. The shine of dangling, pointed earrings sways in and out of my line of vision. Without looking, I know that her toes point slightly out to the sides. She doesn't look pretty or rested or confident; we are too far from home.

I count backward fourteen days. Christine and I were dancing in a huge circle with Spaniards in the streets of Barcelona. Hunched-over old men stood on either side of me, grasping my hands tightly, helping me perform the steps. Cross front, together, cross back, together—I stumbled. I glanced across the circle at Christine, who was hooked up between two old men of her own. We grinned at each other. "Look at us!" her expression said. *Remember this*, I told myself.

"Look at me!" Christine cries. Everyone in our compartment of the train turns to look.

Am I wearing that "goddamned look" again?

"What did you think—that I was gone forever?" I ask her suddenly.

"How can you even say that? I swear to God," Christine leans over the tiny space between our knees and shakes her outstretched hand in my face.

Why is she so afraid? Doesn't she understand me at all? I am not like her; she has to know that by now. The air in the train feels stale and icy. Edinburgh is in the middle of a cold August. Christine falls silent, planning what to say next. I try to do the same.

But a memory forces itself on me: We are sitting on church stairs in a tiny Spanish square munching spicy sausages wrapped in warm tortillas. The scent of garlic and cumin clung to my clothes and hair. I let my head drop back, faced the sun and closed my eyes.

"I'm going over there for a minute," Christine said, startling me. She wore a dark t-shirt, knotted at the side. Her left arm was raised, and her long sharp index finger pointed toward a narrow street off the square. Bracelets fell in loud, tinny bunches toward her elbow. "I'll be back in a little bit . . . OK?" A slimy, toothless young Spaniard, his silk shirt unbuttoned to his navel, stood next to her. A vacant smile spread across his scarred face as he slid his hand into Christine's back pocket and squeezed. "Whatever," I told her.

I dropped my head back again and imagined Christine arriving at the hostel the next morning, still a little high, looking like death. "I need coffee," she would say, and I would walk to the lounge and get her a small cup. "I was so high," she would start, "that I'm afraid I may have slept with that guy." I would nod.

I raised my head and held to my plan on the church steps.

I refuse to go back to the hostel so soon.

Directly in front of me women in long, brightly embroidered dresses performed a dance, raising their arms high into the air, fingers snapping and wrists flicking with flair. The people around me cheered, and I joined in, letting out an "ayy-ayy." Dark barefoot children hopped from cobblestone to cobblestone, counting together "unos, dos, tres." Two hours later I headed for the hostel on foot, alone.

"What if you HAD missed the train?" Christine forces my eyes open again.

I did not miss the train. I would not have missed the train. I feel the chill of Scotland.

"What would I have done?—*no* plane ticket, *no* money, *no* idea how to find the airport in London," she screams, counting her losses on the fingers of her left hand. "You are such a bitch to do this to me. How dare you?"

Don't say it. Don't say it.

"I cannot *believe* you did that," Christine says with hatred.

Say it. Say it. Go to hell, Christine.

"You have been shitting all over me for years," I say slowly.

Her eyes widen. I want to cuff the goddamned look right off of her face.

"*That* is hardly the same thing," she says.

She is right.

We scream back and forth the first hour of our ride to London. When Christine ultimately falls silent, exhausted from her violent sarcasm and careful, abusive phrasing, she sits back in her chair, turns her head toward the window and stays like that for a long time. I can see the tears streaming down her cheeks, and know that she isn't thinking about me.

This is a powerful, effecting, and moving story. As Cathy herself observes in her log, in the course of writing this piece she "learned something about myself, about my friendship with Christine, and about my own writing process."

Cathy writes her log entries in spurts of reflection. While reading the entries that follow, note how her understanding of the piece about Christine grows during the week *because* of her writing about the experience. Using the freewriting prompt given her in the session, the log entries she writes on her own, the discussion with peers in response groups, and the successive drafts of the memoir itself, she works her way through to a significant understanding of the experience—one that might not have been possible had she been expected to have that level of understanding *before* she began writing. This is the kind of active engagement with the process of the text which leads the writer deeper into the subject and which enriches—deepens—the final draft.

Log Entry

Monday

Something struck me last night. I'm not sure who said it, but I was sitting with a group of people at the reception and heard this: "Well, it's a fairly non-threatening session [what session he meant, I haven't a clue], not like that . . . what is it? . . . 'About Men, About Women' thing. I'm not ready for that." Laughter. It made me think. Why did that very session cry out to me as the obvious choice? I actually thought, "God, I hope that it isn't full before my reservation sheet gets there." Why is it that I feel so comfortable with those kinds of issues—and why are other people so scared?

* * *

It was awful last night as I sat here thinking "What will I write about tomorrow?" Pressure. But I promised myself that this week would be

▶

mass chaos, and that I could handle that just fine. It isn't like teaching, where suddenly I realize that I've promised to bring in a personal sample TODAY and feel driven to complete something decent yet rough in an hour. I write better when I let the chaos *slowly* untangle.

*   *   *

I miss living in dorms.

*   *   *

This morning while freewriting Christine's name popped up again. I think it's time to finally write about her. I have tried so many times, and there is just too much there to work with. So I spent nearly the whole day doing discovery work, searching for a road, waiting for "it" to happen. How frustrating. Other people are reading drafts to one another, and I still don't understand enough about my subject to begin anything concrete yet. Finally tonight when I sat down at the screen, something emerged. I don't think it hangs together too well. But surprises did pop up. I love that—especially my sentence: "She was right." I've always loved irony—but will my reader pick up on it?

*   *   *

I sat here at this machine for nearly five hours today—after the sessions were over. That's the first time I've had such a substantial block of time completely to myself, to do nothing but write. This is why I came here.

*   *   *

Is there anything else that I want to incorporate in the piece on Christine/Edinburgh? The whole "HOW DARE YOU" thing could become a much more central image—my first time daring to cross her. I had a thought about contrasting the idea of daring to act that way— and the personal risk—the way I worry about her when she disappears, but she only worried about herself when I vanished. And is there any way to show her utter refusal to forgive me for the same shit I forgive her for over and over and over and over again? How? Is it important? Is it necessary? SOMEDAY I WILL BE OBJECTIVE ABOUT THIS PIECE, RIGHT?

*   *   *

My second "idea" that I expanded on in my morning session was "My first day at Kingswood." I recall some fairly nice images—especially the father toting the enormous box of maxi pads down the hall, and the older girls sitting in the hazy lounge, chain smoking. And I had forgotten all about Joy, my short-lived roommate—the way she unloaded dirty wadded up clothes from her suitcase, and ran everywhere (from the bed to the bathroom to the closet to the dresser to the window to the door—like a bumper car). Maybe my second piece could spring from that idea? Actually I think that I should do some more general freewriting. See what happens.

▷

Tuesday

My first surprise that happened while writing today: The whole concept of disappointment popped up while freewriting. People who make lots of mistakes are more easily forgiven than those who rarely screw up. I feel like I am not allowed to disappoint people.

*   *   *

Something else that surprised me: While freewriting, strange things bred even stranger things—as they do/should—but somehow I connected the fact that Christine has perfect printing, and that it looks as even and ideal as my kindergarten teacher's. And then I recalled my last run-in with [that teacher]. It was at a wedding reception and she was trashed. She hung all over me and my brother, saying "I had you kids so long ago and just look at you now!" I thought she was disgusting—not the same lady who had sent me back to my table to redo my work. I had accidentally drawn a purple daisy.

Wednesday

It is easier to respond to someone's writing in a group of 3–4 than as a whole class. I need to feel a certain degree of intimacy with someone, to look into her/his eyes, before I say anything—criticism or praise. I need to see in their faces that they understand me, and how sincerely I mean what I say.

*   *   *

I have to fight this desire to SHOW everything. I've denied myself the right to "tell" anything in my writing. I want my reader to *figure out* my meaning, not read it. Where is the balance?

*   *   *

I tried to explain this "thing" I have about being literary/obscure to several people today. I'm beginning to understand that most readers need more clues along the way—and more blatant information—than I do. I'm so used to analyzing what I read (looking for images and foreshadowing and patterns) that sometimes I dismiss even very good writing as "heavy-handed." But somebody helped me see that the line is fine. She said: "It's like watching a movie . . . sometimes I think 'How subtle—nice,' and other times I think, 'Huh?' I have no idea what's happening."

*   *   *

Chaos is good, right? Then why do I feel so distraught by the mess my piece is in? I keep cutting and pasting away, but it still sounds scattered. It feels like every sentence has lived on every page at least for one draft by now. Will I wake up in the middle of the night and say "Ah-haa!" No. I'll sit down with it all again tomorrow morning, move things again. Read again. Change my mind, change my mind, change my mind.

▶

*   *   *

How come writers don't trust their instincts more? I tell my students to trust their hunches all of the time. But how many times today have I read someone's piece and said—"This part right here . . ." and they immediately say "I know, I was thinking about that, but I wasn't sure." Sometimes I plug in something I hate, something I know is awful—but it gets me to the point where I at least can print a copy to look at. Then I read it, and take that awful thing back out. Why couldn't I print with a blank space there to fill in? It had to be full first. Hmmm.

*   *   *

It's hard for me to write when it's as hot as it was today. Even in the air-conditioned building I could feel the heaviness, the slowness. And it had direct impact on my desire to write. I waited until it was dark and cool again and wrote in front of my fan.

*   *   *

A memory popped when I was riding on the bus back from Leland today. I watched fields of cherry trees whip by and saw this:

> Dad was driving. Mom next to him. Gary and I were in the back seat, on our way to check out the school in Leelanau. "Mom, did you hear that Liberace died?" I asked. "No, he didn't." Mom knew better than to believe us. Liberace wasn't dead at all. But Gary backed me up. "Mom, we saw it on the news last night, didn't you see it?" Mom said nothing. "He dropped dead right before going on stage at that big hotel in Las Vegas," I said. "The Palace?" Mom filled in the name of the hotel for us. "That sounds right."

I've had students write about family vacations—being packed into cars and having luggage fall off the roof on expressways. I wonder whether I couldn't write about our trips, focusing on the strange relationship we had with Mom?

Thursday

The feedback I got today ran the gamut. I heard "Fix just a few little things," "Cut huge sections," and "I like the way this flows cinematically." So here is where it's up to me. It's obviously easiest to leave it basically as is. And I have to say that I'm proud of how far it has come. This whole incident with Christine has been screaming "Write about me! Figure me out!" for a long time, and I feel like I've finally had the time, the support, and the drive to wrestle it to the floor.

*   *   *

I felt even stronger connections happening between people today. We really trust each other. Some of the women in my group were talking and have decided that we should all try to gather in a central location

▶

every few months to share our writing. Wow. That is so exciting to me. It really inspires me to keep writing—more than ever. I write a lot— almost every day I produce either a long freewrite or 2–3 pages of something more developed. To think that I have a real, outside place to take them is fantastic.

*   *   *

It felt good to print out that final (for now) draft. I set the printer on "high" quality, and watched it push out a dark, serious, real copy. And it took me a little while to think of a title. I wanted something with a twist to its meaning. I chose "The Crossing" because that is sort of what I did to Christine. Also, there are interesting crossings in the story: I step into Christine's traditional role for a moment, and she does not like crossing over into the role she normally imposes upon me. Also, some of the language crosses between us. I tried to fill the story with parallels, and crossovers and twists. So I thought the title suited it well. A week from now I will probably hate it. Big deal.

*   *   *

I've come to the conclusion that I need to do about twice as much brainstorming as I usually do when I write. It took me days and days of thinking almost exclusively about what I wanted to show. I learned something about myself, about my friendship with Christine, and about my own writing process.

*   *   *

Friday

The Friday morning group share session was great. It was nice to hear what the other groups were doing—and I was glad that I had chosen a workshop where we were free to just write and write and write. I don't think that I could have produced what I did if I'd been faced with a specific assignment every night. The prompts we were given helped, but I appreciated the fact that I could go back to the dorm every night and let everything brew, then work late into the night, on what I felt inspired to attack.

The log is discursive, spontaneous, personal; consider all the things it records for the writer:

- discoveries about drafts (she struggles for an appropriate title),
- discoveries about process (she brainstorms more than she realized),
- discoveries of memories and potential material for other pieces (the way the travel on the Leelanau Peninsula recalls trips with her parents),

- discoveries about writing groups (the excitement of having a regular group of readers, the generative power of closeness among group members),
- discoveries about self-chosen topics (she recognizes that writing someone else's assignment would not have been as inspiring).

These are the discoveries that writers make which carry over into their own teaching of writing; they attune the teacher-writer to identify strategies that will lead students to make similar discoveries about what works for them and also help the teacher to realize how some pedagogies enhance creativity and expression and others impede it.

The idea that writing can lead us to understand ourselves better and to understand the haunting, sometimes shaping incidents of our lives may not be academic news by now, but to the individual writer, it may be a revelation that gains its fullest force during the composing process; moreover, it is a revelation capable of repeating itself each time the writer has, in Cathy's memorable phrase, "the time, the support, and the drive to wrestle it to the floor."

Cathy's discoveries about her own writing process and its relationship to her discoveries about herself are significant moments played out repeatedly by teachers writing. When teachers become writers, they begin to recognize more fully what students need if they too are to become writers. For some the discoveries are pleasant epiphanies, for others major revelations, but for most they are sufficiently transforming that they return to their classrooms newly invigorated and determined to give their own students opportunities to experience what the workshop granted them permission to enjoy.

As one workshopper, Maryalice Stoneback, observed in the last entry of her log:

The workshop delivered a twofold freedom:

1. Personal freedom to spend time expressing myself in writing because I am a writer; and,

2. Permission to encourage freedom in my students, whether these students be young or old.

For writing teachers those two freedoms go hand-in-hand, which is what Kathie Johnson meant when she reported in her log about feeling "reconnected" to writing: "I am ready to be a better writing teacher and I know where to start." Or to put it another way, "Gladly wolde they lerne and gladly teche."

References

Britton, James N., et al. *The Development of Writing Abilities (11–18)*. London: Macmillan, 1975.

Dahl, Karin L., ed. *Teacher as Writer: Entering the Professional Conversation*. Urbana, IL: NCTE, 1992.

Daniels, Harvey, and Steven Zemelman. *A Writing Project: Training Teachers of Composition from Kindergarten to College*. Portsmouth, NH: Heinemann, 1985.

Emig, Janet. *The Composing Processes of Twelfth Graders*. NCTE Research Report #13. Urbana, IL: NCTE, 1971.

Graves, Donald H. *Writing: Teachers and Children at Work*. Exeter, NH: Heinemann, 1983.

Hairston, Maxine. "The Winds of Change: Thomas Kuhn and the Revolution in the Teaching of Writing." *College Composition and Communication* 33 (February 1982): 76–88.

Lamott, Anne. *Bird By Bird: Some Instructions on Writing and Life*. New York: Pantheon, 1994.

Murray, Donald M. *A Writer Teaches Writing*. 2nd ed. Boston: Houghton Mifflin, 1985.

Murray, Donald M. *Shoptalk: Learning to Write with Writers*. Portsmouth, NH: Boynton/Cook, 1990.

Myers, Miles, and James Gray, eds. *Theory and Practice in the Teaching of Composition: Processing, Distancing, and Modeling*. Urbana, IL: NCTE, 1983.

Nathan, Ruth, ed. *Writers in the Classroom*. Norwood, MA: Christopher-Gordon, 1991.

Schwartz, Mimi. *Writer's Craft, Teacher's Art*. Portsmouth, NH: Boynton/Cook, 1991.

Steinberg, Michael. "Teachers Writing, Writers Teaching: Serving Two Passions," *Hawaii English Journal*, 1.1 (1993): 5–17.

Waldrep, Tom, ed. *Writers on Writing*. Vols. 1 & 2. New York: Random House, 1985–1988.

I Gladly Would They Learn . . .

1 "The Writing's for Us": Granting Ourselves Permission through Personal Narratives

Michael Steinberg
Michigan State University

"The narrative line is the way we understand the world."
—Toni Morrison

Log Entry

One of the initial steps we took in our morning session was a definition of the elements of good narrative writing. We decided that a strong authentic voice is the most important element, but good narratives also require specific detail, an opportunity for growth and change for both reader and writer, direction or purpose, the ability to make a connection with the reader, the creation of a mood or feeling, clarity, and coherence. Good narrative also must have meaning, and Mike emphasized that the material should determine the meaning. He cautioned us that if the writer attempts to impose meaning it kills the piece of writing.

I found this to be true later in the day. I attempted to begin several pieces; each time I knew exactly where I wanted to go and what meaning I would impart. Only after I gave up on "making" meaning and just wrote did I have a piece worth pursuing.

Some of the prompts we have used with students include reading, the creation of day books, free association, creating a writing environment, freewriting, asking questions with the right hand and answering them with the left, and creating topic/subject headings. It amazed me that I had such difficulty recalling prompts that I've used successfully in class. I think the reason was that many of them were spur-of-the-moment ideas. Next year I'm going to keep a section of my notebook labeled "Prompts" and try to jot these ideas down in one place.

—Janet Swenson

Those of us who teach personal narrative are always telling our students to take risks. "Explore, discover what you didn't know you knew. Dig deeper, write for yourselves," we urge them.

And rightfully so. After all, as teachers we're always complaining about having to read generic, safe student essays. It follows that if we are so convinced of the unexpected surprises and self-discoveries that come from the writing of personal essays, shouldn't we, as teacher-writers, allow ourselves to experience those same benefits? And if we do give ourselves that permission, wouldn't it add some authenticity and dimension to our own teaching, not to mention to our writing?

"Permission." That's the secret word, isn't it? As any writing workshop leader knows, convincing English teachers—especially high school teachers—to write openly and honestly about themselves is not so easy as it would seem. When I first began thinking about putting my session together, I recalled a workshop given by Donald Graves that radically changed my thinking about both my writing and my teaching. With an evangelist's fervor and a Borscht Belt comedian's flair—his sparse hair flying in all directions, tie flapping over his right shoulder—Graves breezed around the room reciting a litany of reasons why English teachers should write: to model for our students what we teach, to help us understand their struggles to write, to realize what we're asking students to achieve. Heads nodded, fists pumped, but when Graves said, "Those are good reasons, but they're not good enough," everyone snapped to attention. "Sure we write because it makes us better teachers," he said. "Sure it helps us understand our students. But it's not just for the kids that we ought to do it. The writing's for us. It's our outlet and our therapy. It's recess and play for big people. And, damn it, we need it more than they do."

Without pausing Graves invited us to write for five to seven minutes. "Write anything you want to," he told us, "an observation, a poem, a meditation, whatever." We stumbled though the exercise, then he paired us with partners. Within minutes the room was alive with shared disclosures, with laughter, and with occasional tears. "This is the first time," one teacher told me, "anybody has given me permission to write about myself."

Unfortunately, that's a sad fact of our teaching lives. Most writing teachers really don't have time to write, even for personal growth and enrichment. Too many classes, papers, meetings, and school and outside activities, they say. It's hard to deny the reality: English teachers are describing some very real constraints. And there are other, more human reasons that writing teachers don't write. Much like our students, we fear that we have little of value to write about. We also are reluctant to disclose our deepest doubts and fears, afraid of incurring disapproval from our peers, friends, and relatives, as well as from *our* teachers.

When I was setting up my writing workshop for Traverse Bay, I took all those fears and avoidances into consideration. I decided that if we wrote personal narratives about our experiences as men and women on subjects like our childhoods, adolescence, aging, looking back, dating rituals, schooling, sex roles, family relationships, friendships, marriages, parenting, career choices, we were bound to discover rich and authentic stories to develop. As for the fear of disclosure, I knew I'd have to create a "safe" writing environment for my group. That's the challenge I set for myself *and* for them. It's the same challenge, I suspect, that all good writing teachers set for their students, regardless of grade level or background.

I like working with personal narrative because the genre invites both seasoned and inexperienced writers to use their imaginations, their experiences, and their own voices. And it encourages them to reflect on their lives and the world they live in. I've found that when writers of any age accept the invitation to write about themselves and their own world, it is much easier to coach them along, to encourage them to help each other, and to trust that they will take ownership of the writing.

I've also discovered that students (of all ages and backgrounds) who can compose confident narratives have an easier time of it when it comes to writing in required, prescribed forms, whether academic, "real-world," or the so-called "creative" genres. That's because the criteria for good narrative writing are the same as they are for writing well in any genre—that is, discovering what you have to say; using engaging and authoritative examples, details, and illustrations; developing an appropriate and carefully planned structure; and creating an authentic personal voice.

Moreover, writing personal narratives has specific, individual benefits:

- It encourages self-discovery and self-insight, offering us the gift of wonder and surprise.
- It allows us to indulge in the sheer joy of tracking an insight or idea and letting it unfold at its natural pace and length.

- It offers us the freedom of our moods: we can be medi-
  tative, serious, critical, outrageous, sarcastic, empathetic, etc.
- It allows us to discover and present our best, our worst,
  our most eccentric and idiosyncratic selves.
- It encourages us to make sense of our lives in order to
  better understand who we are.

Keeping the safe-haven and permission ideas in mind, on the evening before our first session, I held a short get-acquainted meeting with my group of ten women and two men. As an ice-breaker I asked each participant to divide a piece of paper into four quarters, and to list what things they thought they did well and what they liked best about themselves. I also asked them to write short paragraphs on an embarrassing moment and on what they thought they'd be doing ten years from now. Sharing these quick writes—especially the embarrassing moments—got most people talking and responding. Then we spent the rest of the time introducing ourselves and discussing the workshop goal of writing about ourselves as men and women, as well as talking about some of our personal teaching-writing goals for the week.

Despite the successful ice-breaker, I sensed an undercurrent of fear. In addition to the avoidances I mentioned earlier, we English teachers tend to create unrealistic expectations for ourselves. We're supposed to be the "writing experts," and since we've grown up reading "Great Literature," we're always comparing ourselves to our favorite writers. Moreover, like our students, we're rarely encouraged to write for self-discovery or self-exploration. Aside from writing letters to friends, and the occasional journal entry or poem, most English teachers don't write much that's personal or self-expressive.

The next morning, I began the session by handing out two permission-granting passages written by the late William Stafford. They read:

> I believe the so-called "writing block" is a product of some sort of disproportion between your standards and performance. . . . One should lower one's standards until there is no felt threshold to go over in writing. It's easy to write. You should not have standards that inhibit you from writing.

> I can imagine a person beginning to feel that he's not able to write up to that standard he imagines the world has set for him. But to me that is surrealistic. The only standard I can rationally have is the standard I'm meeting right now. . . . You should be more willing to forgive yourself. It really doesn't make any dif-

ference if you are good or bad today; the *assessment* of the product is something that happens *after* you've done it. (*Shoptalk* 76)

For about a half hour, we discussed the whys and hows of writer's blocks. We talked about our own avoidances of writing, and we took comfort in Donald Murray's pronouncement that procrastination is a normal, and necessary, phase of the creative process. For encouragement and support, I handed out a list of the benefits of writing personal narratives. I also told them that if their preliminary writing happened to take a direction of its own, they were free to cut loose from any of my writing prompts and follow the writing where it was taking them. I left the option open because sometimes sticking too closely to a prompt can inhibit the writing.

It was now time to ease into the writing workshop. I invited everyone to browse through the "class library" and borrow anything they wanted to use. Earlier that morning, I'd set up two tables that displayed several folders full of personal narratives. Some were my own, some I'd clipped from the "About Men" and "Hers" columns in the *New York Times,* some I'd taken from other newspapers and from men's and women's magazines, and some I'd culled from Sunday supplements. I also set out several essay collections: Anna Quindlen's *Living Out Loud* (a collection of her popular "Life in the 30s" column which ran in the *New York Times* for several years), Donald Murray's "Over Sixty" columns from the *Boston Globe,* Barbara Lazear Ascher's *Playing After Dark,* Susan Allen Toth's *How To Prepare for Your High School Reunion and Other Mid-life Musings,* Joseph Epstein's *The Middle of My Tether*, and Phillip Lopate's collection, *Against Joie de Vivre.* In addition, I displayed "self-help" writing books like William Zinsser's *Inventing the Truth: The Art and Craft of Memoir,* Natalie Goldberg's *Writing Down the Bones* and *Wild Mind,* Dorothea Brande's *On Becoming a Writer,* William Sloane's *The Craft of Writing,* and Donald Murray's *Expecting the Unexpected* and *Shoptalk.* All of these deal with, among other things, getting writing started and keeping it going.

Following the browsing period, I told those who already had ideas for writing that they could work independently, while those who needed a prompt to get started worked on the following, an exercise borrowed from Stephen Tchudi. It goes like this: two partners brainstorm (in writing) three story ideas each. When they're done, each writer reads all three to his/her partner. The partner then picks one of the ideas for the writer. Each then writes a one-page rough draft; they exchange the drafts for feedback, make some revisions, and write a one-page "final" draft.

By helping each other choose topics to write about, each participant invests in the other's piece. It's a quick and simple way to develop a small support community. A brief caution for teachers who want to do this in a high school classroom: developing a writing community in a workshop for writing teachers demands a lot less front-end teaching than it does in a secondary classroom. Most writing teachers who have signed up for a summer writing workshop have had some previous exposure to writing process. High school writers, on the other hand, generally need much more exposure to writing process pedagogy. In addition, while most teenage writers have limited life experience and very little training in how to reflect or make meaning out of those experiences, adult learners—even reluctant ones—have a storehouse of life experiences to write about. And many are at the stage in their lives and careers where they feel the need to reflect on those experiences.

Along with the collaborative prompt, I handed out a sheet of additional suggestions for getting personal narratives started. (See "Applications in the Classroom" at the end of this chapter.)

I was pleasantly surprised to find that by mid-morning the group had already begun to take its own direction. Though Janet was reluctant to read her preliminary writing just yet, she was willing to listen to other writers' drafts; Debby was reading around in the class library and hunting for a topic; Shirley just couldn't get started; Jeannie already had a draft going, so she took off to write outside under a tree; Mary was ready for small group feedback; and by working with two partners, Pat discovered he was writing something potentially powerful and moving.

Whatever activity they chose—browsing through the class library, writing alone, working in pairs on my story prompt—everyone had to come back a half hour before the session ended to share his/her writing and tell us about the struggles and successes of getting started.

As people began to work, I found I had time to get at my own piece—a mid-life reflection on my thirty-five-year addiction to basketball. It had been almost a half year since I'd begun the essay, so I read through it and made some preliminary notes for revisions. Because I'd spent so much time away from it, I re-drafted a new outline.

When we re-convened, Nancy volunteered to share her piece. She was trying to develop an essay about how she had once tried to encourage a disturbed student, but the student ultimately ended up committing suicide. Her problem, she said, was twofold. As a single woman, she wondered if she was qualified to deal with a teenage boy's personal problems. Should she send him to the male guidance counselor? Her other concern was technical, a matter of craft. Nancy was confused about how to dramatize her feelings about the boy: should she reveal how inadequate and helpless she felt, should she write about herself as the subject, should she focus on the boy's problem? As people jumped in with suggestions, Nancy took notes and began thinking about revisions.

Nancy's personal disclosure—and the discussion that followed—set the right tone for the workshop. Most of us now understood that the "About Women, About Men" idea was pretty open-ended. And we all knew we had permission, if we were so disposed, to write about our most private fears and demons. Not all took that option, but it was important for them to know that the choice was all theirs to make.

Having the full group re-convene for the last half hour allowed us to learn about the different ways each of us begins a piece of writing. The talk-back also sparked a spontaneous discussion of teaching. We agreed that when we teach writing process workshop to teenagers, we need to be careful not to make the "process" seem too mechanical and prescribed. As teachers we often tend to pace, even lock-step, our students into a format. Usually, it's some variation of brainstorming/getting started, rough draft, feedback, revision, next draft, feedback, revision, polishing, editing, and final draft. As we struggled to begin a piece of our own, we soon realized that each of us progresses at a different rate. At this stage of composing, most of us couldn't say with any certainty whether we were still brainstorming, what kind of feedback (if any) we needed, if we'd already written a rough draft, if we were ready to begin revisions, or if we needed to start over.

As we talked more about our writing processes, the teaching implications became clear: we agreed that teachers need to recognize that students—like ourselves—won't all be at the same stage of composition at the same time. This led to a discussion about finding more effective and appropriate ways of individualizing feedback: when, for example, do we use groups, work as partners, have teacher conferences, read drafts aloud, read drafts silently? We also talked about student engagement. Often we expect our students to engage in the writing simply because we are so convinced of its value. But we forget that our students fear exposure as much as we do, and that they are reluctant to critique one another because they are inexperienced and self-conscious about their writing.

We ended our first morning on a note of discovery. The common denominator between our group and teaching a high school class, we found, was our commitment to developing a permission-granting writing environment. But the crucial difference between our situation and that of our students was time—we had only five days to develop a writing community, and to finish a piece; our students have weeks to accomplish this. For that reason I decided to defer further discussion of pedagogy. I didn't want to stop the writing momentum we'd worked so hard at generating.

It's been my experience that a week-long, adult writing workshop takes at least three sessions to jell—or not to jell—as the case may be. With that timeline in mind, on Tuesday we met as a whole group for an hour and talked about our overnight progress. Drawing on the previous day's closing discussion, I asked each person what kind of feedback he or she would prefer. Mary wanted to work alone; Debby was still reluctant to go into a group, so she worked with Pat; Jeannie was cooking along so she kept writing on her own; Janet had a conference with me; Nancy sought out a group of three others that wanted to read their drafts aloud; and Dave (who was writing his story from a female point of view) asked a group of three women to listen to his draft.

By mid-morning, most everyone was in a response group, giving and receiving feedback. Unlike high school students, who often are either too tentative or too generic in their feedback, English teachers invariably discuss things like good leads, main points, specific examples, organization strategies, focus, voice—the real nuts and bolts of writing. As a result, several of the pieces begin to take shape earlier than they would have if this had been a group of teenage writers. Pat, for example, learned that he had drafted a strong introduction to his piece about the funeral of a close friend's father. Mary already had a completed draft on her story about how a childhood spitting contest led her to form a relationship with an eccentric neighbor woman. And Jeannie had discovered that her piece was about the changing relationship between herself and her mother.

We had about fifteen minutes remaining, so I chipped in my two cents' worth. My own essay, I said, was starting to come together. Now that I'd settled on a new beginning and ending, I had another decision to make: How much of the piece was going to be a childhood reminiscence, and how much of it would be about the adult who changed from basketball junkie to middle-aged teacher-writer?

Once again I asked that everyone return for the last half hour, this time to share some of the drafts-in-progress with the whole group. Nancy read hers aloud and we talked about the changes she'd made since yesterday: She had a much stronger lead, and the body now focused on the teacher-student relationship she had with the boy, rather than on her internal reactions to his behavior. Dave read his draft and asked for help on the voice. We all agreed that he had to work at developing a more authentic "female" persona.

After those two critiques, the session broke up. Most of the writers in the group seemed more comfortable with their developing narratives and much more open about sharing and giving each other feedback. It was day three and slowly, tentatively, we were starting to evolve into a community of writers.

On Wednesday, I announced that we all had to have a clean, typed draft for Friday's group publication, and that our drafts should also be ready to display at Friday's "Writing Fair." The moans and groans let me know how my group felt about that. But when I explained that we could still look at our writing as "works in progress," they seemed to breathe a bit easier. That set us off on another teaching discussion. This time we talked about the psychology of letting our students know that their writing is always in progress, even when it's handed in to meet a deadline. It's just one more example, we agreed, of the positive effect of "permission-granting."

We continued to work as we had the previous two days. By the middle of the session, I noticed that most of the teachers were warming up to the give-and-take. And when Debby finally declared that she'd found a subject—an unforgettable character she encountered while waitressing in a small town restaurant—and that she was now ready to present her draft to a group, I felt some of my doubts and hesitations begin to fade. Until now, I'd pretty much left Debby alone until she was comfortable enough with the others in the workshop to trust them and herself with her writing.

Perhaps there's a lesson here for us all. In our zeal to get our students engaged in response groups, sometimes we may have to pull back until writers decide that they want and need feedback. For example, I'm a more experienced and confident writer than Debby. As a result, I'm not afraid to offer a flawed draft for critique while she, on the other hand, is very uneasy about showing a "messy" draft to colleagues. For the first two days of our workshop, I'd wanted to nudge Debby into a group, to get her into the flow of the workshop. But her hesitancy caused me to back off. And it turned out to be the right move.

While we were working in groups, Jeannie sought me out for a conference, Janet was working with a partner, Pat and Mary were copyediting one another's drafts, and Shirley, who was still reluctant to share her own writing, volunteered to critique others' narratives.

After my meeting with Jeannie I found that I had some free time to work on my own piece. By now, I was more comfortable with my beginning, and I was ready to work on finding a structure for the story. I toyed first with chronology, but that didn't feel right. Then I asked Janet and Pat to listen as I read them the essay. Both suggested that I could get around the chronology problem by laying some flashbacks into the narrative. So I began to tinker with that idea.

When it came time for our full-group debriefing, I looked around the room and saw that everyone was buzzing away in groups. I decided to let them keep going. Again, it turned out to be a good choice, because when it came time for the session to end, two groups kept working through lunch. Funny, the power of deadlines.

The deadline anxiety carried over to the next day, because on Thursday morning we got right down to business. No procrastinating, no avoidances, no teaching discussions. All morning, without interruption or breaks, we wrote, shared, and polished our pieces. Some, like Pat's and Mary's, were ready for final proofreading and editing. Mary's lead told about a spitting contest the kids in her neighborhood had conducted from the roof of the eccentric old lady's house. I asked Mary to read her lead to the group.

> I loved the window at the back of our junk room. . . . one of the best things about that window was that it gave me a place to practice for the national Spit Stretching Championship—a rite introduced to me by my older brother and sister.

Afterwards, we had a brief but spirited discussion about ways of hooking our readers' attention by writing fresh, colorful leads.

Pat read next. His narrative was a reflection on the funeral of a friend's father. Here's a short excerpt:

> This is not what I expected. This is not a class reunion. We have not just run into each other at an airport. Frankie, you are standing with your back to your dead father and your sorrowful mother. Frankie, where did you get that suit? You're dressed like Gordon Gecko. What the hell do you do out there in California? How did you get so thin? You're tan. Your shirt collar isn't showing behind the knot in your tie—how do you do that? You look like this all the time, don't you?

Pat's use of double-voice narrative was so skilled that we pointed to it as a model of how to handle that particular technique.

Not everyone was as far along as Mary and Pat. Nancy and Jeannie still needed to do more shaping and polishing; Janet, Dave, and Debby were a day or so from getting their pieces ready for display. As I polished my own piece, knowing it was at least a month or two from real completion, I reminded the group not to forget the draft-in-progress theory. Maybe it was just me who needed reminding, because almost everyone had now reached the point where they'd invested so much in their own writing that they didn't need to hear from me. As a teacher, what you hope and plan for is the moment when your students take "ownership" of their own writing. At the point where you become somewhat superfluous, however, you suddenly find that you have mixed sentiments.

I remember similar happenings when I used to direct stage plays. In the early and middle stages of the process—blocking, learning lines, rehearsing "off book"—the cast depended on my approval, my validation of their progress. But a day or two before the show went up in front of a live audience, the actors instinctively knew that they now "owned" the play. They were, after all, the ones who had to perform it every night. After watching this occur a few times and brooding about my diminished role, I began to realize that for the production to succceed I had to give up control; I had to watch from the wings and let the actors take the play where they would. And invariably, they made better decisions than I would have made.

On the final day we traditionally hold a "Writing Fair," a ritual where all the groups come together to publicly share their work. On Friday morning, our group turned in its final drafts for the class publication. As we were taping our essays up on the wall for the other groups to see, I stood off to the side and observed my group reading each other's work. They were like little kids, smiling, nodding their heads, patting each other on the shoulder, giving each other "high fives." Moments like those are the ones teachers love to savor.

To cap the workshop, every group did a three- to five-minute read-around in front of the entire assembly. When the session ended, everyone hugged and promised to keep writing. Many cried and assured their workshop partners they'd keep in touch. This was what the week's permission-granting had finally come down to—what Don Graves means when he says, "The writing's for us."

In so many of his books and essays on writing, Donald Murray talks not only about giving himself and his students permission to write, but also about "planning for surprise." I've always been a permission-giver, but until this workshop I was somewhat resistant about planning for surprise. Initially, as I watched my group struggle to get its writing started, I wanted to jump in and help. But as the teachers learned to trust their own intuitions, I saw them begin to take risks and respond to the unexpected surprises in their own writing.

Finally, as my group developed into more confident writers, as well as more receptive and critical responders to writing, I began to understand and appreciate the value of what we'd accomplished in our short workshop. I think those teachers learned once again that it is only when we give ourselves permission to write that we can become authentic permission-givers for our students' writing. And like the teachers in my workshop, we need to keep reminding ourselves of that lesson each time we go back to our own writing classroom.

References

Ascher, Barbara Lazear. *Playing After Dark*. Garden City, N.Y.: Doubleday, 1986.

Brande, Dorothea. *On Becoming a Writer*. Los Angeles: J. P. Tarcher, 1984.

Epstein, Joseph. *The Middle of My Tether: Familiar Essays*. New York: W. W. Norton, 1982.

Goldberg, Natalie. *Wild Mind: Living the Writer's Life*. New York: Bantam, 1990.

———. *Writing Down the Bones: Freeing the Writer Within*. Boston: Shambhala, 1986.

Judy, Stephen N., and Susan J. Judy. *An Introduction to the Teaching of Writing*. New York: John Wiley, 1981.

Lopate, Phillip. *Against Joie de Vivre: Personal Essays*. New York: Poseidon Press, 1989.

Murray, Donald M. *Expecting the Unexpected: Teaching Myself—and Others—to Read and Write*. Portsmouth, NH: Boynton/Cook, 1989.

———. *Shoptalk: Learning to Write with Writers*. Portsmouth, NH: Boynton/Cook, 1990.

Quindlen, Anna. *Living Out Loud*. New York: Random House, 1988.

Sloane, William. *The Craft of Writing*. New York: W. W. Norton, 1983.

Toth, Susan Allen. *How to Prepare for Your High School Reunion, and Other Midlife Musings*. Boston: Little, Brown, 1988.

Zinsser, William, ed. *Inventing the Truth: The Art and Craft of Memoir*. Boston: Houghton Mifflin, 1987.

Applications in the Classroom

About Men, About Women: Writing Gender-Based Narratives

Getting Narratives Started

■ In her novel, *Breathing Lessons,* Anne Tyler describes a character who dreams she dies and goes to Heaven. The woman imagines what she will take in her gunnysack to present to Saint Peter at the pearly gates. Some of the items include "misplaced compacts, single earrings . . . a green dress that her brother Josh's wife, Natalie, had admired one day . . . that funny little kitten, Thistledown, who'd been Ira's first present to her in her courting days . . ." To get some memories pried loose, and to get some reflective writing started, ask your class to list what items they'd take in their gunnysacks and what associations they have with those items. Then have them read their freewriting to one another. This is a good starter exercise.

■ Ask each class member to draw a picture of him or herself as a child and share the picture with a partner or partners. Then ask each one to freewrite on a childhood experience related to that period of time.

■ Have your students recall the houses they grew up in and what their rooms looked like. Then ask them to describe the rooms in concrete detail and write a free association connected with any object, possession, or aspect of that room. Have them share the writing.

■ Have your students draw visual maps of their childhood neighborhoods and let them describe the maps to a partner (or group). Then ask them to freewrite what comes to mind.

■ Read selected passages from student or professional narratives, and ask students to write about things like favorite toys, childhood fears, embarrassing moments, mishaps, etc.

■ Ask students to freewrite about past turning points, landmarks, or crucial decisions.

■ Have them freewrite about "firsts": first date, first kiss, first car, first experience with death, first day of school, etc.

■ Have students freewrite about unforgettable characters, enemies, rivals, friends, good and bad teachers, relatives, etc.

■ Have students freewrite about a relationship where they felt betrayed, humiliated, disappointed, hurt, misled, undermined, etc.

■ Ask them to write any of the above in another genre or form: write from someone else's point of view—a friend, parent, teacher, enemy, etc.; write a letter; develop a conversation or dialogue with a friend; do an invented dialogue with a fictional character; write a poem, story, editorial, cartoon, comic strip, song, feature article, etc.

Keeping Narratives Going

■ For all freewrites, I ask my students to reflect on and then write about what they learned from the experience, person, incident, encounter, disaster. This encourages them to think about meaning and main point, and it helps keep their pieces in focus.

■ Together with your students, brainstorm and set specific and agreed-upon criteria for good narrative writing. As they develop their own pieces, have students read and analyze teacher- and student-selected personal narratives, some written by other students, some by professional writers. Discuss them with students, and ask them to find examples of the techniques and strategies that make these narratives effective or ineffective. Also talk about the whys and hows of good narrative writing.

Several of these prompts were adapted from Stephen and Susan Judy's *An Introduction to the Teaching of Writing.*

Log Entry

Mike devoted today's instructional sequence to structure. He feels that chronology is stifling, but it is the most common method. Mike suggested that we attempt to begin scenes at the last possible moment of the scene. He quoted Annie Dillard, who suggests that writers not save good material—they should use it up front and allow other good pieces to come.

As so often happens, I thought that Mike's suggestions were perfectly reasonable, yet when I tried to apply them to my anthology piece—moving the point of crisis closer to the beginning of the piece—it just didn't go anywhere. This is the real value for me of attending a writing class—I WILL DEFINITELY BE MORE EMPATHETIC WITH MY STUDENT WRITERS!

I shared my piece of writing in class, and was surprised at how intimidating I found the ordeal. I waited while someone else read it only to hear deafening silence at the conclusion. I couldn't decide whether to make eye contact with anyone, but when I forced myself to look up, I saw that two women were wiping their eyes. I made notes of the readers' responses, but I found that as I listened I was having problems resolving my reader-response philosophy with our writers' discussion. I felt the chances of recreating my experience for my readers was non-existent, and so my attempt would be to create AN experience for them. I'm reminded of a quote that Mike shared about the person who wished that life was a process of picking up one strand, laying it down, and picking up another, rather than trying to weave many strands at once. I have a hard time believing that I'm able to direct my readers in the process of "weaving" my experience; my hope is to influence the weaving of their own.

—Janet Swenson

WRITING FAIR

Cutting Down Resistance

Janet Swenson

I can't believe that at twelve she still wants to sit on my lap. She nestles in, rubbing her short, freckled nose against my neck. Her long, wispy, blonde hair floats through the air into my mouth and eyes and tickles the hand I use to stroke her back.

I smell the top of her head—only after I became a mother did I realize that sunshine has a smell. The pungent, yet airy smell of light and life mingle on her skin.

I shift, beginning to grow uncomfortable under her lanky, 100-pound form. She moves her long, slender legs in an attempt to accommodate me and prolong my tolerance for the intimacy of this contact. These are her father's legs, the legs of an athlete. Muscles built swimming, running, and playing tennis flex and relax effortlessly under her smooth, tanned skin.

Her arms encircle my neck, and she brushes my cheek with her lips. I turn uncomfortably so that I can peer into her face. Her eyelids are closed and the lightly freckled face enveloped by the clouds of baby-fine blonde hair looks the picture of peace, safety, and contentment.

Then she opens her eyes and, as always, I am startled and afraid when I see my own blue eyes looking back at me. "I love you, Mama," she whispers. Like the soft caress of her hair, the words envelop me like a silk net, and I tremble.

My voice sounds much gruffer than I had intended, "Come on, Megan, get up. I've got things to do."

Reluctantly, she pulls herself up, her five-foot-two frame towering over me. Mimicking my gruffness, she retorts, "You never have time for me! You're always too busy. Never mind, I didn't want to be with you anyway." The side door slams shut, and I can hear the clank of her bike pedal as she throws all of her weight on that first downward stroke.

Feeling much older than forty, I wearily stand, pick up my coffee mug, and swirl the dregs as if I am reading tea leaves. The fault, dear Brutus, is neither in the stars nor in this coffee cup.

I walk into the kitchen, put a more-than-generous squirt of Ivory into the sink, plug the drain, and turn on the hot water full blast. Although it's a hot, muggy day, the steam feels good on my face. I close my eyes, and I can feel rivulets of perspiration running down my cheeks and into the crevices around my mouth; I am only mildly surprised by their salty taste.

The sink is too full. The soapy bubbles undulate over the rim, and I know that I will need to plunge my hand into the sink and release some of the hot water if there is to be room for the dishes. After the initial pain of the immersion, I find that I can grow accustomed to the heat. I carefully release only a small amount of water, then gather the dirty glasses and silverware and plunge them and my hands back into the water and begin to wash.

Looking through the steamy window, I can see her bicycling away from me. Her legs pump quickly and rhythmically like a heartbeat. She leans over into the wind, holding her body as close to the handlebars as she can to cut down on resistance. I can see her hair fall forward, toward the spokes of her bike, the brilliance of the blonde intersecting the silver circle, and I want to throw open the window and call to her. I want to yell to her at the top of my lungs, "Be careful. Be careful. I love you so much. I'm afraid. I love you so much."

Instead, I put my hand on the steamy window in front of me and feel the coolness of the invisible glass that separates us. And then after a moment, I take my hand away, and looking through the handprint that I've left, I see my daughter who is now a very small, indistinct figure on the horizon. I plunge my hands back into the hot dishwater. The painful sensation lasts for only a moment. Then I can't feel it any more.

2 Writing the Outdoors: From Journals to Essays

Robert L. Root, Jr.
Central Michigan University

When you tug at a single strand in Nature, you find it attached to the rest of the world.

—John Muir

Log Entry

This is a great spot to sit. My own patch of sand surrounded by weeds, not too much vegetation or insect life crawling by. A circle of sun to warm my head and keep mosquitoes away. The tall weeds around me sway languidly in the breeze. An oak tree overhead whispers in movement, its acorns dropped and scattered by hungry critters. Some have taken root and the ground is sprinkled with the new growth of infant oak trees . . . Thousands of acorns scattered around me, yet only a few will take root and grow. Makes me think of all the children who will never find success or satisfaction in life. Is that chance too? . . .

Walking down these paths takes my thoughts to Eagle Village Camp in Hersey, MI, where my fifth-graders go to challenge themselves each fall. The path, the trees, the hills, and the sounds are so much the same but the inner feeling is so different. At EV in spite of the peaceful surroundings the focus is on challenge, rope climbs, night walks, group cooperation. My mind is constantly in tune with 25–30 youngsters, trying to stay one step ahead of them and making sure each gets the most out of the experience. Now my mind can focus just on myself and the outdoors and it's wonderful. It feels so free of worry and organization. I wonder if I can recapture this feeling when walking through EV this fall?

Later: WOW! Just a few steps out of the dark overhanging curtain of the woods and into a different world. This is so majestic: rolling dunes down to the silent blue cool of the lake, the squeaky-hinge cries of sea gulls, buzzing bees that sound like trucks, and the luxurious feel of lying down in sun-toasted sand. Why try to put this in words? Can't we just sit and let our eyes feast on the spiking dune grass, the lone towering sentinel of a scrub pine, the freighter gliding effortlessly past

▶

> on the horizon? I remember days much like this sailing across Lake Erie with my family. There are no sailboats in sight today but I can still feel the quiet movement through the water as the wind filled the sails.
>
> **—Debbie LaGuire**

It was not until the second year of facilitating the outdoors writing workshop that I discovered that its central theme had been expressed succinctly and eloquently nearly a century earlier by John Muir. Appropriately enough, the thought was first expressed in one of Muir's journal entries. Muir, like his predecessor Thoreau, his contemporary John Burroughs, and such successors as Gretel Ehrlich, Annie Dillard, Edward Abbey, and John Hay, kept journals throughout his life; indeed, his writing career began rather late in his life, and a number of his essays and books came almost directly from his journals. In designing a writing workshop in which writers create journal entries before turning to full-fledged essays, I have then followed common practice among nature writers.

I find that journals and other expressive, impromptu forms of writing are valuable to all writers because writing in a journal aids discovery of topics and arguments, of details and examples. Journals can draw memories and information to the surface, advance the development of ideas and the understanding of experience. Particularly in shorter pieces of writing, they can stand in for the early drafts of an essay, working through problems that, in longer works, can be resolved only through multiple drafts. A writer like Annie Dillard knows, as she says, "It doesn't hurt much to babble in a first draft" ("How" 19) because the babbling leads her somewhere more coherent and because she knows she can eliminate the babbling in later drafts; less experienced writers at any level (including not only our students but also experienced teachers who seldom engage in writing themselves) are less often aware of this and less often plan their composing to take advantage of it. Journal entries, then, are a way of preparing for coherent drafts and a place to babble safely, without evaluative internal monitors setting off alarms. In all the classes I teach—not only composition but also literature, media, and pedagogy courses—I use journals and other forms of extemporaneous expressive writing, such as logs, exit slips, and freewrites, to lay the groundwork for more transactional writing, such as explications, research articles, and essay exams, later on.

The epigram from John Muir is especially useful to me because it suggests an encompassing definition of a nature writer. Some of the people who have taken the workshop have logged many miles as backpackers and canoeists and draw upon memories of many wilderness adventures; some, however, have only the limited experience of summer camp, family vacations, farm visits, or a view of a bird feeder outside a kitchen window. I establish the boundaries of our subject matter as anything that thinking about the outdoors moves us to write, from the tale of a harrowing wilderness expedition to the memoir of a family outing at the beach to a reflection on a hideaway in the lilac bushes near the front porch.

When I ask students in my own composition classes to draw maps of their hometowns or their neighborhoods, maps that center on their life experiences, they invariably include outdoor sites, from riverbanks, lakeshores, and forests, to parks, backyards, vacant lots, porches, balconies, and rooftops. The mapping triggers memories, which listing and clustering activities develop further, to provide likely topics first to focus on in journal entries and later to develop into personal narratives and reminiscences.

I routinely set composition assignments in motion long before students are required to do any substantial drafting or composing. By initiating or instigating investigation and exploration of certain areas or topics, I can rely on the writer's powers of subconscious incubation to move the composing forward unrestrained by the immediate exigencies of drafting. So in the workshop I use the initial evening meeting to start the workshoppers free-associating about their relationship to the outdoors. I refer my group to copies of "Transfiguration in a Candle Flame" and "How I Wrote the Moth Essay" by Annie Dillard, "Once More to the Lake" by E. B. White, an excerpt from *The Making of Walden* by J. Lyndon Shanley showing how Thoreau converted journal entries to book text, a handful of sharp-imaged poetry, and some very short pieces of my own to help them figure out who I am. They are all artifacts of a kind, pieces to generate the mood of the workshop, models of the range of possibility, but the Dillard and White pieces in particular represent the poles of nature writing between which we can navigate. One is a poetic, highly descriptive essay about closely observed and deeply felt natural events—the death of a moth in a campsite candle—that Annie Dillard relates to her own creativity; the other is a narrative of a trip back to a familiar family vacation spot, in which E. B. White's role changes from the son of bygone years to the father in the present, with some confusion and some stark realizations. The two are classics of their kind, but they are also indicative of the range I think writing the outdoors can cover.

When the workshop begins on Monday morning, I read one of my pieces created in the workshop in a previous year, either one about discovering the rewards of walking slowly and looking carefully or one about canoeing on a placid wilderness river. The pieces are short and less intimidating than the artful essays by Dillard and White, which we discuss in terms of vivid description and the ways meaning arises from incident in both essays. Then we quickly turn to the creation of a mini-journal. The first journal entry of the first hour points us toward slow immersion in outdoor thinking. It looks like this:

Placing Yourself Outdoors

After some conversation today about the nature of writing about the outdoors and some examination of published works, most of this workshop will be divided between times when you're writing and times when we're talking about your writing. To get us started let's take some time to collect our thoughts about writing and the outdoors by producing a journal entry that explores your reactions to this theme. Think about the following questions:

What's your relationship with the outdoors? What have your experiences been like? What moments in your life do you associate with the outdoors? To what extent are you an outdoorsperson? What are your intentions about writing the outdoors? What have you written in the past? What would you like to write in the future? What connection do you see between your writing life and your outdoors life? To what extent do you see yourself as a writer? What kind of writing do you hope to do this week?

Using these questions as a trail head for your thoughts, write for the next twenty-five minutes.

Twenty-five minutes is short enough to keep everyone engaged and energetic but long enough to demand analysis deeper than an initial reaction would allow. The journals usually begin to surface memories, experiences, and ideas: Mary Ellen remembers the summer camp she attended year after year; Sandy conjures up an image of herself bursting out of the Maine woods onto an Atlantic beach; Mike finds his thoughts returning to a canoe trip with his children, while Kathie and Richard think about their own gardens and backyards. For some there are only vague stirrings; for others, powerful and vivid scenes recalled whole.

The follow-up to the journal entry is a conversation in which we introduce ourselves, drawing on the journal entry for ideas and references. The interchange not only helps everyone feel more comfortable with one another, but it also generates a broad range of ideas for writing by voicing responses that trigger more memories and more responses in those listening. It gives me a chance to reassure the uncertain, fortify the timid, free the hobbled, and harness the unbridled.

Then we turn to the second journal entry. It instructs them thus:

Seeing the Outdoors

Our aim this week is not to become specific kinds of outdoors writers—Thoreauvians junior grade, or Future Dillards of America—but to use writing about the outdoors to meet (maybe even help define) our own needs as writers. To do this we need to do some writing outdoors, particularly writing that helps record our sense of a specific place. That's what this journal entry will do. Go outdoors. Find a spot to sit down and observe. It needn't be wild or secluded or overgrown, but it should be outdoors with some natural components. Try to get a sense of the location and record what you see, hear, smell, taste, feel, react to, deduce, infer, experience. Chiefly you're testing your powers of observation, but feel free to let yourself wander in your writing, particularly if your observations trigger "powerful emotions recollected in tranquility". At some point you should try to collect or summarize your reactions to your observations. Be gone for forty minutes. Write twenty or twenty-five minutes.

Happily, the conference center where the workshop meets is in the middle of a little patch of woods, on a campus with a variety of interesting outdoor sites, and a short walk away from one of the arms of Traverse Bay. In our regular classrooms we usually have to draw upon locations in memory and lead students back to them through guided imagery or music or tapes of outdoor sounds; however, there's power in changing the site of writing, even if it only takes them to the schoolyard or a location on campus a few steps away from the classroom building. One of my most successful moments in a twelfth-grade classroom happened when, to counter student hesitancy about a spurt of descriptive writing and the distraction of a heavy rain pelting the building, I sent them to the windows to throw them open, feel the rain and wind on their hands and faces, and write about that moment or any other moment in rain or wind or storm that they remembered. It was wonderful to see the kinds of writing a moment in the rain could trigger.

When my workshop group disperses, each person finds a place to perch without much difficulty; it may be a bench on the beach or a spot on the sand where someone can write with her sandals off and the waters of the bay licking at her feet, or it may be a picnic table among towering pines in front of the library or a tree stump in the middle of the woods around the conference center, or a stretch of lawn in the middle of campus. When everyone returns and we talk about what we've seen or experienced or recalled, the conversation surfaces issues of observation, description, and recall; the writers help one another to find ways of focusing, describing, recording, interpreting. Some discover the amount of detail to be observed in a tiny patch of space; some discover the utility of all their senses; some recover memories triggered by their circumstances or surroundings. Already in the first three-hour morning session they are going deeper into the outdoors (even while they sit in a conference center), and they are beginning to think of themselves as journal keepers and potential essayists.

The first day ends with the distribution of this final journal assignment:

Outdoors

Although time is short in this workshop we can still squeeze in a few more journal entries. Tomorrow we'll wander lonely as a class through a section of Leelanau State Park and you should expect to write a couple of entries there, perhaps from different locations, in different habitats, or on different themes (past and present, outdoors and indoors, north woods and desert, etc.). In addition you might try to write two or three more entries outside of the workshop—if time permits and you get to another location, write an entry there, or use the journal to write retrospectively about outdoor experiences or to react to the writing of others. By Wednesday let's have at least three new entries to draw on as we discuss the direction of the draft(s) you'll be working on throughout the remainder of the week.

In courses in writing that last a semester, the buildup of resources to draw on for later writing can take more time and end up with a larger storehouse of materials; yet here, even hurried, even limited, the few journal entries that those in the workshop produce will be enough to inspire a later essay and, more important, to make the point that having a storehouse, a reservoir, to draw from makes more productive, richer drafts than trying to snatch them out of the air, without preparation.

The following morning we carpool on a field trip to Leelanau State Park, which has an area of trails that give us access to various habitats: sandy beach, marsh, inland lake, dunes, and forest. After a couple of hours of wandering and journalkeeping, we gather on a cedar deck overlooking Lake Michigan to discuss the day's entries and observations and then take in the other section of the park, a stony promontory capped with a historic lighthouse. The locales are various enough to generate comparisons and trigger reminiscences. The dunes recall other dunes and other shorelines, and as John stands skipping stones he begins to remember teaching his daughter how to throw, triggering a chain of memories involving his own youth on Lake Superior and his experiences with his daughter on inland lakes; for Sandy, the Atlantic shoreline memory grows more vivid and surfaces the family conflict that had led her to wander off in the first place; for Renata, a short flight of stone steps entrances her, and as she describes it in her journal, she begins to recall her own arduous experience with stone work. For others the setting is merely a backdrop to other thoughts, a place for Kathie to ponder a walk in the garden with her aging, ailing father or for Jeanette to remember the comedy of errors her honeymoon camping trip turned into. We return to Traverse City. Some people find more time later in the day to wander outward again or closet themselves for an additional entry or two. All develop journal entries unique to themselves, prompted by the places where they write, the ways they start, the stream of associations they start flowing, the people they have been.

The third morning begins with the final handout to set in motion whatever all their preliminary writing has led them to. Usually something has emerged which separates itself from the rest of the material, demanding the most attention, seeming to be the most urgent or the most vivid—of all the vacations at the beach a certain summer is most important because of the way it brought two sisters together; of all the camping trips, this one stands out for everything that went wrong; of all the days spent outdoors over a lifetime, this moment at the kitchen window watching the birds at the feeder seems the one that best encapsulates certain feelings about nature. The handout tries to help them decide what to begin developing.

Writing the Outdoors: An Assignment

We've managed to write a couple of journal entries over the past few days, all focused on the outdoors in some way. We've also looked at the ways Annie Dillard and Henry David Thoreau managed to draw upon their journals for their essays and books. Today and tomorrow should be spent trying to develop drafts of some outdoor writing we can share on

Friday. Beyond that we are free to go in whatever directions we want to go in our writing.

For example, the thoughts and ideas and expressions in the journal entries may have led you to consider writing an essay, a memoir, a Michigan Memories column, a poem; perhaps the journal is just a jumping-off place. If so, we'll work on planning and drafting that work this morning and revising it tomorrow morning.

For another example, perhaps one of your journal entries or a sequence of journal entries can serve as the nucleus of a particular piece. In that case you'll be working for the next two days on the development of that piece, making connections and transitions and revisions to create a unified work.

Or perhaps the journal entries themselves lead you to consider the journal as the work you want to develop. In that case you'd be working to polish the previous entries and add new entries to flesh out your thinking about the themes and ideas you'd articulated earlier. You'd use today to generate further entries and tomorrow to work on the preparation of a display text.

If these options seem indecisive and wishy-washy, it may be because the real value of the workshop (dare I say of writing itself?) is to help you to use writing for your own purposes, to produce the kind of texts you want to produce, to make your writing serve your life and not the other way around. Decide what you want to work on—there's no reason you can't work on more than one—and let that project be the focus of our activities for the next two days.

The handout is a lead-in to brief small group conversations about likely projects followed by a whole group preview, in which everyone gets a chance to suggest what they intend or hope to write; the conversations generate further ideas and clarify intentions. Choices are made among topics and commitments are decided: Jan elects to work on a cycle of Leelanau poems; Tom intends to develop his humorous description of himself as a "bug beacon"; Renata chooses to tell about her experience building a stone wall across her yard; Richard wants to write about his backyard and the baseball diamond the neighborhood kids played at; Debbie finds that her memories of family sailing center on a cruise where she resolved the conflict between "my Peter Pan desire to be forever young and securely surrounded by my family" and "my eagerness for independence and the autonomy a teaching job would provide." Then people get down to planning and drafting.

After allowing an hour or more to get something accomplished, I tour the group, which may have broken up to find more private places to compose, and monitor process, reading manuscripts, consulting on plans, responding to text—the kind of workshopping I might do with work in progress among my students. Toward the end of the morning I call everyone together again and let them work in small groups on the text produced so far. They advise one another on structure, on development, on places that need more detail or more clarification, on places that delight or surprise or move them, on beginnings and endings. Then they are released for the day with the admonition to bring a full draft in the morning.

The final writing day is a day of revision, in which each person gets to (has to) read their draft aloud and the large group responds with encouragement and suggestions for revision. Usually there is something to praise, an image that evokes a feeling, a scene that has some power, a turn of phrase that gets at the writer's intentions; when we hear Kathie describing how she startled two deer in an orchard and "stretching full length in their bed, I lay, usurping their home, until the moment cooled," we feel a thrill of delight and recognition. Usually everyone has some tightening up to do, some potential redirecting or restructuring, some places that could stand clearer syntax or more concrete imagery: we haven't understood some of the process of building the stone wall and need more detail; we haven't quite gotten the relationship between the orchard where Kathie found the deer and the garden where she walked with her father and need more description. We make those suggestions and provide the praise. The remainder of the morning is focused on revising text and conversing about the revisions in small groups or impromptu conferences. Then we work together for a group reading that would be made up of snatches from everyone's work; the quote from Muir provides the thread that binds the excerpts together.

By the time they leave for lunch with afternoon workshops and an evening gathering ahead of them, along with final effort on their works-in-progress, the writers are at the comfortable place in writing, the place for finetuning, polishing, enhancing their revised drafts, with little memory that a few days ago many couldn't imagine anything they could write about the outdoors. Now some of the conversation is about second or third pieces they could write later in the summer, as well as requests and offers to read those intended drafts. Some are already thinking about the distant school year ahead, intending to show their students all their journal entries, notes, and drafts on their outdoors essays, typing errors, messy handwriting and all, including a pristine, immaculate presentation text, thus modeling the composing process and taking the risk of sharing that they so often ask their students to take. Others are brainstorming the logistics of a modified version of the workshop in the courses and units they teach—creative writing, composition, American literature, ecology and environment; they're thinking of woods, fields, ponds and parks, readings in Thoreau, Aldo Leopold and Rachel Carson, extensions, alternatives, derivations—"Writing the Indoors," "The Urban Outdoors," "Industrial Spaces." Like students talking about homework and course materials, they're generating the materials for their own learning and writing, their own teaching.

In the end, on Friday morning, we display our writing, both polished drafts and works-in-progress, and attach comment sheets for reader responses. The work of the week usually shows up in an anthology, *North Words: Writing the Outdoors,* but those who take the course for credit often turn in additional essays and poems within a month after the workshop ends. The workshop gets us all longing to be outdoors, and we find a way to get away, write journals, compose essays in more leisure which get at other things we want to remember and share. The workshop theme, it turns out, is hardly limiting at all—the essay topics range from canoeing the Boundary Waters and backpacking the Porcupine Mountains, revisiting a childhood summer camp, and discovering kinship on an ocean shore to building a stone wall across a yard, walking in a garden with an aging parent, and attracting bugs on nature walks. They are rich in powerful moments—Sandy describing the scene on the Atlantic shore when she and her sister became friends:

> And then in this peaceful setting she began to sing . . . . Her voice was clear and strong, not at all the voice of a child . . . . We lay there on our warm rocks, in that spectacular setting and with the whole world as her audience she gave the performance of a lifetime.

Judy finding in the shoreline a metaphor for her own life:

> My sisters build sand castles and converse, and I join their activity until something within calls me away. I walk the shoreline, alone and in silence, feeling forever caught between the safety of sandy beach and the compelling current of deep waters. I have rejected the limitations of Mama's blanket and I have explored the mystery of unknown depths, but I have never learned to swim.

Debbie discovering in a moment at the tiller of the sailboat the reassurance of her own independence:

> I was the captain and the master of our forward motion. This was true sailing. I made slight adjustments to port or starboard for optimum speed, I stood masterfully with feet braced for balance, and we surged over each rollercoaster swell. The uncertainty of each upcoming dip gave the future a thrill of anticipation and fearful pleasure.

Richard stepping out of memory into the present with deepening awareness of the meaning of the past:

> Still, I know that there will be times when I will again stand here, gazing at the mound, seeking again the patterns buried forever under the sod. The lawn spreads lush beneath my feet as I, for old time's sake, walk the covered basepaths once more. Crabapple, walnut, plywood, home.

And they are rich in evocative description and humor and memorable images. They are about solitude and communication, death, divorce, regeneration, solace, growing old and being young, friendship, love, experience, and memory. In writing the outdoors, we write about all the things we write about anyplace else, because, after all, "when you tug at a single strand in nature, you find it attached to the rest of the world."

Reading the Outdoors: A List of Classroom Resources

Abbey, Edward. *Desert Solitaire: A Season in the Wilderness.* New York: McGraw-Hill, 1968.

Bergon, Frank, ed. *The Wilderness Reader.* New York: New American Library, 1980.

Dillard, Annie. "How I Wrote the Moth Essay—and Why." *The Norton Sampler*, 4th ed. Ed. Thomas Cooley. New York: Norton, 1993. 15–23.

———. "Transfiguration in a Candle Flame." *The Norton Sampler*, 4th ed. Ed. Thomas Cooley. New York: Norton, 1993. 9–12.

Ehrlich, Gretel. *The Solace of Open Spaces.* New York: Viking, 1985.

Finch, Robert, and John Elder, eds. *The Norton Book of Nature Writing.* New York: W. W. Norton, 1990.

Hubbell, Sue. *A Country Year: Living the Questions.* New York: Random House, 1986.

Huser, Verne, ed. *River Reflections: A Collection of River Writings.* Old Saybrook, CT: Globe Pequot, 1988.

Leopold, Aldo. *A Sand County Almanac, and Sketches Here and There.* New York: Oxford University Press, 1949.

Lueders, Edward, ed. *Writing Natural History: Dialogues with Authors.* Salt Lake City: University of Utah Press, 1989.

Lyon, Thomas J., ed. *This Incomperable Lande: A Book of American Nature Writing.* Boston: Houghton-Mifflin, 1989.

McPhee, John. *The John McPhee Reader.* Ed. William L. Howarth. New York: Farrar, Straus, & Giroux, 1976.

Muir, John. *The Wilderness World of John Muir.* Ed. Edwin Way Teale. Boston: Houghton-Mifflin, 1954.

Murray, John, ed. *Nature's New Voices.* Golden, CO: Fulcrum, 1992.

Olson, Sigurd. *Songs of the North: A Sigurd Olson Reader.* Edited by Howard Frank Mosher. New York: Penguin, 1987.

Perrin, Noel. *First Person Rural: Essays of a Sometime Farmer.* Boston: David R. Godine, 1978.

Shanley, J. Lyndon. *The Making of Walden.* Chicago: University of Chicago Press, 1957.

Trimble, Stephen, ed. *Words From the Land: Encounters with Natural History Writing.* Layton, UT: Gibbs M. Smith, 1988.

White, E. B. "Once More to the Lake." *One Man's Meat.* New York: Harper, 1978. 215–21.

Applications in the Classroom

Writing the Outdoors: From Journals to Essays

Journalkeeping

■ Take students outdoors to an on-campus site or a park to write about what they see around them, including as much detail as possible. Ask them to close their eyes, listen for three minutes, then write about what they hear and feel. Have them record whatever the experience reminds them of.

{*Extension:* Let groups of students in specific locations read their journals aloud to compare the language that they chose, the things they noticed, and the varieties of description they could use.}

■ Give students a guided imagery experience in the classroom where they close their eyes and picture themselves outdoors, and then write about where they were, what they were doing, and what it was like.

{*Extension:* Play an audio tape of nature sounds, preferably without music, ask students to listen with eyes closed, and after a few minutes write a detailed description of what they imagined as they listened to the tape. *Alternative*—use a natural experiences video.}

■ Ask students to pick an outdoor place they've never been and write an imagined descriptive narrative about what they would see and experience there.

{*Extension:* Ask students to explain separately why they imagined the outdoor place to be like that, then have them research the place to compare their descriptions to reality. Many outdoor locations can be learned about in travel videos.}

■ Assign students to write several more journal entries while sitting at very different outdoor locations, observing, and remembering.

■ Ask students to make a map of their outdoor experiences and highlight the locations they remember best, then write lists or clusters about what they remember. Developed journal entries could follow.

■ At an art museum or through art posters, have students write journal entries about their experiences inside one or more of the paintings.

■ Open the windows of the classroom and let the students stick their heads outside for a moment, then write about what they experience through their senses as they do that.

Essaying

Any of the journals above could lead into essays and formal written texts, drawing on the details and the description of notes and journals. In addition, classroom-published anthologies of student writing could include:

■ A collection of essays on childhood outdoor experiences in that particular community or among students in that particular classroom.

■ A student-researched and written guide to outdoor activities in the area, including locations, descriptions, history, personal experience—individual work composed, shared, collated, edited, and published by the class.

■ A collection of essays about the outdoors in the lives of older family members—parents, grandparents, ancestors—or older citizens in the community.

Log Entry

Trip is over. Beautiful scenery, especially from dunes looking over the beach. I am realizing the importance water plays in my life and my attachment to it. All of my meaningful outdoor experiences have been related to some body of water, from childhood homes on Lake Erie in Ohio to an island near Detroit, crewing on a sail boat to sitting on top of a hill, here at my parents' condo overlooking East Bay. The beach path pulled me forward out of the woods earlier at the state park and the serenity of walking through the trees could not compare to the joy of sighting water ahead. Now I watch the bay water turn from a paint box blue to slate gray as the sky darkens. I feel I'm only babbling on these pages and am trying too hard to write the right things. So glad

▶

Annie Dillard says it's OK to babble at first. But where is this leading? Especially after reading such seemingly effortless pieces by Dillard, White, and Root, I know I have a long way to go. But my goal is to be a better writing teacher and I hope I'll be learning through practice this week. I have often felt frustrated at forgetting events and feelings from my past. Journal writing would sure be a solution for that. I want my "life to accumulate" and not just pass into obscurity. I want to hang on to my experiences and emotions so I can pull them back out and re-digest and re-evaluate. Can I stay committed to journal writing and not be embarrassed at the thought of anyone else reading my ramblings?

—Debbie LaGuire

WRITING FAIR

The Sail
Debbie LaGuire

June, 1973, and I'd moved back to my childhood bedroom on a placid street in Gross Ile, a protected island community near Detroit. Student teaching, exams, and graduation behind me, I had left the independence and carefree living in a grimy apartment near MSU to return once more to daughterhood in the arms of my family. The blue walls of my bedroom contained relics of my past—four treasured Ginny dolls, a creaky child's rocker—and eyelet curtained windows overlooked ghostly memories of juvenile play and friends. In this room my Peter Pan desire to be forever young and securely surrounded by family conflicted with my eagerness for independence and the autonomy a teaching job would provide.

Throughout the early summer I nervously awaited replies to the more than a hundred letters of application already sent. I sought my father's advice (sometimes grudgingly) on the most professional-looking resume and letter formats. My mother's encouragement nudged me toward knocking on closed doors in hopes of future possibilities. The few interviews I sweated out were occasions of bated breath and anticipation for all, but ultimately led to disappointment at no results. The depression of a hopeless and jobless fall hung in the air like the persistent humidity of the airless, torrid days.

▶

Life around me swirled normally, though gingerly, due to my increasing irritability and peevishness. Living like a child while struggling for adulthood provided many occasions for snappishness and annoyance. My six-year-old brother was a constant reminder of the immaturity I was straining to leave behind.

My father's announcement of our upcoming annual family sail across Lake Erie caused an inner groan. I felt torn by conflicting desires and needs. I knew I was a valued asset and my father depended on my help with preparation, hoisting of sails, adjusting of the rigging, and carrying out other orders from the captain that I had performed as a loyal crew member in the past. But the tug to stay home alone and unregimented, close to the expectant ring of the phone, was tempting. I relished the possibility of tasting independence, eating my own food, being on my own schedule with my own thoughts for company. I could see disappointment in my parents' eyes as I voiced this alternative, and ultimately I acknowleged the fact that I was needed and so condescended to set sail with my family.

We hoisted sail early one morning after the usual impatient chores of stowing gear, adjusting rigging, and motoring away from the dock and into the channel. The early hours were still and the skies a hazy grey as we examined the telltales for signs of a breeze. The silence was marred by the annoying snapping to and fro of the main sail and jib as we strained to catch the fickle and elusive wind. Several times during the first days we resorted to the bane of any true sailor—the motor—which churned us noisily forward. I performed my duties grudgingly and slept on deck each night, symbolically trying to separate myself from the family togetherness in the cabin below. I stubbornly refused to admit any pleasure in the gentle rhythmic rocking of this oversized cradle.

The wind freshened near the end of our trip as we turned for home and began to tack from port to starboard. The sun blazed through our hair while chasing the vicious black flies away. My father turned the tiller over to me and I was joyously in control as we heeled over and sliced powerfully through the blue-green water. The main sail was taut, the jib adjusted, and my spirits soared. I was the captain and the master of our forward motion. This was true sailing. I made slight adjustments to port or starboard for optimum speed, I stood masterfully with feet braced for balance, and we surged over each roller coaster swell. The uncertainty of each upcoming dip gave the future a thrill of anticipation and fearful pleasure.

Miles from shore we were amazed to see a translucent, silver-white butterfly join our crew. Its fragile wings fluttered gracefully

▶

about the cockpit. Our eyes watched the incongruous appearance with curiosity. Back and forth it darted, searching, searching. At last it came to rest on my arm and perched contentedly for long languid moments. The peaceful moment seemed frozen in time and the only sound was my mother's whispered prediction that this was surely an omen of good things to come. We were all smiling as this "omen," newly refreshed, began its take-off for another journey.

It was soon after our return that I was offered—and enthusiastically accepted—my first teaching position. Back in my bedroom, still sun-darkened from the family sail, I knew I could not, nor did I want to, move forward into my future without tightly treasuring my secure and loving past.

3 Of Road Kill and Community History: Exploring the Past and Present through Writing

Stephen N. Tchudi
University of Nevada–Reno

Log Entry

I would like to develop my ability as a story teller. I hope to be inspired by the beauty of the land as we walk and tour and listen to the local people tell stories of the region.

I have selected a book written by an 80-year-old man. He is recalling his youth growing up in the Upper Peninsula. I've completed two short stories. Interesting tales of his childhood. One story was about gypsies coming to town and how they traded horses and used them for bartering. It ended with a humorous note. The other was about a haunted house which was a brothel. He discussed his trip there with a friend and they were led to believe that ghosts now lived there. Later he found out that it was a wild Canadian lynx that was screaming while they were there at night. He has a great sense of humor. I'm beginning to feel like I could tell stories about my childhood too.

—Linda Meeuwenberg

It was turtle season in Michigan, that time of summer when painted turtles take to the highways and byways. You might think they would be content to stay in the swamps where they were born, but something impels them to seek other marshes, perhaps deeper puddles or bogs with a richer supply of turtedibles. And always, these greener pastures seem to be on the other side of the road.

I was driving the lead van, tootling down a back road in Leelanau County, when I spotted a turtle in my lane and steered toward the center of the road to miss it. Unfortunately, the driver of the following van didn't spot the turtle. Unlike the Oklahoma tortoise in Steinbeck's *Grapes of Wrath*, merely grazed by a passing vehicle and crawling on, this Michigan turtle took a direct hit from a steel-belted radial at fifty miles an hour and was turned into road pizza.

Somebody in my van asked, "Why did the chicken cross the road?"

Someone else knew the answer: "To show the turtle that it could be done."

The turtle squashing was the only flaw in an otherwise perfect day. There were a dozen of us in the vans, high school and college English teachers returning from a field trip, heading for our home base at the Traverse Bay Writing Workshop. We had been museum hopping, exploring historical museums in Michigan's "Little Finger," the Leelanau Peninsula that stretches forty-five miles northwest of Traverse City. I was teaching a workshop that drew on the culture and literature of Traverse Bay as a starting point for writing.

Planning for the Workshop: The Road to Traverse Bay

My interest in and preparation for this week-long course had begun several years earlier in a Michigan State University seminar, "Reading and Writing about Michigan." I had wanted to show students that regional history and culture provide an extraordinary resource for teaching. The students had developed a rich collection of teaching units on Michigan topics such as Great Lakes shipping, defunct Michigan railroads, waste disposal problems, the auto industry, the state's French heritage, and Michigan's legacy of poets, novelists, dramatists, and film writers.

When I was invited to teach a workshop at Traverse Bay, I proposed to translate some of these teaching ideas into action. Specifically, I announced that my workshop would explore the pedagogy of community resources in the Leelanau Peninsula/Traverse Bay area.

To prepare directly for the June course, I made a practice run to Leelanau in March (no turtles visible). I visited a half dozen small museums—the community museum in Leland, a lighthouse museum in Northport, and the visitors' center at the Great Lakes National Seashore, for example. By prior appointment, I was able to meet with the curators and directors to discuss my plans for the course and to learn about the kinds of resources they could make available. I also reread David Anderson's *Michigan: A State Anthology*, an excellent collection of materials containing everything from diary and journal entries by little-known settlers to works by some of the state's better known contemporary writers. I also collected resource materials about the state and cataloged these in my "Michigan Box," a portable library of maps, pamphlets, brochures, novels, state histories, and books for young readers gleaned from university and tourist agencies.

The Workshop: Writers on the Road

Thus prepared, I headed for Traverse City during the last week of June. Our class met both mornings and afternoons, Monday through Friday. Each morning I began the class with a reading from the Anderson anthology, perhaps the story of a Great Lakes or Traverse Bay shipwreck, some poems by Michigan's poet laureate Will Carlton, or one of the Hemingway Michigan stories. After the initial response to literature, my students would dive into the Michigan Box. People were free to read and respond to their choice of materials. They might focus on the Michigan lumbering or mining industries, on the First Michiganders, on the French explorations, or on contemporary problems of underemployment in Michigan's "up north."

Everyone kept a response journal to share with the class, and each member of the group worked on a longer piece of writing to be presented at the end of the week. I encouraged the workshoppers to consider imaginative approaches to writing about Michigan history and culture: They could create poems, plays, stories, biographies, editorials, photo essays, or any other form of discourse that would help them explain their understanding of the region, its history, and its people.

Each afternoon, we loaded up the vans and set out to visit museums. After providing an overview of the kinds of resources we would examine—a logging exhibit, a graveyard of ships, an exhibit of photographs—I asked the participants to think about questions they wanted to ask, what they wanted to learn from the field trip. I hoped they would approach these museums as readers and writers of the culture, not just as ordinary tourists with cameras hung around their necks.

Our field trips included:

- The Great Lakes National Seashore, where we tromped the sand dunes, learned of seashore reclamation projects, and studied exhibits at a museum celebrating the accomplishments of the U.S. Life Saving Service.

- The Leland Historical Museum, then featuring a display of commercial and homemade fishing gear and lures, an exhibit which also helped clarify the role of fishing as industry and sport in northern Michigan.

- The Northport Lighthouse Museum, where we interviewed the eighty-year-old son of one of the early lighthouse keepers and heard yarns of dark and stormy nights at one of the wildest spots in northern Michigan.

- The Traverse City Con Foster Museum, where a curator and a docent dressed in period costumes role-played Michigan historical figures—a strapping French lumberjack and a Swedish cook in a logging camp.

The writings that grew from these individual and collective experiences were diverse, falling into three broad categories:

1. "Gee Whiz" pieces, where the writers marveled at what they hadn't known before. For instance, many members of the class were deeply moved by stories of life-saving heroics. They were flabbergasted that young men of eighteen or nineteen would risk their lives in early winter snowstorms, rowing out to ships sinking in the surf, stringing up breeches buoys at calculated risk to life and limb. My students wrote poems and stories about those heroes, retelling their stories, celebrating their achievements.

2. "Writing in Role," where my students became some of the characters they had read about or studied at the museums—a French logger or voyageur, the wife of a Great Lakes sea captain, a lumberman reminiscing about the good old days of the Michigan tall pines.

3. "Making Connections," where through fiction, drama, poetry, and nonfiction, workshoppers used their understanding of history and culture to explore issues and problems in Michigan today. They wrote pieces on ecology, commercial growth and development, their own feelings for the forests and lakes, and their concerns for their own students and the world in which they are growing up.

As is the tradition in the Traverse Bay workshops, we brought our materials together for a grand "show and tell" on the final morning. Photographs were mounted on poster board, along with brochures from the places we'd visited. We cut and pasted quotes from the writings we'd read, and we polished and displayed our own writing. In addition, each member of the group prepared at least one of his or her pieces for publication in a class anthology, duplicated and distributed after the institute closed.

Mapping the Trip to the Classroom

The reader may have observed that the class did *not* include a formal component dedicated to pedagogy. I felt that through learn-by-doing, hands-on explorations, teachers would naturally engage in discussion of classroom implications. Sure enough, in our drives to and from museum sites, each of our vans became a mobile seminar room where we reflected on pedagogy.

Naturally, participants had some reservations about "practicality," about how easily the approach we were following at Traverse Bay could be adapted to their classrooms. It's one thing to cavort in the idyllic settings of northern Michigan Bay with a dozen motivated teacher-writers, quite another to consider using this approach in classes of thirty to thirty-five elementary, secondary, or college students. Would there be enough reading material and community resources? Would there be enough interest among the students?

To explore the question of resources, I described my own experience creating the Michigan Box. Poking around in a small community library, for example, I had unearthed over one hundred titles dealing with Michigania. Running my fingers through the card catalog at a local elementary school, I had found over fifty titles. I offered my view that even underfunded school and community libraries have similar materials to create a rich and diverse book cart or Michigan Box.

We brainstormed for other kinds of resources. In addition to those available free from state historical and tourism agencies, we thought about obtaining materials via:

- Local chambers of commerce and tourism promotional groups.
- Community history societies.
- The archives and files of the local newspaper.
- Photo albums and diaries brought in by the students themselves.
- School yearbooks, magazines, and newspapers.

We also discussed the human resources that are available in *any* town, large or small:

- Senior citizens who would be delighted to reminisce about days gone by.
- Parents, who can discuss more recent history.

- Teachers, ministers, lawyers, politicians, and others who have a sense of community history.
- File clerks, registrars, surveyors, public utilities workers, police, and fire protection agents, all of whom may have knowledge of local and regional happenings.
- Painters, writers, storytellers, and folksingers, many of them easily located close to home. (In Michigan, both the arts and humanities councils have strong artists-in-the-schools programs, including a number of scholar/writer/performers with extensive knowledge of state history.)

And we discussed the physical or "artifactual" resources that are available:

- Buildings, new or old, each with a historical tale to tell.
- Parks, recreation areas, and wildlife centers.
- Public institutions with their archives and honor rolls.
- Town and community maps, newspaper photo archives.
- Objects forgotten in community warehouses and the storeroom at city hall; stuff stuffed in attics and basements.

The group raised some questions about the role of museums in the program. How vital are they? What if you don't have a museum close to your school? What if the school budget doesn't permit hiring buses and drivers for long field trips?

Attacking the bus problem first, I handed out copies of *Michigan Museums and Historic Exhibits*, a publication of the Michigan Historical Museum that describes over three hundred small museums in the state. People were surprised to learn about underpublicized museums in their own regions, sometimes within walking distance of their schools. It was clear that even if one had to book a Yellow Bus, one didn't necessarily have to drive to Detroit or Chicago to visit a helpful museum. In fact, several people remarked that they had come to prefer the local museums, museums you can get your mind around, to the big city blockbuster museums where kids have trouble finding the coatrooms, much less understanding massive displays.

We also discussed the importance of preparation for museum visits. Teachers shudder at the thought of three dozen kids running around a museum, ignoring the exhibits, irritating the other patrons and the museum workers. Although many museums have project sheets for students to complete, many of us felt these were unsatisfactory, too often forcing students to dash about filling in blanks on odd bits of historical or cultural information. We agreed that advanced preparation is the key, and we reviewed some of the strategies and possibilities:

- Whenever possible, museum visits should be linked to ongoing teaching units, supplementing the text. Try to avoid the "one-shot" visit that is isolated from instruction.

- Use reading as preparation. Have students read articles, newspaper clippings, and literature that is relevant to the materials they will be seeing.

- Use writing as a warm-up. Have students reflect on what they know about the museum's topic and what they want to find out. Have them go to the museum with a list of questions in hand.

- Preview the museum yourself and give students an overview. Just as it can be disastrous to show the class a film you haven't previewed, don't take the students to a museum where you are a stranger.

- Arrange in advance for special attention for your group. Tell the museum director you don't want the ordinary "cook's tour" of the place. Ask if your group can have a focused visit that emphasizes your particular topics or interests.

- Use writing during the museum trip. To keep the kids from going wild, plan a group meeting after you've been in the museum for an hour or so. In a cafeteria or education room, have the students sit quietly and write for ten or fifteen minutes.

- Use writing after the trip. Have the students do some debriefing, in writing, soon after the trip. Then have them do imaginative writing: stories, poems, skits, and the like.

Throughout the Traverse Bay week, I stressed that one need not always do a formal unit on community history in order to draw on such resources. In fact, I think it may be preferable to infuse regional culture throughout the year, rather than concentrating it in a single unit or special week of study. Thus, when we have our students read Wordsworth-on-nature, we can take them outside to appreciate the possibilities in their neighborhood. When we study world literature, we can invite community members who are Greek or Chinese or Vietnamese or Armenian to come to class to describe their roots and traditions. When students write essays or expository papers or research papers, what better source of topics than their own home town?

As our Traverse Bay week drew to a close, we discussed adaptations of our work. None of us left with the naive view that we would simply transplant our own experiences into the very different soils and climates of our classrooms.

But we did carry away seeds.

The Follow-up: Bringing It All Back Home

During the following school year, I spoke to or corresponded with most of the teachers in my course to find out how they had used the learnings from our seminar.

Responses varied with individuals and schools. A couple of people said they hoped to make applications but simply had not had the time or curricular opportunity. Others said they had done work on local history or family history projects, though they were limited for one reason or another in opportunities for field trips, even short ones.

My prize pupil, one who showed the applicability of the approach in a real-world senior high school setting, was Ann Ransford of Caro, Michigan. Caro is located in the "thumb" of Michigan's lower peninsula, a region that has suffered chronic recession as farming has declined and as industries have left for warmer climates and cheaper labor. It is a small town, certainly not the sort of place where the casual observer would say, "Ah, what a gold mine for historical study!"

But Ann and her senior English classes discovered that Caro is, in fact, an historical mother lode. Students in average and honors classes researched community issues, problems, and resources. They interviewed farmers and community leaders; they made trips to historical sites of both white people and Michigan Indians; they poked around in the files of the Caro library and newspaper. Over several months, they collected data, maintained journals and diaries, and composed their materials in essays and papers and displays.

I was able to attend one of their show-and-tell sessions and was impressed by the range of projects and the richness and quality of the writing produced by these young people. As I interviewed the students, they reported to me almost uniformly that they enjoyed their research and found it much more engaging than research papers they had done in the past. Several kids commented that the community history project had given them a great deal of confidence about going to college: They now *knew* how to learn on their own, how to scrounge around for materials, how to synthesize their ideas.

Perhaps most important, the project had given them a sense of belonging to their own community. Caro is not the sort of town that college students return to for employment after graduation. On the other hand, many Caro kids never leave at all, staying on after high school to work in family businesses and farms, in the remaining local industries and shops. Ann Ransford's teaching had shown both groups that there was and is a lot more to their home town than they had imagined.

I credited Ann Ransford for their enthusiasm, though she, in turn, attributed much of her success to her participation in the Traverse Bay project. We mutually back-slapped.

And that, in turn, allows me to bring this essay full circle by revealing that it was Ann Ransford who drove the second van. It was she who hit the turtle and helped give our Traverse Bay group the symbol that appeared on the back page of our published writings:

References

Anderson, David. *Michigan: A State Anthology*. Detroit: Gale Research, 1984.

Michigan Historical Museum. *Michigan Museums and Historical Exhibits*. Lansing: Michigan Tourist Council. 1984.

Ransford, Ann. "Michigan as a Content Area for Writing." *Language Arts Journal of Michigan* 7.2 (1991): 37–48.

Tchudi, Stephen. "Museums and More." *Language Arts Journal of Michigan* 6.2 (1990): 75–83.

Applications in the Classroom

Of Road Kill and Community History: Exploring the Past and Present through Writing

Writing Topics for Use in Museum Work

- Be the artifact. Write about life from its point of view in time and place.

- Do an anthropological analysis of an object: Where was it made? Who might have made it? What was its purpose? What does it tell you about the needs of the people who made it?

- How would you make one today, using modern materials?

- Write a letter to a museum director who is pressed for exhibit space, arguing that this object should be either saved or tossed out.

- Keep a journal or "split column log" of your museum visit, writing down your reactions to what you have seen.

- Write postcards from the museum to friends, telling what you've seen.

- Go back in time to the era of the artifact and write a description of life for a person your age at that time.

- Write a script for a documentary radio show about this object.

- Write about an artifact in one of the following discourse forms: speech, editorial, letter to the editor, imaginary diary, joke, riddle, song lyric, telegram, newspaper article, advertisement, bumper sticker, satire, fantasy, science fiction, directions.

- Interview a museum guide about what is important in an exhibit.

Creating Contexts for Community as Content Area

- Create a book cart or reserve collection in the school library on the broad subject of your visit. Provide reading days or times for students to explore this collection and to come up with questions to answer at the museum.

- Collect magazine and newspaper articles connected with the museum and its collections. Let students help build an in-class library.

■ Scan TV listings for related documentaries on the Discovery Channel, Public Broadcasting, and Arts & Entertainment, and check the school or district media center (and/or local video stores and libraries) for documentaries or other videos which could prepare students to visit.

■ Create a classroom museum of artifacts, photos, anecdotes, posters. Decorate the room with photos and captions from students.

■ Bring in local authors to talk about research and read their work.

■ Have students write personal inventories of community memories, experiences.

■ Use on-site visits as occasions to discuss research and readings (agriculture on a Centennial Farm, history in a reconstructed village).

■ Give a field trip exam, such as going to a historical museum and cemetery, using writing-to-learn techniques to gather information and reflect on experiences, and then develop more polished forms such as reports, letters, dramatic monologues.

From Ransford, Ann, "Michigan as a Content Area for Writing," *Language Arts Journal of Michigan*, 7:2 (Fall 1991), 37–48, and Tchudi, Stephen, "Museums and More," *LAJM*, 6:2 (Fall 1990), 75–83.

Log Entry

Monday was a very busy day. We went to Sleeping Bear Dunes and visited the restored Coast Guard Lifesaving Station. I found the presentation by the retired park ranger to be fascinating. She was an excellent story teller and shared stories of famous shipwrecks and discussed the methods used to rescue people from the violent waters.

    The pictures were very interesting. I got the feeling that those were brave men who had to be very agile and physically fit. They also had to repeat drills so that they could get into the water in five minutes. They had to make quick decisions regarding the type of boat to be used and where to shoot the flares. I would also think that these men thrived on the thrill of a rescue. They were not paid well and appeared to serve in this capacity out of a sense of duty and pride in saving lives. Very heroic!

    On the ride back to Traverse Bay I began to ponder about the women in their lives. Where were the women that loved these men? I remember the ranger pointing out the little houses that their families stayed in and I recall seeing only one picture of a woman. She was tak-

▶

ing a ride in the Breeches Buoy for a demonstration. The Captain's quarters were pointed out and it was stated that he lived there with his family. However, there wasn't any evidence of a woman's presence that I can remember.

It must have been a difficult life for them. I can imagine the flares being sent off and the alarm to alert all the crew of an emergency. The men were well trained to respond immediately. They had no time to spare. What must that have been like for a woman married to one of them? What if she was carrying a child or had children to care after? What was she feeling as she watched him leave in a small wooden boat into the angry water? . . .

—**Linda Meeuwenberg**

WRITING FAIR

Violets in the Windows
Linda Meeuwenberg

Jane sat down with her steaming mug of coffee at her little table. It had been a busy day and she needed time to sit and reflect on all that had happened. The cottage she had moved into was beginning to feel like home. It was rewarding for her to see her personal belongings hanging on the walls and strewn about the cottage. Countless other couples had shared these little cottages over the years. Tomorrow she would tend to hanging some white cotton curtains with ruffles. She had made these herself and had them stored in her cedar chest. It was always fulfilling to move into a new cottage and make it a home for herself and her husband, Jon. He was a lifesaver with the U.S. Coast Guard Service. He had just been transferred to the Glen Haven post.

One of her personal treasures hung over their kitchen table. It was a pen and ink drawing of a sailing vessel which had won an award in her last year of high school. Her two African violets sat in their new home above the kitchen sink. One was full and bright with dark violet blossoms. The other was beginning to bud with white flowers and was full of dark lush foliage. These were her three most treasured possessions that went with every move. They provided a sense of security whenever she moved to a new location. It was not easy having to uproot oneself from a home. Jane was beginning to ease that reality in her life

▶

by having these cherished possessions placed around her. She started to think of it as an exciting adventure into a new chapter of her life. She took great pride in her ability to prepare a cozy nest for her and her husband. It was a thrill to be married to a man of the sea. She had met Jon at the local store she tended in Muskegon. Her father owned the store and she spent her summers clerking and stocking shelves with supplies for the local lumber people. Jon had come to town by a freighter from Chicago. He had a dream to work near the water and Muskegon provided a perfect place to learn logging. He was intrigued by the methods used to plot a course across the lake. He gained a special respect for the lake and its ability to be serene and calm or in a few minutes as violent as any great body of water. He began to dream about life as a captain on a ship. He had plenty of time to dream on his trek up to Muskegon. By the time he arrived in Muskegon he wasn't sure he wanted to pursue a life in logging anymore. Ships fascinated him. He began to become consumed with thoughts of sailing.

Once in Muskegon he began to talk with some men at the local cafe. He was intrigued by a man who had served as a life saver in the Grand Haven Life Saving Corps. He would listen attentively as he told stories of his rescue missions. He seemed to show a genuine pride in his accomplishments. Saving lives from shipwrecks was a heroic act that the logging stories just could not begin to compete with. Jon felt himself becoming drawn to the sea and asking questions feverishly to find out how he could gain an opportunity such as this.

That was ten years ago and he had been serving his country as a lifesaver for the past six years. He had to move four times during that period of time. He was pleased that his wife didn't seem to mind the idea of uprooting herself to move where he was transferred to. She had a real sense of adventure in her blood too. Every place they moved she seemed to have a special talent for making it appear like they had lived there for years. She would busy herself with making a little wooden shack look like a charming doll house. He truly loved her for providing this kind of comfort for them.

She seemed to enjoy listening to the tales of the sea as told by the other lifesavers. She would spend her time writing and keeping journals of their activities. She particularly liked spending time with the captain and his wife. Whenever they had free time she would have them over for coffee or a glass of dandelion wine. She would prompt them to talk of their lives together on the sea. She would walk down the beach to find a secluded place to sit and dream and write. She had published a book of poetry and was beginning to receive a small royalty

▶

from it. This was helping to supplement their income. A lifesaver was not a highly paid position.

Tonight as she sat over her steaming mug of coffee she was recalling the events of the last two days. They had left Grand Haven to move up the coast to Glen Haven. They came by a freighter and the lake was not kind to them. It was late October, which was a month of a high number of shipwrecks each year. They spent the night on Manitou Island until the water allowed them to get to Glen Haven the next day. She was consumed with thoughts of what their lives would be like here. She had already met the crew this morning. She seemed particularly fascinated by the captain. He seemed strong and disciplined, but yet had a gentleness about him that reached out to others. The crew seemed to admire his ability and never questioned his decisions.

She looked around her cottage and was pleased that it looked like a home already. She was anxious for Jon to arrive. He was due to be off duty at midnight. She had a warm stew simmering on the stove to warm him when he came in. Tonight he was assigned to walk the beach searching for vessels in distress. She was pleased that it was a clear night with stars shining brightly. There was a brisk wind but not much sign of any stormy weather. It was now 11:45 P.M. She began setting the table. She had saved a special candle for this occasion and placed it in her cherished candle holder that had been her grandmother's. She set it in the middle of the table and lit it. She was anxious to hear of Jon's first night walking the beach patrol for the Glen Haven Post.

4 Making Poetry: In Search of the Delicate Balance

Gloria Nixon-John
Troy High School, Michigan

Log Entry

We share in the morning session and I am fine tuned to listen. Some people hide in poetry, others reveal. I can hear those who want to pretty things up or bury ideas in words. Gloria conferenced with each of us. She's adept at seeing the hidden and grasping the whole, larger idea. . . .

I want to get back to the idea and process of sharing. I have seen and felt the magnitude of sharing. I look forward to getting feedback on my work. Some are nervous about this process, but I like to hear what my writing does when it lands on my audience. My students, especially in creative writing, need to do more sharing. On the days when they have writing time, and don't use it, it would be far more productive to have response groups in action. I will try the process I experienced in the writing center. Students must take more responsibility for their writing and their classmates' writing.

—Laurie C. Kavanagh

I know that I am moved to write poetry when I am trying to make sense of the world, when the beauty or horror of life on the planet penetrates my skin, when I can't find the answers anywhere else and nothing else will do. Therefore, when someone enters my poetry workshop, I assume that he or she has gravitated towards this art form for more than art's sake. Through his struggle for a first line, Michael Gannon, one of my students in my 1991 Workshop, put it this way: "I need to write poetry in order to make some honest, ordinary, important statement that clarifies my life." Statements like Michael's (and there have been many) remind me constantly that some self-indulgence is important to the process of poetry writing. But knowing how to keep the focus on the workshop agenda, along with the life struggle that has prompted poetry, is also important, or any poetry workshop will quickly become shoddy group therapy or uncomfortable voyeurism. Workshops, like poems, need balance.

No matter how often I speak about poetry or poetry writing, I end up speaking or writing about balance—not just the balance in terms of the use of language or unraveling of meaning, but also the balance needed to deal with the student of poetry. And while one might think that the adult poet is more open to suggestion, more willing to take chances than the younger poet, such is not always the case. In fact, many beginning adult poets (especially those who teach literature or language arts) seem to have a more difficult time finding their own voice, perhaps because they are so familiar with classic literature or style that is rooted in a previous century.

One of my first tasks, then, is to familiarize the student with many good contemporary poets. So, at our first official meeting, I begin with a reading list or even copies of a few good contemporary poems. And I always feel a need to share my favorite contemporary poets with my students, probably because I like to see and hear certain poems over and over again. Most importantly, though, I try to include a variety of styles in the suggested reading list. I include everything from minimalistic poetry to the rather cryptic works of poets such as Joseph Brodsky. I also make certain that women (Mary Oliver, Adrienne Rich), minority (Gwendolyn Brooks, Lucille Clifton), and non-Western (Issa, Bashō) poets are represented on the list as well as the more bizarre surrealistic poets, such as Dobyns or Edson.

Then too, I often use my own poems to facilitate discussion because, at some point, it becomes important for my students to know that I swim in the temperatures and tides of which I speak, or they will not even be willing to go wading. A word of caution: There is always at least one student who feels that we are somehow betraying the poetry masters (Homer, Milton, even Sandburg or Frost) when we look at more modern poets or when we treat poetry writing as an evolving art; but such students usually learn that their own poetry must be separated from the old masters or rooted in life as they know it. And while the classics can model many important elements of good poetry, limiting the discussion to the classics produces a limited model for the modern poet.

Here are a few of the poems on my suggested reading list:

"An Old Whorehouse," Mary Oliver

"Rain," William Carpenter

"An Old Man's Song," Russel Edson
"Cemetery Nights," Steven Dobyns
"Diving Into The Wreck," Adrienne Rich
"The Mother," Gwendolyn Brooks

Windows of the Past

At our first official class session, we do little more than discuss what we feel are the special qualities of these very diverse pieces. Like good English teachers, the workshop participants generally discuss language, metaphor, or theme, and that is just fine for starters. But I know I must get them to write or recall the poems in their own lives, and I know that the writing must happen quickly, almost magically, as our time is rather limited and some positive reinforcement must occur relatively soon. So on that first day of class I also ask students to revisit a mood. I take them on imaginative journeys through the doors and windows of their pasts. I take them into closets, into rooms that have troubled them, and I help them deal with the darkness, clean out the cobwebs, and let the air in. I also use a series of journal prompts—prompts that seem to help my students peel away the layers of concerns, joys, and troubles in their lives. And in so doing, they somehow find their life poems, their concerns, and their voices.

For example, I might prompt with a line like:

Close your eyes and imagine a window in your past.

Or I might provoke with questions like:

What is it that you know with your heart that your mind denies?

What is it that you want but cannot have?

What is it that causes you pain? Dress yourself in the pain. Go out to dinner wearing it. Taste the pain!

I sometimes prompt by giving the student a first line for a journal write, a line like "This is a time in my life in which . . ." or "There is one thing that makes men and women more alike than different, and that is . . ." with instruction to let the writing take its own course. Or I might simply send my students outdoors into the world with instructions like "Go outside, find a comfortable spot in the grass, and look between the blades of grass. Describe what you see. Trust yourself. Just let go, just write!"

The window exercise always works:

Think about a window in a place that has some significance in your life. It may be a window of the past. Visualize the window.

Decide if you are standing inside or outside of the window (in other words, are you looking into a place or out of a place).

Title the piece either "Inside Looking Out" or "Outside Looking In."

Close your eyes if closing your eyes helps you to visualize the window. Imagine that you are standing by the window and select one object on the other side of the window that has some special meaning to you or that you just enjoy for some reason or another. Describe that object in one line or less. The line need not be a sentence.

Next, imagine that you open the window enough to hear the sounds on the other side more clearly. Describe these sounds in one line or less.

Open the window a bit more. What do you smell on the other side? Describe what you smell in one line or less.

Stretch your imagination now, and pretend that you can reach out to touch anything you want to touch on the other side of the window. Touch it. How does it feel? Write one line or less describing how it feels.

Taste the object you just touched on the other side of the window (whether it is edible or not). How does it taste or how might it taste? One line or less please.

Now as a final step:

Pretend that the window is gone or that it never really existed.

Write a line or two about your life without the window.

Notice that I really haven't asked for poetry, per se, as I feel that the first task is helping the student find the substance of a poem and a comfortable voice.

In other words, I prompt, and the writer begins by collecting thoughts and feelings and insights, then later sifts through it all to find the special ideas and words or phrases that just might end up in a poem.

Here is one workshopper's sample of the "raw material" that resulted from the window prompt:

WINDOW - WOOD / COTTAGE / FRONT
    inside looking out
    white painted child's rocker on
    grey porch floor
    rustling birch leaves
    water (plashing) waves on stones
    old pine needles baked with cedar

> bitter sharp earthy crunch
> papery curls on old tree bark

HOLLOW SOUL—DEADENED SENSES—"NATURE"LESS
　　　　　　　　　Laurie C. Kavanagh

The Shape of the Poem

On Day Two, we discuss the physical characteristics of a poem (rhyme, rhythm, line lengths, and typography in general), and we look at a variety of styles from traditional rhyme and prose poems. I revisit some of the poems on our reading list for this discussion. Mary Oliver's "An Old Whorehouse" works well because it is accessible, yet profound, and it has a very simple, rather free structure. It also meets all of the criteria (of a good poem) that I eventually discuss in the workshop so I can refer back to it easily once it has been shared.

> *AN OLD WHOREHOUSE*
> We climbed through a broken window,
> walked through every room.
>
> Out of business for years,
> the mattresses held only
>
> rainwater, and one
> woman's black shoe. Downstairs
>
> spiders had wrapped up
> the crystal chandelier.
>
> A cracked cup lay in the sink.
> But we were fourteen,
>
> and no way dust could hide
> the expected glamour from us,
>
> or teach us anything.
> We whispered, we imagined.
>
> It would be years before
> we'd learn how effortlessly
>
> sin blooms, then softens,
> like any bed of flowers.

The poem is not only a reference point for discussions of poetry and a model of concision and detail, but also a point of departure, an example for people to move away from in the forms and themes of their own poetry.

Before I give the students some time for writing and reshaping their first pieces of writing, I mention that by the next day they will be expected to share their efforts thus far. Sometimes the first opportunity for sharing happens in small groups, or we open the floor to those who wish to read their first draft to the whole group. I let the class decide how to proceed. I encourage all the students to react to the poetry—to discuss the positive aspects of the piece, the lines that seem special to them for one reason or another, the feeling and mood that the poem creates.

Over the course of the next several days, I slowly produce a series of proofs by which the students in the workshop might measure their writing in order to achieve the delicate balance I spoke about earlier. I try to start with the most obviously shared need, but basically the theoretical proofs I present are as follows:

1. Is the poem accessible, yet surprising? Does it surprise, yet remind? That is, does it allow us to tap the common experience in an unpredictable way? Does it take us somewhere familiar, but show us something new when we get there?

2. Is the poem rhythmical, yet conversational? That is, do we at least have some access to the beat or rhythm without being overpowered by the rhythm?

3. Does the poem meander enough to keep us interested? Or is it rather linear?

4. Does the end of the poem justify the beginning? Do we understand where we have started and ended up in this piece?

Once everyone seems to have made some progress or some discovery about their own work and with the aforementioned proofs in mind, we revisit some of the poems that we read early on. I like to linger over "Rain" by William Carpenter, not only because it is so well constructed, but also because it shows us the man's journey to a self-discovery that is both joyful and sorrowful at once (a thematic balance).

When the students return to their poems (in groups or privately), they are asked to focus on the balance, to aim for balance, and to strive for at least one poem by the end of the week that meets most of the criteria suggested. No one ever finds it easy, but all seem to want to try, and all succeed to a degree.

Workshopper Laurie Kavanagh visited her window several times in order to edit her poem. "Blood Ties" resulted when she imposed our criteria with regard to balance. Notice that Laurie has visited her past and her relationship with her sister in a nicely-executed metaphor.

BLOOD TIES

My sister carries her scars
inside. Sometimes I stumble
around our past, relive an
injury and find her turned
into herself, intact but
motionless like dead animals
along lonely highways.

We conspired as our parents
tried to give us bridge
lessons. Laughter erupted,
I dashed outside. She
remained and pushed the
glass door closed, unaware
I would turn, stretch out
my hand to keep us together.
Caught by the cool night winds,
the door slammed,
silenced the evening with
sharp, bitter splinters.
She was curled on the couch
when we returned from the
hospital, my hand wrapped
in white gauze, our parents
pale and exhausted. They
thanked her for cleaning up
as if gratitude could wash
my blood from her memory.

Laurie C. Kavanagh

The following two poems by workshop members resulted from a rather simple prompt that extended the window prompt, asking students to look into the window again at a specific season or special family event.

IN FEBRUARY

Three geese in February
Break the cemetery silence, a
Clear cacophony from the frigid sky
Strikes the mounded earth.
Too soon you fly North, too soon.
Fools! Seeking heaven
Ahead of time
As did he.

Mary Ellen Kinkead

AUGUST, 1965

You sit arms folded,
caressing your fragile arm.
A grasshopper's eyes behind dense rims
frightened me as a child. I

study your face. You've opened a gate,
hurried down a worn path.
You cluck your way through dead
conversation. I watch the ghostly mimic
with amusement then alarm. Then
like a child's escaped balloon
you drift in summer clouds.

Carol Taylor

I like all of the poems above because there are surprises within each poem. "In February" surprises us with noise in the cemetery. Grandmother has eyes like a grasshopper in Carol Taylor's poem. "Blood Ties" surprises with a mysterious sense of the shared pain that these two sisters experience. And yet all of these poems anchor us to the ground, to our common experiences of loss and connectedness.

As the workshop comes to a close, both I and my students have more of a sense of beginning than a sense of closure. And yet, it is very difficult for us to leave the celebratory community that we have built around our own words. Many of us continue to communicate by mail over the poems we shape. Some even return for a second or third workshop. Once in a while, a workshop participant sends me a poem or two that one of their high school or college students has written in response to an idea that came out of our workshop, and that is the biggest thrill of all, because I can see my work as a teacher and poet rippling out far beyond my own circle of influence.

Those ripples begin with being a struggling poet myself, one in awe of good poetry no matter the source. Searching my background in an attempt to trace my attraction to poetry and poets, I can only guess at the sources. Perhaps I can credit Miss Waters, my third grade auditorium teacher, who insisted that I memorize and recite poetry to the class. Or perhaps it was my musical training and fascination for rhythm and rhyme. Or, then again, perhaps it was my mother who encouraged me to examine things carefully and was apt to say, "Look at the red of that flower. No, really look at it, smell it too, get close, look at it, touch it!" These early attempts to connect with poetry led me to a sense of how to create a verbal music as a means of connecting with experience.

Other poets and critics have since confirmed for me how vital this sense is. In his collection entitled *The Sargentville Notebook*, Mark Strand places the poem in a realm he calls ineffable, claiming that "the poem is a winding course . . . between love and self, between words and supremely aggressive wordlessness" (5). Elsewhere, Strand says that "poetry invents itself . . . formalizes emotions that are difficult to articulate" ("Slow Down" 36). Poet and critic M. L. Rosenthal tells us that "the poem's character arises with a subjective world of revery, memory, and traceries of association" (xi). Robert Pinsky believes that good poetry (or at least his favorite poems) seem to involve a bridge or space between the worldly and the spiritual, related in ways nearly impossible to unravel (27).

Strangely enough, however, the students who come to my poetry workshop have a pretty good understanding of the "impossible" or vague nature of poetry. That is, the beginning adult poet seems to know that he or she must rise above the subjective world, must accelerate or transform the language in order to relate his or her own uncommon version of some rather common experience. This doesn't happen as easily with most high school poets.

Sometimes I need to share one of my own poems with high school students first and explain the history behind my poem. For example, if I wrote a poem about my mother working in her garden, I might want to tell a little about my mother, my relationship to her, and to her work in the garden. I might have to fill in the details of my subjectivity.

It all sounds so impossible, and yet it comes together as naturally as people do. In fact, it seems all I really need to do is suggest the struggle and show my reverence for good poetry and a willingness to attempt to write poetry myself. And they come to poetry both willful and willy-nilly, and they speak through poems one word at a time with a power that is both elusive and sensual, in a place where the past, the present, and the future seem to merge.

References

Brodsky, Joseph. *A Part of Speech.* New York: Farrar, Straus, Giroux, 1980.

Brooks, Gwendolyn. *The World of Gwendolyn Brooks.* New York: Harper & Row, 1971.

Carpenter, William. *Rain.* Boston: Northeastern University Press, 1985.

Dobyns, Stephen. *Cemetery Nights: Poems.* New York: Viking, 1987.

Edson, Russell. *The Wounded Breakfast.* Middletown, CT: Wesleyan University Press, 1985.

Oliver, Mary. *American Primitive: Poems.* Boston: Little, Brown, 1983.

Pinsky, Robert. *Poetry and The World: Selected Prose, 1977–87.* New York: Ecco, 1988.

Rich, Adrienne. *Poems Selected and New.* New York: W. W. Norton & Co., 1950.

Rosenthal, M. L. *The Poet's Art.* New York: W. W. Norton, 1987.

Strand, Mark. *The Sargentville Notebook.* Providence: Burning Deck, 1973.

———. "Slow Down For Poetry." *The New York Times Book Review,* September 15, 1991. 1, 36–37.

NOTE: A special thanks to Stephen Dunn, who helped me shape my own practice and poems. His influence is obvious here.

Applications in the Classroom

Making Poetry: In Search of the Delicate Balance

More Prompts

■ Have students re-visit a place as Mary Oliver did. They might re-visit a family cottage, a previous home or town, or an event. Write about the visitation in any genre in a diary or journal as a letter or poem. Try a story in first person, then in third.

■ Instead of a window journey, take students on any number of journeys using sensory recall—a road trip in a car, bus, or train; a futuristic trip in a space ship to Mars; a historical trip to the signing of the Declaration of Independence or to Pearl Harbor.

Group Work

■ Write a collaborative window poem. I call this assignment "Stained Glass" because each student adds a piece. Arrange each piece into a collection or one long poem in parts. It might help to suggest a theme prior to writing (for example, you may want to suggest that each group member look through a window into their kitchen or out a front window).

Research/Writing/Speaking

■ Have students read a variety of contemporary poems and have them examine the poems for their qualities, discuss them, and find some quality we have not discussed. Then have them write about the results and present a mini-lecture on the new quality they have discovered.

Visuals/Displays

■ Students may wish to illustrate their window poems or place them in symbolic frames. They could also swap poems with each other and draw or print a visual representation of another's poems. Put all the visual results in a gallery arrangement. Invite others to the gallery for a reading and tour.

Log Entry

The second piece of writing that came easily and quickly was an ending to the poem "Ten, Twenty, Thirty, Forty." I struggled with this poem all week and hashed it over thoroughly at the afternoon writing center in conference with Mike Bacon. But I couldn't figure out how to end it. The poem itself is sort of a fun/sad statement about the significant impact the early forties have had on my body—the deterioration has caught me off guard somehow and seems to be happening without my consent.

The ending came as a result of ideas discussed in Gloria Nixon-John's poetry workshop about the feminine perspective, how important it is and how it needs to be stated when and if it's clearly a part of our thoughts. Well, Mike had suggested earlier Wednesday that I needn't refer to Chronos in my poem as the God of Time—that's a given. Good point. Then I was talking about Chronos toying with me and Mike suggested I refer to him as Kid Chronos. I wrote the suggestion down, but told Mike I disliked it because it sounded like a boxing image to me.

Well, I took these two ideas home—stared at the poem and continued to juxtapose the boxing image of Kid Chronos and the idea that this poem really is done for other 40-year-old women. The following solution came leaping out of my pen when I had finally focused on my audience:

> *What Chronos doesn't know*
> > *rapidly changing*
> *Is how the* ^ *image* ~~sm~~
> > > knows me intimately, w
> *Smiles back at me,* ~~the~~ *kindness and compassion*
> *A sort of*
> > ~~The~~ *big sister I never had*
> > > *se*
> *Who*^ ~~knows~~ *wisdom and serenity*
> *Remain*
> ~~Are~~ *unmarred by mere physical frailties*~~y~~*.*

—Liz Webb

WRITING FAIR

Ten, Twenty, Thirty, Forty
Liz Webb

My Bod
Comes to a carefully kept appointment
With Chronos, who,
Discovering the remote control,
Fast forwards me through my early forties,
And laughs,
As eyebrows that used to be plucked in graceful arches
Grow bushy,
And eyes go without eyeliner
Because tri-focals now reside in the area,
And without the specs,
Eyebrows to be plucked,
Lids to be lined
Books to be read,
Music to be played,
Recipes to be concocted
And junk mail to be discarded,
All blur;
White crow's feet
Track across my summer tan;
A receding gum line exposes tooth roots
Who beg for Sensodyne;
Nape moles mushroom;
Tendonitis weakens a forearm
Aching to play tennis;
Liver spots creep darkly onto my hands;
The sun reflects someone else's shadow,
Thicker than mine;
A spastic colon gets so nervous
At the mention of a Prime Rib Special,
It shudders;
And a recurring yeast infection
Requires delicate medical attention
While a ripening libido
Craves a little rowdiness

His laughter
Echoes through the halls of the athletic complex,
Howls from my morning mirror,
And startles me in store windows.

▶

Should I stop going to the athletic complex,
Should I drape my mirror?
Should I throw a tire through the store window?

What the kid in Chronos can't know
Is how the rapidly changing image
Smiles back at me,
Knows me intimately
A sort of big-sister-I-never-had
Whose wisdom and serenity
Remain unmarred
By mere physical frailties.

The Bee Watcher

Laurie C. Kavanagh

I am the bee watcher
while they hunch over and
scribble vocabulary tests.

The crisp, warm September
day and perfumed bodies stir
the bees, lure them into
my classroom. I

stand guard over
the nervous and allergic, papers
harboring poems, folded
in my hand.

Just the same the
honey bombers dive too low,
buzz their nectar fields. I,
keeper of tender blossoms,
swat them away.

It Hurts

Laura A. Wilson

I'm not sure I want to be a poet.
Poetry does things to you;
Things you can't control.
Poetry makes you ugly.
If my cosmetologist knew how many nights I've gone to bed

exhausted by revisions without three-step cleansing
she would make that face you see when you tell someone
your dog died.
Poetry is bad for your back.
Everywhere I went this week I carried my memories,
four hardbound school yearbooks, three scrapbooks,
two reunion booklets (ten and twenty) and
one unwritten epitaph.
Poetry pain makes your inside beautiful.
That's what really matters.
My mother's wisdom when she would gather and pull my hair
by my request into my favorite Pony Tail,
"It hurts to be beautiful."

---

rachel ritual
August 18, 1965
Carol N. Taylor

Frail frame planted on the couch
you sit arms folded,
mindlessly caressing your fragile arm.
Grasshopper eyes behind dense wire rims
frightened me as a child.

I study your face.
You've opened memory's gate—
hurried down a well-worn path,
to dwell in a favored place.

You chortle and cluck your way through—
lip-sync long dead conversations.
First with amusement , then alarm,
I watch the ghostly mimic.

I'm losing you.

A child's balloon,
you drift in summer mind clouds.
I briefly stop your private play.
Rachel past becomes Grandma present.

"What are you thinking about?"
"It's your birthday. Here's five dollars.
Buy yourself some warm socks."

▶

The Auction

Susan M. Wolfe

Staring out over strange and familiar heads
With faces blurred and barely there
They meander about the pear tree, barn and boxes.

Rusted horseshoe on the granary wall
Turned over with the luck running out
Guinea hens cackling with every bid.

Spring air coming in gently
Over the last remaining snow
Inhale deeply and hold . . .

Going
Going
Gone.

5 Shape, Sound, Form: Crafts from Which to Sing a Poem

Anne-Marie Oomen
Lake Forest Academy, Illinois

Ruth Nathan
Consultant, Novato, California

Log Entry

What an experience this week promises to be! I like to write—or I guess it would be more accurate to say that I play with and at writing. I can't squeeze out the time to be serious about it at this point. Between teaching school full-time and working on a master's program part-time, there's precious little time left for me to do anything else. But my day will come.

I write with my students when they are writing, but that is a different type of writing. It's usually limited to a 50-minute time period because I never get the time to revise a piece. By the time I could do that, I have thirty others needing my attention and my own writing just sits there to be considered at some later point.

So it's with mixed feelings that I face this week. I'm excited about finally getting a chance to work on writing of my own. And the sessions that have been described sound great! But I'm as nervous as my own student writers about having to present my own writing for group sharing and critique. The fact that we're ALL English teachers only makes matters worse, I think. It makes me feel that even rough drafts need to be pretty perfect. I expect that somewhere along the line in all this, I'm going to experience again what my students feel like when I say "Okay, let's put the chairs in a circle and share some of the work we did yesterday. Who'd like to volunteer?"

—**Diana Smith**

Teach poetry? We don't think we teach poetry. Rather, we may teach some things about poetry—to trust our writing to give us ideas for poems, to give ourselves pleasure by understanding shape, sound, and form as it functions in poetry, to observe and emulate good poetic work. These are the things we can teach. Maybe. What we know for certain is that we teach *poets*, that is, any person (student or teacher, ourselves included) who is ready to enjoy the taste of words as much as the taste of food. In this case, "we" are fifteen teachers and writers and two practicers of poetry who have come together at the Traverse Bay Summer Workshops. We start, that first morning, with writing—not poetry—just writing.

Three Kinds of Journals

We start poetry with journals because they give us raw, unstructured grist and because they are familiar. They also generate a lot of writing, the kind we need to make poetry. Depending on the type of journal writing, journals teach us to observe, help us find our place or setting, and center on the senses—all characteristics of good writing.

Our teacher-writers begin with "Focus Outward" journals, which Ruth learned from Donald Graves. This written observation consists of ten minutes of writing about anything happening around us in the here and now. Before they write, we note the difference between observation ("I see a willow tree.") and inference ("It's an intense tree.") or evaluation ("It's a good tree.") and we encourage them to practice observing in journals. However, even though each writer begins by focusing on observation, the writing can lead anywhere. A Focus Outward journal entry forces us to start with sensation, and it gives us pleasure because we are involved in the act of creation on its simplest and most accessible terms, by recreating with words. As we share these first entries, as we would do with our own students, we are always surprised at the variety. Here we are, all present in the same room, hearing the same sounds and breathing the same air. But our individual recordings reveal rich differences. By practicing this kind of observation, our world gets bigger with detail and we become more aware of how we sense it.

After that, we teach Focus Inward. Instead of present external experience, we focus inward on memory of a past experience. We ask our teacher-students to brainstorm: "List experiences which you understand now but didn't understand when they happened." Then we share them because we know one memory will trigger another. When I say "first kiss," someone says "first car." Then someone says "first time," and everyone bends to their list with a smirk. We encourage them to borrow ideas from each other because we know that no one will write any memory in exactly the same way. People enjoy this warm-up list because they get ideas from each other—a simple pleasure which fosters trust. Then we ask our students to choose one they like and write as much as they can remember about it in ten minutes. We reassure them that often the writing itself will trigger details about events.

This Focus Inward journal also focuses on observation but adds reflection, meaning. What is it that we know now that we didn't once? And why? This writing is good preparation for poetry because it will cross the line into the abstract but remain anchored in experience. Whether we know it or not, we are avoiding one of the weaknesses inexperienced poets often give in to—the Overwhelming Abstract. It's also a rich journal experience because we often need to discover what we have actually learned, and this writing may give it to us.

The last journal we teach is one we playfully call Focus 2001. Anne-Marie brings her hat collection and we try them on, trading until we each find one we like. Anne-Marie puts on several hats, reciting a poem with each hat. Each time she says the name of a person she imagines wearing the hat, a person she imagines speaking in the poem. Then our writers invent the names of the people who wore their hats. They may write about the invented person or they may write in the invented person's voice. We ask them to put this person in a setting: time and place. They may write about an event which happened to that person or an introductory biography or whatever the hat triggers. Focus 2001 is simply a journal which uses an object as a starter for inventing a character. The object could be anything from gloves to rocks, but we think hats are the most fun.

The purpose of this journal is invention. What we have learned over years of writing is that the poet often writes from personal experience, in the confessional mode. But the poet can also write from an invented perspective, just as the fiction writer does. No poet is required to write from only his or her own experience. Sometimes this invented experience or character is better for new poets because they are more free from themselves. The writers simply ask, "Who wore this?" "Who made this?" or "Who held this in her hands?" And they write. For example, one of the hats in the collection triggered these lines, excerpts from a long poem titled "Love" by Suzanne Dodge:

> Beatrice was a wife.
> Weekdays she
> mashed potatoes,
> stirred gravy.
> Half past eleven,
> "Ready for Grandpa."

Home for lunch
exactly at noon.
"My mechanic from the
Ford dealership on
Huron Street."

Eventually Suzanne discovered that the poem was linked to her grandmother but it didn't begin with that awareness. The lines came at first from simple invention. She was making it up. That is the charm and justification for Focus 2001.

Sharing Leads to Line Breaks

We move to reading our favorite poems, coffee in hand. From Shakespeare to Allen Ginsberg to the Language Poets, we share. Our workshop students have brought their own to read and many times they know one or two by heart; in the secondary classroom, we would assign students to track down poems or discover new ones from time to time. We share consistently through the week because we want them to be immersed in the shapes and sounds and forms of poems, and also because we want to trigger questions. Eventually someone asks, "What makes these poems?"

The answer, though not foolproof, is the most obvious: We identify poetry first by the way it is placed on the page—its shape. We go on to a simple demonstration. One of us writes the following sentence on the board: "The boy fell head over heels in love with the girl." We ask them to take this sentence and make three differently shaped poems from it. For example, one student writes:

The boy
fell
head over heels
in love
with the girl.

We talk about what the line breaks do and how they change emphasis. This first poem breaks lines following the natural rhythm of spoken language.

Another student shapes:

The boy fell
             head
                  over
                       heels
in love with
the girl.

This second version uses word arrangement to visually reinforce meaning.

A third writes:

The boy f
                e
                    l
                        l
head over heels
in love with the girl.

Here, shape may actually create meaning because the word "fell" breaks into its individual letters which fall on the page. Because shape hits the eye first, the gesture of the letters makes meaning as well as the word.

Our students begin to look at the opportunities of line breaks. With new awareness, we review poems we have read. We ask students to take any of their Focus Outward journal entries and shape them into something that looks like poems. It's not threatening; we're just playing. Here is how one student managed it:

> *What the Lake Said*
>
> Jan Mekula

Be Patient. Waves roll in
    and then recede again;
let go.
Be still: water waits
    and sand is silent. Listen.
Be.

In the shape of Jan's poem, our writers observe the action of waves. They also notice words which stand alone, "let go" and "be." The word "be" carries great weight in the poem because it is placed alone at the end. The poet created a crescendo at the end of the poem because of the way she shaped the words. Students don't have to know much about crafting a poem to see how her line breaks help a poem mean more.

The Way Poems Sound

A student will usually comment on the journal poem, "But this just looks like poetry; it isn't really a poem." Not yet, perhaps. What is missing are the other dimensions of poetry. How do we craft those? Anne-Marie introduces sound because sound is pleasurable and easy to observe. Ruth teaches people the names of the devices of sound: vocabulary opens eyes as much as exercises do. (Stephen Minot's chapter on

sound in *Three Genres* is a good resource.) We explain words like assonance, consonance, alliteration, onomatopoeia, and slant, imperfect,
and internal rhyme. We ask them to explore their journals for examples
which they have written, often by accident. We all listen together, discovering alliteration, assonance, or internal rhymes in our own writing.

For example, Jan Andre showed us these lines about beaches.

Water flutes the shore,
Suits pinch bottoms,
Rafts smooth waves . . .

She had written the assonant "ooo" sounds in *flutes, suits* (also internal rhyme), and *smooth*. Another teacher-writer pointed out how those
sounds make us say the words more slowly, just the way the lake
affects us.

To follow up, we give them a version of a classroom exercise that
can be done with any number of different poems to raise consciousness
about form and language—offering selections of words to choose from
in an attempt to complete existing poems. In a copy of Robert Frost's
"Spring Pools" with substitute words added, we ask them to make
selections among the alternatives with sound as well as meaning in
mind. For example, here are the first two lines: "These pools that,
though in forests, (still, yet) reflect // The (total, arching) sky almost
without defect . . ." The correct words are *still* and *total*. By the time
they have finished working through the other word choices in the
poem, students notice that sometimes the poet followed rules of sound,
sometimes he didn't. Sometimes they agree with his choices and sometimes they don't. Though the shapes and sounds are necessary to know,
the poet decides how and to what extent they are applied.

Day Two: Rhyme Time

By the end of the first day, our teacher-writers are attempting their
own poetry. If they have not written poetry before, which is often the
case, many of them will begin by trying to rhyme their poems. Rhyme
is what the new poet most often identifies as a characteristic of poetry
because it's a quick way for them to find the familiar. However, their
first comments about their own rhymed poems often reflect dissatis-
faction. They see quickly that they usually don't rhyme the same way
more experienced poets rhyme. One student stated it best when she
observed, "Mine sounds like a Hallmark card, but I thought I started
with something better than that." Using that kind of remark as a
springboard, we teach rhyme.

We explain that perfect end rhyme is not wrong, but it is often difficult because English is such a rhyme-poor language. We encourage both students who like rhyme and those who don't to try different kinds of rhyming devices and observe what happens. We look, for example, at lines like these by Marie Ponsot, "A dancing is a trance she takes. // Sweating cleanses." Most students quickly realize that internal rhyme (*dance* and *trance*) breaks the sing-song effect of the predictable end rhymes we use in verse—rhymes such as *moon* and *tune, car* and *bar, cow* and *now.* Finding fresh and interesting rhyme, avoiding cliché or overused rhyme, and varying rhythm are also ways to break the "versey" quality of rhymed poetry. Internal rhyme, slant rhyme, eye rhyme, masculine and feminine rhyme, and the devices of sound keep a poem's music but divert the reader (and the writer) from rhyme which dominates meaning. We encourage them to play with rhyme and rhyme scheme, but not to be bound by it.

The Beat Goes On

Usually the discussion of rhyme and rhyme scheme is inseparable from a discussion of rhythm. Sooner or later one discussion spills into the next. Rather than talk about rhythm in general ways, we do exactly what we did with sound. We give names: iamb, anapest, dactyl, trochee, and what we call the emphatic foot, a spondee—a good basic starting list. We love these names, but we also know that here many aspiring young poets stopped aspiring and started hating poetry.

So we ease our teacher-writers into this element the way we would in a secondary classroom, with a very simple exercise on the heroic couplet. This couplet holds a complete idea which is closed because the end rhyme finishes the idea. It's obvious in this one by Pope:

> Know nature's children all divide her care;
> The fur that warms the monarch, warmed a bear.

We ask them to count syllables (in the heroic couplet, ten to a line) and break them into beats (usually five iambs). They write an emulation first.

> My mother's clothing all got lots of care,
> what she did wear, we all did later share.

Even if the rhythm is not quite relaxed, the couplet is easily managed, because it's small enough to be non-threatening. Many people can follow the rhythm of iambic pentameter as soon as we tell them to clap the emphasis. Many elementary teachers are familiar with clapping rhythms because they use it to teach syllabication.

Then teacher-writers choose another journal entry and break it into ten-syllable lines, adjusting as necessary to get two lines. We discover buried rhythms and note where they revised for rhythm. The following lines are from Nancy Sypien's list poem of "Things Rory Left Behind":

> A big green top with no one to spin for,
> A blue blanket with no one to cover.

We listen to the rhythm. Other writers note the repetition of "with no one to," and how that repetition actually creates rhythm. We spend long minutes trying to discover the haunting emphasis in Jan Andre's lines, "He who had nothing, offered me kindness; // I who had much, returned nothing." We finally decide it comes from the pause, a caesura, in the second line which, because it forced us to break the rhythm, brought attention to that line, thus reinforcing meaning. This is the kind of discovery which moves teacher-writers into the pleasure of crafting poetry.

We ask everyone to write a few ten-syllable lines, leaving rhythm as an option, and we are always rewarded by teacher-students who didn't think they could do it but who listened trustingly and found they were able to create rhythm, or better still, found that they had used rhythm in their journals and transposed it to poem as in Laurie Cooper's lines, "My inward eye // in quiet times // reflections reveal // a myriad."

We play with rhythm—but not too much today. We let them know that traditional rhythm is one choice among many. We ask them to write some more poems, giving them optional starters like list poems and some patterns which are simple structured prompts. We ask two things: trust the information to surface in their work, and come back with observations on their own progress. They go to the lake to write.

Day Three: From Rhythm to Rhythm

On the third day, people return both ecstatic and frustrated because they hear differently. So do we. We applaud that realization and we teach another way of getting to rhythm which is not so technical but which is a fast and dramatic way of showing how we hear the sounds of language. We tell them rhythm works everywhere, in all kinds of writing. Anne-Marie reads a piece of good prose and points out rhythms. Ruth continues teaching about rhythm through a practice called "copychange." It's very similar to the couplet emulation exercise. She starts with a paragraph of prose. She writes it out on a sheet of lined paper, skipping every other line. In the lines between she writes in the same pattern, paralleling the syntax and using the same part of speech but changing the subject. Anne-Marie demonstrates with this sentence:

> The woman's name came to me after I had stared at the cat for about five minutes, staring without thinking at the puddle of cat on the rug.

Here is a copychange of that sentence:

> The tree's branch fell on me when I had laughed at the lawnboy for a week, laughing without caring at that lump of a lawnboy on the grass.

Here is an even more free example:

> The hat's feather dropped into her hand after she had been lost in the room for an hour, lost but looking hard for the feather from an ostrich she had never met.

We ask everyone to find a short passage and try a copychange. There is an immediate response. First, they feel the rhythms of the language better because they are separating rhythm from the original words. Second, their own ideas are triggered by the original rhythms. As ideas surface, they demand a rhythm different from the one they heard originally. It's a brief and dramatic demonstration that each of us does hear rhythm and can create and recreate it.

Once again, we pass out collections of poetry and favorite books of poetic prose. Louise Erdrich, Toni Morrison, Annie Dillard, and Ernest Hemingway are good examples of prose writers with a strong sense of rhythm. We send our teacher-writers to the lake or woods, asking them to try copychange or to simply write again with more trust and pleasure in rhythm and sound. We don't drill, because we suspect poets find their way to the elements when they need to. It's enough to expose them to the ideas behind rhythm, give them demonstrations of what the language is doing, and let them stamp their feet and clap their hands. On this day, when our teacher-writers return to the center, we make fast copies of poems and run a workshop for the last part of the day. What is most wonderful about this day is the way even the first drafts have changed from the first day.

Day Four: The Way a Poem Thinks

We move from shape to sound and finally to form. Learning about form is both difficult and rewarding. At first, form may seem confining, a series of structured lines, but we also know there is pleasure in understanding how form shapes and inspires an idea.

For this now very daring group, we choose carefully from dozens of poetic forms. Our goal is not merely to give a working knowledge of a particular form; we hope to show how form works to shape sense. We chose the haiku (Hokku), not because it is easy (it is, in fact, hard to do well), but because at Traverse Bay we are surrounded by nature, in the middle of a small woods, only a block from the bay. The haiku is often about nature or seasons, and in June, when teachers often rediscover being outdoors, the haiku is a natural form.

We read haiku, passing them around, sharing our favorites, relying on our ears to pick up the rhythm and sound. We explain there are gaps in the Haiku—a turn, change, realization which (in the English form) usually occurs between the second and third line. We choose a subject—fireflies. We ask teacher-students to write the word in the center of a sheet of paper and surround it with words or phrases which describe it. We collect all the descriptions, write them on the board, count syllables, change phrases, and listen for the right sounds. Here's one we invented:

> Twilight firefly
> Captured in a mason jar
> Pulsating spaceship

A student says, "That 'pulsating spaceship' is like punctuation for the idea described in the first two lines. That's the turn." A good description, "punctuation words." We look for this same feeling in other haiku. Then we invite our students to write. We warm our coffee and do the same. Fifteen minutes later we have haiku coming out of our ears. Here is an example from Nancy Sypien which shows the rhythm break, the gap between the first and second line:

> Blinking snapping light
> Captured in the woods at night
> Lightning in a jar!

The "haikia" is part of a longer poem often written by several poets. This collaborative tradition is perfect for us. We teach the tanka (two lines of seven syllables) and we offer students an opportunity to write the ryenga, a cycle of alternating haiku and tanka. They do as the Japanese would have done, passing on sheets of paper and responding to the previous writing. Because the haiku must "say what it sees," we share a lively hour which introduces a delightful form and re-establishes our focus on imagery.

The Leap!

We continue to encourage our writers to see how form and idea are linked, how form can shape idea. We teach the sonnet, basing our teaching on the connection between sonnet and haiku. We remind them of the haiku's two parts and we claim something similar occurs in the Italian sonnet. We make a chart which traces the rhyme scheme, rhythm pattern, and stanza breakdown for a traditional Italian sonnet, sometimes called the Petrarchan Sonnet. We explain that traditional Italian sonnets have fourteen lines in rhymed verse. The traditional subjects of the sonnet are love, death, and time, but modern sonneteers have used many others.

However, the important part to remember is the two-part structure: the octave and the sextet. The eight lines (octave) describe a problem, a conflict, or an idea that needs a comment. The sextet, the remaining six lines, offers that comment or solution or solves the problem. The sonnet loosely parallels the haiku in this way: In each case the first part sets up the situation, whether it be about nature or love. The second part offers our minds a different direction—a surprise, an answer, an insight to whatever question the first octave poses. The class listens closely, understanding both forms better because of this parallel.

We look in our journals for ideas which seem to be asking for a form, perhaps the sonnet, perhaps the haiku, perhaps something else. Here are some observations: "The entries I made on the first day in focus outward all lend themselves to haiku, they all describe and then describe some more"; "I was writing about getting older and my dad seeming to get younger. I think it would make a humorous sonnet, two parts like opposites." And then: "What do you do when you have an idea that's more than two parts?" This is a question we have been waiting for because it tells us that the writers are looking for form as an integral part of expression. They see form functioning in the craft of the poem.

To answer that specific question, we introduce the Elizabethan sonnet, which also has fourteen lines, but this poem thinks in three quatrains and a couplet. In the Elizabethan sonnet, the three different verses often explore the three different aspects of a problem or idea.

Or, in each verse, an idea is advanced. The couplet concludes, resolves, or comments on the idea. In a way this sonnet follows the patterns of the old three point-essay, with the couplet paralleling a conclusion.

We challenge them to try form, to look at their ideas and see how form makes idea sensible. One teacher-writer who does not want to write a sonnet says, "I didn't know form shows the way a poem thinks." That's all we need to hear. We wanted them to see how form and idea are linked, how writers may find pleasure in shaping idea—that form may even give meaning to an idea. We tell them they don't have to follow all the rules, but to write freely, being aware of form.

Day Five: Publishing the Trust

After sonnets, we turn to publishing. We talk about being poets—what poets are, how we all can be poets, and how it is often craft which separates the accomplished poet (whether student or teacher) from the unaccomplished poet. We believe the art of poetry is choosing the subject, the craft is choosing the shape, sound, and form—knowing the techniques that make a poem. What we are teaching is the craft of poetry, how to handle the idea. But what we believe is that everyone has the poetic thought, even when they are the small thoughts of every day: leaving the house to go to school, watching the lake, performing a household chore, arguing with another person—activities to which both students and teachers can respond.

On our last day we reflect as we prepare to publish our anthology and participate in the final presentation, the writing fair, with the other groups of writers. We have returned to the pleasure principle, creating a new whole of the work we have done through the week. We take our poems to the fair.

References

Behn, Robin, and Chase Twichell, eds. *The Practice of Poetry: Writing Exercises from Poets Who Teach.* New York: Harper Perennial, 1992.

Frost, Robert. "Spring Pools." *The Poetry of Robert Frost.* Ed. Edward Connery Latham. New York: Henry Holt and Co., 1979.

Koch, Kenneth. *Wishes, Lies, and Dreams: Teaching Children to Write Poetry.* New York: Vintage, 1971.

Minot, Stephen. *Three Genres: The Writing of Fiction, Poetry, and Drama.* Englewood Cliffs, NJ: Prentice-Hall, 1965.

Ponsot, Marie. "Curandera," *The Green Dark.* New York: Knopf, 1981. 45.

Applications in the Classroom

Shape, Sound, Form: Crafts from Which to Sing a Poem

■ Show students how to review their journals for poetic material. Teach the journals—Focus Outward, Focus Inward, Focus 2001—as starters for poetic ideas.

■ Write a sentence on the board and show how to create line breaks by following the natural rhythm of the voice. Then ask students to break the sentence in different ways to demonstrate free verse rhythms. Discuss.

■ Identify devices of sound in your students' poetry. Ask them to find additional examples in each other's work.

■ Copychange a favorite poem. Ask students to select a poem of their own to copychange. Encourage breaking away at some point.

■ Assist students in observing fresh and unusual ways to use rhyme by pointing out internal rhyme and imperfect rhyme. Invite them to find it in their own poetry.

■ Adapt a journal entry into blank verse by shaping the entry into ten-syllable lines. Assist students in identifying rhythm by teaching them to clap (or snap) the emphasis.

■ Research the library media center for poetry. Ask students to bring poems they like and make observations about the poems. Assist students in naming various poetic devices.

■ Review the poem starters in Kenneth Koch's *Wishes, Lies and Dreams* or *The Practice of Poetry,* edited by Robin Behn and Chase Twitchell.

■ Create poems inspired by literature students have read by assuming a character, describing an incident, exploring an insight.

■ Provide some of your favorite poems, and talk about what you like.

■ Invite a local poet to come and read his or her works with your students.

■ Publish students' work by getting it on a "communal disk" and create a chapbook that will be published in the classroom.

Log Entry

Often the best thing about classes, workshops, and conferences is the people we meet. We go to these educational meccas for varying reasons: certification, general interest, to get away from the family for a few days, or to renew ourselves personally. Ultimately we all go away renewed and refreshed. What we come away with is a pile of handouts, wonder-

▶

ful ideas, and goals we'll never find the time to meet. But we will go away reassured that we don't walk alone, don't suffer alone, don't struggle in isolation. We'll be reassured that others suffer the same sorrow and frustration with those kids that can't be reached. We'll be reassured that administrators everywhere are either ignorant or senile or both. We'll have shared the joy of realizing that the Class of '91 was an outstanding group, not just in our own schools, but across the country. It must have been something in the air or water when they were born. We'll feel good about our schools because things are inevitably worse in some other school. Yet we'll harbor a lingering jealousy over that district that seems to have everything that we don't. Essentially we'll come away with memories of friends we'll never see again.

—Katherine Steinbring

WRITING FAIR

Choices
Nancy E. Dean

She stood before the bureau.
Her long thin fingers brushed against the purple gloves
as they reached for the hat.

Sturdy
black felt.
No gaudy veil to flutter in her eyes!
Starched
black lace her only compromise.
Narrow
band of ridged braid lent this crowning glory a regal air.

It
WAS
the perfect choice.

Her long thin fingers touched the purple gloves as she grasped
the sharp, black-beaded pin.
She worked methodically, quickly securing the cap of black to the
smooth brown form.

▶

Her long thin fingers rubbed against the purple gloves as she
clutched the narrow pearl-handled mirror.
Methodically, quickly, she examined her work.
The corners of her lips revealing a pleased feeling.

Her long thin fingers stroked the purple gloves

One
Last
Time.

She turned quickly, methodically.
She WAS NOT,
after all,
a purple-gloved woman.

Poem Rider
Jeanie Mortensen

At certain
Satin moments
Fragments whirl
Like plaster ponies
Fierce and fine;

Silver-haltered images
Flash, blur, reappear
Like high stepping
Air dancers;

Rhythmic phrases
Of unspeakable precision
Nearly connect
In palpable
Prance patterns
Amidst the tangled
Jangle
Of round organ notes;

Lean lines,
Snorting and fire-full,

Propel me,
Carousel me,
Windblown and breathless,
Toward another
Brass ring.

Faux Pas

Barbara J. Rebbeck

Back then,
my French teacher
would tell us the story
of her immigrant mother
who walked around
with her head all cluttered
with the debris of two languages.
(One as easy as the smell of bread
rising through Paris streets at dawn;
the other lost like tourists in front
of bakery girls, stuttering out an order.)
This simple peasant read things all wrong.
A "For Sale" sign
warned her "very dirty."
At sixteen, we all laughed
and went on with our verbs.

But yesterday at the bookstore,
I saw volumes of someone's poetry
piled high on two outside tables,
not even saved from a raw March day.
I looked down and saw that old Lady's
"For Sale."
Some dirty trick.
Some poet's life,
marked down,
pages flipping in the wind.

6 What We Talk About When We Talk About Writing Fiction

John Smolens
Michigan State University

Log Entry

The first morning session with Smolens was very interesting. He paired us off, and we blindfolded our partners, then led them around the picnic tables and trees, while holding their hands. We placed a stone or a twig in their hands and had them touch trees and this Calder-inspired metal piece of not-art. It was interesting to feel the texture of the ground, which I hadn't noticed while sighted. Sounds and other senses were more intense. The exercise was also fun because it caused us to break down the barriers between us and made it easier to work together. We then wrote two short freewrites and then a longer piece after our break, which we then responded to with our partners. . . . In the Writing Center John slashed the jeans piece and offered some good criticism: customized culture, recycled jeans, and other ideas. We talked about using third or first persona and the advantages of each.

—**Tom Watson**

Setting a Direction

The term "short story" derives from the reader's perception, for although a story may indeed be brief, in many cases a matter of only a few pages, it is seldom the product of brief effort. Most story writers take a remarkable amount of time to finish one short story; often hundreds of hours are devoted to a work of fiction that is only a few thousand words long. The exception is someone like Hemingway, who wrote three of his earlier stories in one day; most fiction writers require not only numerous drafts but also considerable gestation periods to resolve the various questions that each composition raises. It is not uncommon for a story to take months, even years, to complete. In an average school semester even the best students should expect to finish no more than three or four stories; even the most modest accomplishments in classrooms take weeks. Thus I had no expectation that the members of my Traverse Bay Workshop would complete a story in the five days we worked together. My goal was to help them get started; if they left Traverse Bay with a clear sense of direction, I felt the workshop would have been successful.

I begin with the assumption that they feel they have a story to tell—where these impulses to create a story come from cannot, and possibly should not, be identified, for there is a certain mysterious quality, an unknown factor, in story telling; it has its own quiet, its own dark, its own voice, and to function properly it is better left alone, not to be tampered with by the meddling hands of analysis. That assumption made, I wanted my workshop to consider three issues that in my experience fiction writers at secondary, college, and post-college levels must address when they begin the process of writing a story— point of view, voice, and structure. When I was a boy attending parochial school in Greater Boston, the Sisters of Charity had a very simple formula for what a story was—character, plot, and setting—but that, to some extent, applies more to the final result. At the beginning, when a story is just a notion in the writer's mind, things such as character, plot, and setting cannot become reality (fictional reality: on the page) until the questions of point of view, voice, and structure are considered. That's what I hoped we'd accomplish at Traverse Bay.

Preparation

Because we really only had four days for the workshop (the final day, Friday, being devoted to the Fair), extended conversation about the readings wasn't part of my plan; however, at times we need examples to refer to as a means of illustrating a point. I made up a packet which included three short stories that serve, among other things, as examples of different uses of voice and point of view.

- "The Fat Girl," by Andre Dubus, provides an example of third-person narrative that succeeds in not just relaying the exterior of the main character's life, but delicately peels back the superficial layers to expose her interior life.

- "Snow," by John Smolens, is a story which, I hope, is told in the believable voice of a former high school basketball player. Selecting voice is one of the unique aspects of writing—we can mimic, imitate, brag, lie, sing in a way that we often can't in daily conversation— and when the voice in a story is successful, it's usually because the writer has fully realized it, has clearly come to terms with its limits.

- "City of Boys," by Beth Nugent, is marvelous to read for any number of reasons, but students always want to talk about the language, which is so alive, unique, spirited. It's the kind of story that says *Break free—write something different, quick, and passionate.*

I also included the following:

- "An Interview with Allan Gurganus," by Anne Bowling. *The Oldest Living Confederate Widow Tells All* had recently been published to outstanding reviews, and I used Gurganus' interview with Anne Bowling to emphasize the notion that success in fiction writing requires patience, nerve, discipline, and a kind of grace. Mr. Gurganus talks about the thirteen years of "preparing the tools and honing my skills" before the idea for his 720-page novel struck.

- Excerpts from *The Writing Life,* by Annie Dillard. *The Writing Life* is a poem written to prose writers. In the opening pages Annie Dillard talks about writing from within; I know of no other book on writing that comes close to what she does. In that slender volume there's a quiet, centered voice that every writer has heard at some point. She seems to have listened to it long and hard, and managed to record it for the rest of us. There are so many fine images, such as how she came to understand splitting wood, which was a matter of thinking the axe blade through the log to the block. And she gets at the heart of the matter through anecdotes such as the following:

    A well-known writer got collared by a university student who asked, "Do you think I could be a writer?"
    "Well," the writer said, "I don't know. . . . Do you like sentences?"
    The writer could see the student's amazement. Sentences? Do I like sentences? If he had liked sentences, of course, he could begin, like a joyful painter I knew. I asked him how he came to be a painter. He said, "I liked the smell of paint." (70)

Day One

A fiction workshop comprised of teachers presents a unique problem: They are already accomplished writers who are well-versed in literature. In my Traverse Bay writers' group we had teachers from elementary up through high school; they had devoted their careers to literature—children's literature, English literature, American literature—and it meant that they were coming to this workshop with a lot of experience. Not surprisingly, some of the workshoppers brought samples of their fiction with them to Traverse Bay. Two women had been writing and illustrating children's literature, and one man had been writing short stories. Some of the others, on the other hand, claimed to have never attempted to write fiction and seemed quite naturally afraid of the idea.

We went outside, finding a pleasant, secluded section of campus that had a number of picnic tables under some oaks and maples. Our first session started out with conversation. These people knew all too well that a period of introduction is necessary in all classes. We talked about where we were from, using the traditional pocket map of Michigan's lower peninsula (the palm of the right hand) to locate home towns; we talked about families, about our students, about what we taught, about what we liked to read. We were honing in, and after about an hour they seemed ready—and a bit nervous. Asking people to write is one thing, but asking them to write fiction is something else. There's a unique risk involved in creating a character, a scene, telling a story, and they fully appreciated the presence of that risk.

I asked that they find a comfortable spot and work in their notebooks for the next hour or so. As for prompts, I merely suggested the following: start with a scene; use first or third person; take it from your own experience; don't feel constrained by accuracy; you may *lie through your teeth*—which came as a relief to some. Focus on a particular moment in a character's life: the place, the concerns, the internal voice of the character at that moment. Rather than length—number of words—I told them to think in terms of writing for a particular length of time. I often do this with students; as these teachers all knew, the first question students ask when a paper is assigned is "How long?" I always respond by saying that length has nothing to do with quality. I try and redirect this natural concern and ask them to write for specific periods of time. I asked this group of teachers to write for an hour and a half; then we would reconvene to discuss what we had gotten down on paper.

We spread out, some seeking one of the picnic tables in the sun, others sitting on the ground with their backs against a tree trunk. Within minutes I looked up from my own notebook and saw all six of them bent to their task.

About an hour and twenty minutes later, I asked them to wind down in their writing. When we gathered at one of the picnic tables some of them were breathless, as though they'd been running a race. We spent the remainder of the morning session talking about what we had written, where we had started, why we thought we could start there. One member of the workshop, Ellen, was writing about a woman named Marie who was attending her grandfather's funeral. We talked in particular about how well the details set the tone in the first few paragraphs, which described driving to the service.

When we only had a few minutes left I read to them the opening paragraphs of the three stories in our packet:

> *from* "The Fat Girl"
>
> Her name was Louise. Once when she was sixteen a boy kissed her at a barbecue; he was drunk and he jammed his tongue into her mouth and ran his hands up and down her hips. Her father kissed her often. He was thin and kind and she could see in his eyes when he looked at her the lights of love and pity. (Dubus 233)
>
> *from* "Snow"
>
> When I was in high school, I was blind for a day. The program was called Helping Hand, and in preparation for the arrival of several blind students the other volunteers and I had to spend one entire school day blindfolded. From homeroom through all seven class periods we had to keep the blindfold on and get around school without anyone's assistance. After being blindfolded, each of us was given a cane. (61–62)
>
> *from* "City of Boys"
>
> My little sweetheart, she says, bringing her face close enough for me to see the fine net of lines that carves her skin into a weathered stone. You love me, don't you, little sweetheart, little lamb?
>
> Whether or not she listens anymore, I am not sure, but I always answer yes, yes I always say, yes, I love you.
>
> She is my mother, my father, my sister, brother, cousin, lover; she is everything I ever thought any one person needed in the world. She is everything but a boy.
>
> —Boys, she tells me. Boys will only break you. (Nugent 3–4)

When I finished reading and looked about, it seemed as though they were in a trance, and as we ended that first session they appeared lifted up by what they had written and by what they could write.

Day Two

The second day we met outside again—another beautiful day—and after only a brief period of discussion, we spread out and got to work. They seemed eager to get to their notebooks; some said they had done work overnight.

After the first hour of solitude, I asked that we pair off and that each couple exchange what they had written. As I walked around and listened in on conversations I heard them talking about characters, scenes, sources for stories, turns of phrase. What was most striking was how excited and nervous some of them seemed. Though they were experienced teachers who had frequently created classroom situations similar to what we were doing here, they seemed to be carried along on a kind of natural high of discovery. Having their partner laugh at a line they'd written or nod at a passage of description seemed only to fuel their enthusiasm. This was particularly true for those who had never attempted to write fiction before, and when we got together as a group for a wrap-up discussion, they talked first about how good this all made them feel and how their partners' responses had given them all sorts of new ideas.

I asked them to take several minutes to write to their partners, explaining how they felt about the fiction they'd read: where they thought it was going, how they felt about the characters and the language. I asked them to consider three questions:

- Who is telling this story? Describe how the point of view affects you as a reader.
- Does the language suggest a clear, distinct, consistent voice?
- Though it's unfinished, can you summarize the story thus far?

After exchanging these notes we discussed "The Fat Girl"; we discussed how fiction sets boundaries, in this case the life of a young woman who was overweight and had long had the secret habit of eating candy bars. The workshoppers began to apply this to what they were doing: they talked about how they could keep their story in one clearly defined place (though not only in the physical sense), and that there wasn't the need for such a host of characters. The first two scenes in Ellen's story, for example, moved from a funeral to Marie's grandparents' house, yet in both she evoked a small town in Michigan. I tried to emphasize something that the novelist John Yount used to stress when I was working with him in the graduate program at the University of New Hampshire: fiction writing is a process of elimination—of determining the 90% that you can't or shouldn't write—and then doing the remaining 10% as well as you can.

During the last portion of the class, I asked them to experiment, to take a passage from what they had written so far and rewrite it in another person—first to third, third to first. For some of the workshoppers who had never written a short story before, and who had quite naturally started by writing about a personal experience in the first person, it was a revelation to see what simply shifting to the third person can do. Inherent in the third person narrative is a greater sense of authority, and we talked about the sense of distance third person provides, how it allows the writer to take more control over the events, to place a character (previously the narrator) in a larger context.

Day Three

The following day, we began with a discussion of another story I'd asked them to read. "City of Boys," by Beth Nugent, is, among other things, a splendid exercise in voice. It led us to a discussion of our characters' voices. Everyone claimed they could "hear" their characters. Thus I asked them to begin the day's writing session on a fresh page in their notebooks; I asked them to write in the voice of one of their main characters. They did so for about a half an hour; then we read them aloud to each other. There were grandmothers and teachers and grocers and town ministers; there were accents, and there were anecdotes told in voices quite different from that of the author.

Time to work alone: I asked them to go over what they had written in their stories thus far, revising for voice. When we reconvened about an hour later, I asked them to share their revisions with the partner they'd worked with the day before. From their conversations it seemed they had all discovered that several voices can be used in a piece of fiction, that the narrative voice may be quite different from the characters' dialogue, or that a first-person narrative may be told in a very distinctive voice. For example, in "City of Boys," there is a sentence that could only be from this particular narrator who creates a kind of sensual geographical landscape:

> Where I live now is also a city full of boys, and coming here I passed through hundreds of cities and they were all full of boys. (5)

In their own stories I wanted them to find such passages, sharpen them, build upon them. Voice tends to come and go in early drafts, much like a distant radio station on a car radio, fading in and out as you drive. By identifying where they had found voice, the workshoppers could consider exactly what they had done in those passages in terms of language, image, cadence, perception, then attempt to invest that voice throughout the story. Voice is something that often seeps into a work of fiction: the first signs may be a turn of phrase, or even something that is omitted from a line, causing it to toy with the reader's expectations. The writer must recognize that unique voice, *hear* it, in order to use it throughout the story.

Day Four

Thursday it rained, which was convenient because it allowed us to use a classroom in the arts building, where we'd have access to a chalkboard. For the first hour the workshoppers paired off again, though finding new partners to read their stories. When we reconvened I started by talking about structure. I suggested that it would be helpful to block out the stories, so the writers could see what they had in this first typed draft (like my undergraduates, they all claimed they could see so many things in their writing once it was typed). I asked for a volunteer—someone who would "block out" their partner's story. Jill volunteered to do Ellen's story. I drew a large block on the board and asked what the first "movement" of the story was—a word I used because I didn't want to suggest that this blocking process was only a matter of counting scenes.

Jill had determined that there were essentially four blocks in Ellen's story:

> block 1: Drive to the funeral
> Main character Marie; driving with husband and children to funeral
>
> block 2: Funeral service for grandfather
> a) flashback #1—Marie (age 12) and grandfather fishing on Lake Michigan
> b) After the funeral—family and friends gather at grandmother's house for a sumptuous meal
> c) flashback #2: recollections of Marie's wedding day, which took place in yard of grandparents (grandfather gave her away in ceremony because her father had died when she was very young)
> d) Leaving grandmother, who gives Marie a package
>
> block 3: Grandfather's gift
> Some days later and Marie's life is beginning to get back to "normal." She finally decides to open the package, which is from her grandfather. It contains a series of letters her father wrote him while he was in the service during World War II, photographs of her father and grandfather, and a newspaper clipping about her father's death in the war.

block 4: Marie walking in woods
Later that day, Marie is walking in the woods with her children, feeling a new kind of grief—for her father, whom she didn't know at all, and a kind of acceptance and joy because she realized her grandfather was giving her something she'd always been missing.

We discussed the story's structure, particularly the funeral scene with the two flashbacks, and why they all formed one "movement" belonging in one structural block.

Then I asked each of them to block out their partner's drafts and explain how they saw the story's structure. When writing a first draft we tend to get lost in the telling of a story, giving little thought to development and proportion. I never encourage students to write an outline before starting a story (I never discourage it either). Instead, I suggest that once a draft has been written, to block it out to see what you've got. It's remarkable how many problems can be revealed—the kinds of problems, such as chronology, repetition, and inconsistency, that would give readers trouble. Blocking out stories gives a workshop something concrete other than the draft itself; one draft blocked out on a chalkboard usually asks everyone to think about their story from *outside* its telling.

Day Five

Friday: The Writing Fair. For their presentation my workshop decided to read each other's fiction to the audience. It helped ease the tension of reading one's own work to an audience, and it was interesting how each reader attempted to interpret the voices in the stories.

Reading each other's stories aloud was an extraordinary conclusion to our week together. Too much of what we do as writers is solitary. We need a certain amount of isolation, of course, but unlike many other artistic pursuits, writers rarely seem really comfortable in a community of their peers. We write alone. We usually read alone. We rarely hear what our readers think. I have often envied musicians for their sense of community. A composer must, of course, have solitude to write new pieces, but often the ideas derive from sessions with other musicians. And then there's simply the joy of playing together, of several musicians playing different instruments—piano, bass, drums, guitar, horn—but in a way that the audience will come to appreciate the expression of each performer, as well as the unity of the whole group. On Friday our workshop read as though they were a group of musicians, and the result was inspiring, harmonic, humorous, and downright pretty. It even had a good beat.

References

Bowling, Anne. "Interview with Allan Gurganus." *Novel and Short Story Writer's Market '91*. Cincinnati: Writer's Digest Books, 1991.

Dillard, Annie. *The Writing Life*. New York: Harper & Row, 1989.

Dubus, Andre. "The Fat Girl." *Selected Stories*. Boston: D. R. Godine, 1988. 233–47.

Nugent, Beth. "City of Boys." *City of Boys*. New York: Alfred A. Knopf, 1992. 3–21.

Smolens, John. "Snow." *Yankee*, January 1989. 61–63, 108–9, 111–12.

Applications in the Classroom

Blocking Out a Story

■ As a classroom activity, blocking out a story works well when conducted in pairs.

■ Swap a draft of a story with a partner; read; develop a sketch of the story's movement in terms of connected blocks. Each block should contain a short phrase, the equivalent of a subtitle, describing the essence of that portion of the story.

■ *Show & Tell*. Each student will show the sketch to the rest of the workshop (who have not yet read the draft), and tell them the story and why there are so many movements.

■ The telling of another's story (without assistance from the author, even if they must be tied and gagged in the corner) to an impartial audience can be an illuminating experience for a writer. The author will learn how clearly the intended movement of the story got through in the present draft. Often the author will be told that there is a stronger sense of structure where she had not yet seen it.

■ Ask the author to respond to the sketch and description of the draft, to offer explanation, to ask questions.

■ Ask the workshop to keep a writing journal, where they address what they're trying to do in the stories they're writing. Part of this journal should be devoted to blocking out the story, and discussing how its movement changes during the drafting process.

Log Entry

We workshopped my jeans piece in this morning's session. I received some excellent feedback, some that I can work into the piece. John's session is turning out to be very good. He's very subtle and sensitive to the feelings of the group. His is not as bold as some of the other sessions; yet, he achieves the same result, which is getting people involved in the craft of their writing. I'm looking forward to working with him this afternoon in the Writing Center. I wrote a rough draft of Eco Lottery, a story about when finally everyone in the USA has become a millionaire. It came from an idea I have been kicking around for a year or so. . . . Smolens and I talked more about the differences and similarities between the personal narrative and fiction. It's not so much a matter of voice or style, but rather that of technique. Simply said, fiction is more of "he said, she said" and movement of discernible characters. Maybe I can find a way to infuse my personal narratives, my strength, into a short story by letting them be the narrator's voice. This is what I'm trying to do with the Eco Lottery piece. So far, it has been slow going with the dialogue and easy going with the narrative part. What I need to do then is let one of the characters think and/or say the personal narrative stuff, except that some of it is pretty heavy. Maybe I'll try to do it the way Vonnegut does and let me be the narrator and have relatively weak characters act out the plot.

—Tom Watson

WRITING FAIR

Bell Bottom Blues

Tom Watson

Twenty-five years sneak up on you, like wearing a tight pair of jeans without underwear: callouses form on your ass, while you dance the decades away.

I remember standing in line for tickets for the Rolling Stones show, anticipating a night of getting my fair share of abuse. I was wearing my second favorite pair of jeans, as usual without underwear. I would be equipped with my number one, cool jeans for the show. But in line with the rest of the faithful, my Levi's were regulation tattered, broken in just right, so it didn't look like I had spent yesterday shopping at Sears. They were bell bottoms, of course, and the cuffs were a

▶

bit torn and frayed from dragging on the ground. For the show, I wore my flare bottoms, which had a higher rise and fit tighter below my knees. I didn't need any material flopping about my feet, while I was dancing or was compelled to make a quick getaway from the surging of the crowd.

I had gingham knee patches on the bell bottoms, stitched on haphazardly during some mescaline-inspired evening. Like Led Zeppelin's Robert Plant, I had a worn, faded spot where the tip of my penis had rubbed against the material. When the denim finally wore through, I sewed a piece of an American flag on the fly as a patch. The flares had patches also on the ass, a collage of different materials, like bits of comic strips and corduroy, sewn on top of each other. The flares had tears at the knees, but weren't totally ripped. But I was totally ripped by the first riffs of "Honky Tonk Woman."

Jeans, more accurately denim, composed most of my wardrobe. I was comfortable in almost nothing else, physically or politically. When a pair of Levi's finally wore out through the knees, I sheared off the legs and had a pair of cutoffs, which served as the *de rigueur* summer attire and swimsuit, when I was forced to forego skinny dipping. I also had a denim shirt; the best were made by Wrangler, that had imitation pearl snaps instead of buttons, even on the sleeves. In time, the elbows wore through, and my "old lady" sewed on denim patches from a dead pair of jeans.

Recycling jeans was culturally hip. In keeping with the consciousness of saving the planet by not wasting precious cotton, we made lots of clothing from used denim. The "old lady" made blue jean ties from faded elephant bells. She sewed bits of sun- and crescent-shaped colored leather and embroidered clouds, trees, and maybe a rainbow on the ties. I wore a denim porkpie hat, made from scraps of old jeans. There were tiny silver bells and beads sewn into the seams of the fabric. I even had a denim wallet, that I bartered for a home-made tie-dyed shirt in the parking lot of a Grateful Dead concert. I lost the hat somewhere over the years.

I knew a woman, biblically, that made dresses from old pairs of Osh Kosh overalls. She split the seams of the legs and sewed in added denim from a used pair of hip-huggers to make a bouncy skirt. She tatted a bit of lace or colored cloth on the bottom hem and crocheted the skirt and chest pockets with silver thread, or attached pieces of fur to produce a kind of wearable sculpture. Even the shoulder straps were decorated with Indian cloth, like the strap that supported Pete Townsend's guitar.

My jeans were old friends; each pair fit differently, but I wore them all without underwear. Jockey shorts just didn't make it when quick disrobing was necessary. We were all supposed to be naked anyway, and jeans were a handy concession to humanity. It was a little joke I played on the world. Denim daydreams.

I wonder now about the crafted nonchalance of wearing perfectly broken-in new jeans. I had to rush home from the store with my new Levi's and begin the ritual of washing, bleaching, softening, and shrinking them in the dryer before I would take to the streets in my new "old" jeans. Newness was disdained, except for the latest Stones record, for reasons that were righteously clear to me then. Now, I regard the hypocrisy of rebelliously conforming to the wearing of the "uniform," old jeans, as innocent contradiction in a world hopelessly contrived. We customized them with our patches and beads, but the jeans were standard issue, much like the dungarees of workers decades earlier.

Today, I can buy a pair of "Instant Old Jeans" from Levi for about $35.00, but I don't. I still like to condition my jeans "naturally," the way I used to so long ago. When I go to a concert now, I wear my jeans without underwear, which reminds me that once we could be naked in a world much more innocent than ours today.

Denim served me well. The fabric was tough enough to withstand a week of dancing and running around, before I had to wash them for sanitary reasons and to shrink them back to the fit, that invincibly snug feeling in my ass, that told me I was never going to die.

7 Courting the Notion: Anecdotal Writing for Self-Enrichment

Alan Weber
Central Michigan University

Log Entry

For writing, I chose the session with Alan Weber on writing anecdotes and personal narratives. He originally asked what we hoped to get out of our sessions and I said that I'd like to gain more confidence and security with my writing. I figured that with personal topics I would, at the very least, be familiar with my subject, so it seemed fairly safe. He offered some really terrific exercises and ideas for starting to write, some great ways to generate topics for us and for our students. It was fun to see the other group members get excited about it. We had plenty of time to start on our own pieces so I holed up in the library to avoid distraction. I started three different pieces, two fairly similar, but started to become frustrated. We met back as a group and were then to share what we had done with someone else. My partner was very supportive and gave me some wonderful ideas. As much as I originally dreaded reading my work aloud, she helped me a great deal and I already feel a little better about my writing.

—Tracey Thompson

No matter what our backgrounds and perceptions are about writing, all of us have stories to tell.

The purposes of this week are to help teachers enjoy writing, see themselves as writers—not necessarily professional writers or even exceptional ones, but merely people who write—and gain a perspective from which they will be able to see their students as people with stories to tell. My hope is that they fall in love with the act of writing, much like people fall in love with other non-work-related activities like gardening, golfing, quilting, and playing music. For this reason, and because most people find them the easiest to write about, my workshop is structured around anecdotes. They provide a comfortable access for people to explore humorous situations, playful capers, and nostalgic memories.

The evening before the workshop begins, our group meets to introduce ourselves. As we whip around the room, it is apparent that the ten members have varied writing backgrounds. A few people, like John, are accomplished narrative or academic writers who just want time to produce a new piece or polish a working draft. Mary Ann and Phyllis are ardent letter writers or journal keepers who wish to experiment with extended formats. Others have put pen to paper only when balancing their checkbooks, making shopping lists, or correcting papers. Sarah, a middle school science teacher, shakes and perspires when discussing the prospect of sitting down to write.

After the introductions to each other, we discuss the week's morning schedule, which will include time for individual writing, sharing, and discussion of writing topics and technique. Before we break up for the evening, I give them a copy of John Updike's "A&P" and ask them for Tuesday's session to mark three passages which they find rich in telling details. I also ask them to write down in one sentence what the story is about. I end by explaining that I will be an active member of the group and write every day. Like other group members, I will share my work and submit a finished piece for publication in the anthology.

Day One

For our whole group gatherings, we decide to meet at the picnic tables nestled under a stand of mature pines. We arrange the tables in a circle and spend the first forty minutes on Monday participating in group-building activities. These help people gain trust with one another so that future sharing sessions are comfortable. They also provide people with playful writing prompts which help them reach into their past. In the first activity, we form pairs and each member recounts a lifelong fantasy or describes a favorite childhood toy. Mary tells about her Barbie dolls, John describes his ideal woman, and I detail my fantasy about traveling to Africa. In the second activity, people form new pairs and tell each other brief stories (anecdotes) about their first kiss.

After we laugh with Mary Jo about a wet first kiss in sixth grade, we regroup and discuss where writing ideas come from. People talk about getting inspiration from reading memorable novels like *Alice in Wonderland* and *Lonesome Dove,* from bad experiences like illnesses and acne, or from humorous situations which were not funny at the time they occurred. From Donald Murray's book, *Shoptalk,* I share quotes from famous writers about finding subjects to write about. Donald Barthelme advises to "write about what you're most afraid of" (80); McKeel McBride says, "I get pieces, flashes of an idea, an image, and I won't know what it means, but I'll be fascinated by it" (86), and Gabriel Maria Marquez states, "I suppose that some writers begin with a phrase, an idea, or a concept. I always begin with an image" (86).

In order to find our own writing ideas, we next fill out a sheet listing 120 common and bizarre topics, and we put a check by those of which we have some knowledge or experience. These subjects range from candle-making and wild flowers to falconry and foraging. At the bottom of the sheet we each mention two areas of expertise that have been left off the list. We also state something that we have done that we believe no one else in the group accomplished. Sarah states that she has been to India, and Diane asserts that she has made thirty quilts. John proudly attests to his golfing prowess.

Next, we randomly exchange our sheets. The responders scan the checked items and the two statements at the bottom of the sheet and asterisk what they feel are the three most interesting topics, ones that they would like the author to write about. My partner wanted to hear about my interests in golfing and jazz music. She also put a mark by my unique experience of ascending Machu Picchu in Peru.

After the sheets are returned to the respective authors, each person takes a manila folder and writes the heading "Possible Topics" at the top of the inside left panel. Then, they list three or four topics that they would be willing to write about. I suggest that they review the checked items on their sheet and the topics we previously discussed in the group building activities.

The group departs to their individual writing spots. Some people go back to the dorm; others remain at a picnic table under the pines; a few find comfort amid the ambient noise of the cafeteria. Traverse Bay's lapping water and sandy beach beckons the sun worshippers. One person sits in her car and writes.

At 11:30 we regroup. Each person states the topic about which he or she wrote. Two or three volunteers read their pieces. Cheryl describes the experience of going to her first summer camp. Sarah tells about her introduction to parenthood. The supportive group feedback produces nervous but reassuring smiles. The session has strengthened everyone's confidence to write about a different topic for ten minutes later that day.

Day Two

On Monday a few people mentioned that they were having difficulties getting their writing started. So, on Tuesday morning we begin with a discussion about ways that we can overcome writing paralysis. People mention a number of strategies: switch writing tools, dictate your thoughts, write directly to an audience, pretend you're writing a letter, and be silly. We then read through Donald Murray's list (in *Write to Learn*) of 25 tricks that experienced writers use to get started writing. We mark the three that we consider using when writer's block strikes.

We apply one of these tricks in a ten-minute expressive writing assignment. This third writing start allows me to model some conferencing techniques and provides the group with another playful way to visualize their memories. The prompt for this assignment is:

Picturing Your Bedroom

Close your eyes and get in a comfortable position. Picture yourself as a fifteen-year-old standing in the doorway to your bedroom. Look directly across the room. What do you see? Is there a window, a dresser, a chair? Scan the room until you see your bed. Where is it located? How big is it? What color is the bedspread? Does it match the curtains? What objects do you notice on the dresser? Peek into the top drawer. Are there any precious or lurid things tucked away from snoopy parents, brothers, or sisters? What do you keep in the bottom dresser drawer? Is the floor carpeted or bare? Look at each corner of the room. What do you see on the floor? Open your eyes and spend ten minutes writing about your bedroom or memories associated with it.

After ten minutes, people exchange papers and respond to the following questions at the bottom of their partner's papers: What do you want to know more about? What details painted a strong image for you?

Three or four people read the reactions of their partners. Susan wants to know more about the dolls sitting atop Tracey's dresser; Diane questions me about the baseball cards I stash in my bottom dresser drawer. We laugh at Mary Jo's vivid description of her fish-clad drapes and matching bedspread. We discuss the importance of showing an action or mood rather than telling about it. Near the end of this discussion, I share a quote from Graham Greene:

Adjectives are to be avoided unless they are strictly necessary; adverbs too, which is even more important. When I open a book and find that so and so has "answered sharply" or "spoken tenderly," I shut it again: it's the dialogue itself which should express the sharpness and tenderness without a need to use adverbs to underline them. (Murray, *Shoptalk* 160–61)

We next share our favorite showing details from "A&P," a tale of adolescent sensibility. This story is effective because Updike crams it with so many vivid images. Diane states that one of her favorites is, "She was a chunky kid, with a good tan and a sweet broad soft-looking can with those two crescents of white just under it, where the sun never seems to hit, at the top of the backs of her legs" (187). Mary loves the visual imagery of ". . . and then all three of them went up the cat-and-dog-food-breakfast-cereal-macaroni-rice-raisins-seasonings-spreads-spaghetti-soft-drinks-crackers-and-cookies aisle" (189–90).

Our discussions of Updike's use of showing details leads us to consider how he makes his point. We share our impressions of the story's main idea and how every story needs what the movie director, Sydney Pollack, refers to as a spine, that idea which focuses the details and provides the backbone to the story, its theme or thesis.

After our discussion, participants share one of their pieces with at least two other people during the individual writing time. People fan out to their private writing niches. I spend the remainder of the morning reading and responding to manuscripts, nudging a few writers to expand on an idea, and listening to others as they explore different ways to verbalize an image. My own narrative about checkout lines has to wait.

Day Three

One of the purposes of the workshop is to show writers that they don't have to create a finished product every time they write something, that some topics lay forever stagnant while others need time before they can be brought back to life. Thus, we begin Wednesday with our fourth expressive writing exercise. This time I introduce Gabriele Lusser Rico's technique of clustering. Usually half the people have taught this strategy but few have applied it to their own writing process. I first model the strategy with the entire group by clustering around a specific kernel word. Last year we clustered "purple." In other workshops we clustered around a mood like "ornery" or an object like "leaves."

From the associations in the cluster, people write for about ten minutes. After we respond to a few readers, we formulate open-ended questions that would give us helpful information about our work. We create a long list which includes "What would you like me to expand upon or talk more about?" "What are your feelings after reading the first paragraph?" "If I shorten the paper, what should I delete and why?" The group applies these questions to a few of the papers just created from the clusters.

The group marvels at clustering's ability to create diverse associations in a fanciful way. Yet, most group members are feeling the pressure to choose one piece of writing that they intend to revise for publication on Friday. While most have made their topic selection, Sarah is toying with the idea of extending her cluster. Before we break for our individual writing time, people share their choices. Cheryl has decided to concentrate on a short story based on a teenage caper rather than to polish her camping vignette. John wants to stick with his farm anecdote; Phyllis thinks she will create a series of postcards or "written snapshots" about the Traverse Bay area. Tracey likes her essay about a flag burning incident. I have chosen a humorous narrative that explains the reasons checkout lines at big stores frustrate me.

The remainder of Wednesday morning, people revise their major piece or form small groups and conference with each other. While egos are still fragile, most people invite suggestions about ways of improving clarity or solving stylistic problems. We meet at 11:30 a.m. and receive more feedback from the entire group. Now the writing ignites all sorts of emotions. We cry during Mary Ann's narrative about her year in an orphanage. We reminisce with Diane about her childhood memories of playing in the garage. We laugh with Máry when she reads her lead paragraph about her third grade teacher:

> My third grade teacher who made my life a living hell some thirty years ago has finally kicked the bucket, gone six feet under, croaked, bought the farm, bit the big one!

Day Four

People who fall in love with an activity usually create routines or habits, so they have time to pursue that hobby. Our group begins Thursday by reflecting on the writing habits we have acquired during the week. Most of the group likes to write alone and in quiet, but a few like Cheryl and Mary prefer some kind of sound around them, even voices. Some have no preference for time of day; others are like Saul Bellow who "generally writes for three or four hours at a sitting, mornings as a rule." We compare our preferences for time and place with the rituals of famous authors quoted from Murray's book, *Shoptalk.* Many identify with the pain described by Harry Crews:

> I get up in the morning, that's one of the hard parts, drag myself over to the old typewriter and sit down, that's even harder, and then I tell the Lord, "I ain't greedy, Lord, just give me the next 500 words" (50).

We decide to shorten our habit of writing individually so that we can meet back together at 11:00 A.M. But before we scatter to complete our revisions and final editing, someone raises the topic of the classroom applications of the workshop. Though these teachers have been immersed in their roles as writers, they still are preoccupied with their return to the classroom, even though the summer has only started. They have realized that everything they have been doing in the workshop can be taken back to their students. The fantasy or toy prompt, the topic list and partnering, the bedroom prompt, the clustering, and the resources in literary writing—all of these are relevant to helping their students select their own topics, tell their own stories, and recognize that they have a lot to write about.

Our conversation leads us to broach the topics of grading, grammar, and evaluation. We discuss mechanics and grammar exercises assigned apart from the students' actual writing and concur that writing improves if problems are addressed in the context of the students' own writing. We talk about evaluation, which helps students while they are writing and discourages blanket letter or number evaluations. While listening to the teachers talking, responding to one another's ideas and concerns, it occurs to me that these teachers who write can brainstorm a lot of powerful and valuable teaching ideas more quickly and effectively than a workshop leader can invent, collect, and disseminate them. Likewise, a group of students who write can solve one another's problems in ways no single writing teacher is likely to cover. Even as they go off to their writing, the teachers are thinking of ways to create a classroom atmosphere where students can see themselves as writers and enjoy the self-satisfaction of writing.

When we gather at the picnic tables for our last whole group session, people are anxious to get feedback about their revisions. John reads his anecdote about gathering eggs as a boy on a Minnesota farm. He asks for ways to trim the piece from four to two pages. The group asks questions which encourage John to verbalize about his intent. As he becomes clearer about his audience, he sees possibilities from the diverse suggestions offered by the group. His final decision to delete the section about his grandmother solves the dilemma. We help Mary Ann clarify the reasons she was sent to the orphanage; with Phyllis we brainstorm various format options. The morning ends with sighs of relief and accomplishment.

Day Five

On Friday morning we display our writing for the other groups taking part in the Traverse Bay Project. We attach comment sheets to our polished drafts and any works still in progress. For our ten-minute presentation, we open with a humorous rendition of the song, "Memories," and follow with each of us reading a snippet from his or her own piece relating to some remembrance. Diane's excerpt reminisced about her garage:

> It had the same dimensions and purpose as others [garages], the potpourri of tools, implements, toys, and paraphernalia, the same spider webs. It did have one additional feature, however—it acted as the breeding ground for our imaginations.

As I reflect about Traverse Bay, I think that spot under the pines acted as the breeding ground for our writing imaginations and confidence. We were proud of our finished products and felt like writers. However, the anecdotes which we published in our anthology were not the important outcomes of our week together. The publication merely provided a framework which allowed people to play around with writing and experience its power and enjoyment. I'm not sure if everyone fell in love with writing by Friday, but the idle conversations made me believe that most were courting the notion.

References

Murray, Donald M. *Write to Learn,* 2nd ed. New York: Holt, Rinehart, Winston, 1987.

————. *Shoptalk: Learning to Write from Writers.* Portsmouth, NH: Boynton/Cook, 1990.

Rico, Gabriele Lusser. *Writing the Natural Way.* Los Angeles: J. P. Tarcher, 1983.

Updike, John. *Pigeon Feathers and Other Stories.* New York: Alfred K. Knopf, 1962.

Applications in the Classroom

Courting the Notion: Anecdotal Writing for Self-Enrichment

Helping Students Find Topics

- Relate to the class how you choose your own writing topics.

- Have the students interview grandparents, uncles, aunts, and other relatives to discover family stories, rituals, and remembrances.

- Have students go through the yellow pages of a telephone book for writing topics.

- Bring local writers into your class and have them describe their process for selecting topics.

- Conduct mini-lessons on clustering and brainstorming, so as to provide students with strategies to discover new writing topics.

- Provide students with a sheet which asks them about their greatest fears, favorite toys, scariest moments, and funniest happenings.

- Develop writing prompts for short pieces of expressive writing, so students might focus on what they know. For example: Describe or relate a "first" in your life (first date, first kiss, first car); detail a bad habit you enjoy; tell a stranger about a family or personal ritual.

- Have students keep a list of possible writing topics somewhere in their writing folder.

Helping Students Share Their Writing

- Create cooperative response groups to provide feedback for individual papers.

- Develop feedback sheets which response groups can use to talk about a piece of writing.

- Have students respond to writing in pairs by praising it, asking a question about it, and giving a personal reaction to it.

- Have students develop questions which they can ask about a written piece.

- Structure groups so the author asks all the questions and the group only responds.

- Have groups talk about a piece of writing with the stipulation that the author says nothing.

- Ask groups to only ask questions about a paper and to refrain from making any type of statement about it.

- Develop questions to ask students about your own writing; then, have the students answer these same questions in relation to their own writing.

Log Entry

Each morning we share our works-in-progress and explore new prompts for ideas. Today Al presented two general areas. First we discussed our personal writing rituals. The responses were varied and interesting. We found that some people prefer a particular physical position or environment. Some needed isolation, others needed to move around. We started with lists, fast-moving ideas, and precise revisions before putting to paper. Someone noted that our students were just as different as we were when it came to rituals. We discussed ideas for our classrooms like developing a writing center or allowing students to go into the hallway or even outside to work in their individual ways. The second idea Al presented was an activity on clustering. We practiced this then shared our writing, and I was amazed to see again the variety of ideas generated from the same seed or kernel idea. After some time in discussion several people shared their work and were anxious to get feedback. Our group is very honest but supportive. This session was very informative and helpful.

—**Tracey Thompson**

WRITING FAIR

Postcards

Phyllis M. Gabler

Dear Mom and Dad,
    I remember . . .
On the way in to T.C., we used to joke about Acme: if we blinked, we'd miss it! You know, the small green hut that held the greasy spoon restaurant is still there, although in ruin. Dad went there the day I was born to brag that at 52 he still could cut the mustard. It's now near the vast Grand Traverse Resort area. Unbelievable that this small, dead stretch is making money, making people happy and making Acme a destination for tourists.

Dear Mom and Dad,
    I remember . . .
Many the time Dad would wake me in the cold chill before the daylight to get ready for fishing the "big ones" in the calm morning waters of Grand Traverse Bay. Mom would help me pack a "snacks only" survival

▶

box for us because we WOULD return with our edible trophies. Frying those so quickly after caught—heaven in each mouthful. Richard fries his fresh-caught fish for me now and the tastes are the same, recalling wonderful memories for me. However, I've retired as a caster of nets.

Dear Mom and Dad,
    I remember . . .
Preparing for the Cherry Festival was an event: selecting a special "cherry" outfit to wear, baking cherry cobbler to eat when we got home, setting up our folding chairs in the same spot on Front Street by Mr. Peterson's store. Year after year the same, yet uniquely exciting we would wave to new faces in the parade line: celebrities, politicians, neighbors. The once two-day festival is now a week long . . . more parades, more contests, more people, more . . . commercial.

Dear Mom and Dad,
    I remember . . .
Picking the cherries at our friend Leaver's farm was an experience in learning the prejudices of the world. It was shocking and not quite clear to me how and why the Mexican migrant workers would live so tightly crammed in the squalid tents and makeshift cabins. How could they be allowed to walk the streets drunk and loud and take over the town in the evening for the few weeks they were here? Now, there are ruins of the migrant shacks along the farms and little Mexican influence. And little of the humanness that went with the rite of cherry picking.

Dear Mom and Dad,
    I remember . . .
Mission Peninsula was a very poor, hard-working community of cherry and fruit farmers, extending right to the tip. The land was cheap; no one was interested. Well, Rich and I have bought retirement property on the West Bay shore area. In fact, we wanted something on the water-front, but it was too overpriced for us! The shared frontage we'll have in the subdivision makes us happy enough and we'll have a view of T.C. at night. It's funny—I'm coming home to retire. I have the special memories of us here and will be making more with Rich.

Dear Mom and Dad,
    I remember . . .
The vicarious, licentious feeling you allowed Pam and me to share going to the beach. At fifteen, I shouldn't have been able to drive to T.

▶

C. State Park legally. The string bikini Mom crocheted for me that summer was the first two-piece, bare-body suit I ever wore. The beach
scene was a grownup rite you knew I was ready for. You also knew
how little traffic I'd encounter on the road and how few people would
be at the beach. But it was BIG TIME for us. Licentious feelings are gone
since I cover up from head to toe. And driving to the beach? It's
bumper to bumper—no chance for an accident.

Writing
Ann Knauer-Bizer

Blocked
The flow of my writing is being damned
Breaks in the wall
Ideas leak through
Drip, drip, drip
Inspiration;
     a river rages on the other side
Churning, burning,
     whirling

The force is undirected
Only drip, drip, drip
Moving swiftly at first
     Pounding forward
Stopped
Solidly the barrier stands
But those leaks,
     those leaks continue
Sliding through;
     Fall into the pool
Then suddenly lost
     Surfacing again
Sometimes drowned,
     Sometimes blended
       with other droplets
Combining
     but then stagnant
The power has vanished.

8 Inviting Success: Ways into Writer Engagement

Paul Wolbrink
Spring Lake High School, Michigan

Log Entry

There has always been divergent thinking when it comes to whether the best writing is produced through personal choice or if mini-assignments produce more provocative directions. One thing is certain, however: to write and share that writing is crucial to personal growth. Writing is an exposure of self, and we have not truly written until we have been heard. To give our words *voice* also gives them *wings!*

I did not come to this week of workshops with that thought in mind, but as Paul Wolbrink advanced that idea in our get-acquainted time this evening, it made sense. It was the type of sense that I know in my heart but try so hard to avoid. There is a fear . . . a soul-shaking, eye-darting inhibition that shouts silently, "No, I won't expose who and what I am!" If I can override that strangulation of free expression, I *will* soar!

In this setting I am being assured of acceptance and am encouraged to be spontaneous. If there are no expectations to excel, no awards given for the "winner of the week," then I can break free to say what I need to say. I can give my thoughts a written outlet and a physical voice.

Ah, the last is a point I need to note. I need to give my students that same outlet and voice.

—Maryalice Stoneback

In ideal circumstances the English teacher is free to create situations which make writers of non-writers, which *invite* success by placing students in circumstances where words come easily, and where the words that come are good words—keeper words. In my most idealistic moments—on some balmy August afternoon at some beach far away from my classroom—I would take this even one step further. The teacher's job is not merely to foster success, but to make success inescapable. She must find ways to beat back the sense of failure that so often visits writers, and instill in failure's place the feeling not only that one *can* write but also that one has something worthwhile to say.

Imagine a writing classroom where all product and even process concerns are thrown out the window. Existing methods of evaluation, both of students and teachers, would be replaced by a single standard, the Writer Engagement Index. In a WEI classroom, the mark of a good teacher would be the extent to which she was able to involve her students in the act of writing. How excited did they get? How deeply did they care? Did they reach a point where the adrenaline really started to flow? Did their pens get hot, moving swiftly across the page? Were they so absorbed that an hour passed without them realizing it? If someone took what they'd written, crumpled it up, and threw it away, would they race to the wastebasket to retrieve it? With the Writer Engagement Index, the object of writing shifts from trying to please others, typically the teacher or classmates, to trying to please oneself, the writer. The only measure of success is the degree of pleasure, involvement, and ownership a writer feels. A WEI-driven teacher, then, does everything within her power to motivate writers, wants only to get her students deeply *into* writing, to take them far under the skin of language and make them believe that they are capable writers with something valuable to say.

Thoughts such as these accompany me in late June as I aim the car toward Traverse City. I meet the people in my writing group for the first time at the opening session on Sunday evening. They're mine for a quick half hour, sandwiched between the general introductory remarks and the wine-and-cheese reception. Rather than use this brief time for get-acquainted games or a preview of the week's activities, I prefer to get directly to the task that awaits us, writing the first of thousands of words. I know that in the days ahead we'll come to know one another well through our writing. I would rather, in these important early moments together, simply be writers seated at the table, unencumbered by knowledge of geography, position, prestige, or publication. Thus it is that within two or three minutes of gathering, sitting equally at tables positioned in a circle, we begin writing. I start with snaphorisms.

Snaphorisms and Surprises

I discovered the literary device of the snaphorism quite by accident one afternoon. As I walked past a colleague's classroom, I noticed the daily quotation on her chalkboard: "The mind is like a parachute—it works best when it's open." Moments later in the faculty office, I scrawled two other solutions: "The mind is like a parachute—if you don't give a rip, you'll go downhill fast" and "The mind is like a parachute—when things get so tough you feel like bailing out, it's the only thing that'll save you." Even now, several years later, I distinctly recall the satisfaction I felt at writing these lines, because I had written, inside of three minutes, something I liked, effortlessly.

Snaphorisms, I soon found, occur elsewhere. As it turns out, the snaphorism is a staple of humor as well as truth. Pay a visit to the local greeting card shop. The set-up line appears in big letters on the front of the card. "A birthday is like a cold toilet seat—," the bold print announces, or "A true friend is like moldy bread—" or "Honey, my love for you is like a flat tire—." The punch line, of course, appears inside.

Writers can profit greatly from working with snaphorisms. As trivial as they might seem, the snaphorism replicates in miniature so much of what is elemental to writing. It confronts the writer with a problem to be solved, forces the writer to discover a linkage where none seems to exist, and requires careful phrasing. The snaphoristic line, properly rendered, is spare and quick. It needs attentive grooming. Moreover, as in my own high school classes, I find snaphorisms to be effective community builders, giving twenty strangers in a room a rich source of entertainment and shared experience after only three minutes of scribbling in response to some seemingly absurd comparison ("Success is like toast"; "Love is like a garage door").

The most important benefit of snaphorisms, however, is in their ability to surprise the writer. For the writer, it's happened so easily. He invests little and expects nothing. But his mind, quite unbidden—and this is a moment we should attempt to duplicate again and again in writing classrooms—takes him places he never expected to go. All week I'm shooting for that moment of surprise, the instant when a writer, meandering along, carelessly filling the page, feels the adrenaline rush of an idea begging to be let out.

Because wine corks are being pulled in an adjoining room, I switch to some other small piece of writing with the capacity to surprise and assign a couple of one-minute poems. Everyone gets sixty seconds (you can cheat toward eighty) to finish a poem. I provide these starts: "I know now I'll never . . ." and "Every house should have an empty room, a room where . . ." (both borrowed from Jack Ridl of Hope College) and "The score was 10–9 when the burgers arrived . . ." (borrowed from Lee Bradley). We read some of the one-minute poems aloud, just listening, noticing together lines that seem to work well. After each writer reads, we snap our fingers appreciatively—a round of snaps. Then just before we leave, I give an overnight assignment, another small piece of writing. I ask them to compose a title for this poem:

> The mound of snow
> at the corner of Broadway and 100th
> freezes and thaws
> thaws and freezes

It seems straightforward, but it's tricky enough to provoke a half-hour of poking through possibilities. We agree to meet the next morning at nine o'clock and walk into the adjoining room to sip and socialize.

Mapping and Memory

The following morning, the Monday that kicks off the week, we return to our places in the circle. Technically, it's our first day together, but we're already beginning to feel comfortable with one another. Although I haven't said much about the structure of the workshop or what I hope we'll collectively accomplish in the days to come, I suspect they have a notion of where we're headed. I ask that we postpone the discussion of potential poem titles and get straight to the writing. I tell them we're going to churn out words without regard to quality, and make them recite a pledge "that what I write will be not at all my best work, not remotely indicative of my capabilities." The pledge, of course, confers permission. For the next five days, no one will need to apologize and we are freed of nay-saying goblins and bogeymen.

We begin by drawing maps of our childhood bedrooms, back when we were four or six years old. We include doors, windows, and basic furniture. After we finish, we share it with other writers, one on one. We give the full tour, taking a good five minutes to report everything. The act of drawing and speaking about it positions us in that long-submerged past. Then I give a series of prompts (adapted from some by Stephen Dunning) at intervals of five to eight to possibly ten minutes, whatever seems right. We sit in silence, writing. When another prompt comes along, everyone switches to the new subject matter, except those who've been pulled so deeply into what they're writing that they cannot bear interruption. The prompts include:

- ■ I am _____ing . . . (Writers are in their bedrooms. Give them just the two and a half words, I am something-ing, and let them spin away in whatever direction the verb takes them.)

- You are standing at the window looking out at something.

- Out in the yard, some inanimate object speaks to you.

- The thing you valued most in your room was . . . (Draw an "X" on the map to show where it was located.

- Someone is in the doorway of your room. He or she is angry. Write what the person is saying.

- Nights, . . . (Just the single word at the head of a sentence.)

- Someone comes to visit.

- Tell something you did that you've never told anyone before.

- In one of the above, you were not telling the whole truth. The whole truth is . . .

At this point we stop and read over what we've written. We find two or three patches that seem interesting and turn to partners with whom we earlier shared the map. We read the patches aloud, everyone reading one-on-one simultaneously. When we've finished, we might jot on our papers a story the other person told us. Or we might, to get more interaction and build the community, go around the room telling stories, in this case not our own stories, but retelling one told to us by a classmate.

For the remainder of the morning we stay in our childhoods, writing headlong to keep pace with the onrushing prompts. We do this for the better part of three hours, always pushing, always trying to maintain the white-heat atmosphere. By the end of the morning, students will have written the opening page of a half-dozen short stories. They'll have generated a quiver of poem fragments. Just like my high school students, who build their own responses to the same prompts in the opening days and weeks of my classes, the workshoppers can't be told this in advance, of course. It would silence their pens. They're just ambling across the landscape. They have no expectations for their writing, and in the absence of expectations, free of the burden of being literary, they find their way to the reservoir.

Somewhere near the end, I might throw out a few philosophical turns:

- What do you know now that you didn't know then?
- What did you believe in at that time?
- What mattered most?
- What do you believe now?
- What was the hardest thing you had to do then?

These turn the writer away from narrative and descriptive detail toward reflections upon the significance of their experiences.

There's nothing magical, by the way, about a childhood bedroom. I know from experience that it works well. But at other times I've positioned students in their fourth-grade classrooms, having them instead map the route to school.

Whatever the prompts we've written to, I ask workshoppers to arrive the next day with two pieces of writing, a prose piece—either a story or an essay, two pages at the most—and a poem of no more than twenty lines. I'm careful to say "arrive with" rather than "write" because the writing has already been done. The task is one of selection and arrangement rather than rewriting. Indeed, it can be a rule that nothing except names can be changed, or that added new material will appear in brackets. This helps to sustain the lighthearted, experimental, throwaway mood—everyone's just messing around.

Prompting the Process

On Tuesday morning we entertain one another for a few minutes with titles for the mounded-snow poem. Then we pick up our pens and begin writing again. I know that everyone is anxious to get to the poem and prose piece that came out of the previous day's writing, but I want to put it off for a moment. On this, our second day together, I have two objectives. I hope to sustain the high output of the previous day, maintaining the satisfaction and forward motion of filling pages quickly. But I also want to build among us the sense of trust and community so important to the development of a writer. I prefer to do the writing first, taking advantage of the high-energy, caffeinated part of the day, then to share for an hour, then to do both toward the end of the session. We warm up with simple journal exercises that offer the promise of opening into much larger pieces of writing, bigger than the fifteen or twenty minutes we invest in getting a good start. I'll choose from prompts such as these, often providing a generic first line ("Once upon a time . . ." or "It happened like this . . .") to remove the burden of starting:

- Write about a time when you were particularly aware of the night sky—when the sky seemed especially close, when you lay on your back looking at the stars, or when you watched an eclipse. Perhaps it was the Northern Lights, a comet, a meteor shower, satellites, searchlights, or maybe just a good storm crackling around you. Remember where you were, who you were with, what it looked like, what you talked about, what you were thinking, what you could hear and smell and taste. Write about the way things *felt.*

- Write about a unique alteration that has occurred to your body since the time you were born. Not the obvious weight gain or hair loss or wrinkle onset, but a scar, a broken bone, some surgical repair or removal. Describe how it happened, who you were with, what people said, what you did, what others did, how it felt, and so on. What image comes back first? What do you see when you think of that time?

- Borrowing from Peter DeVrie's *Slouching Toward Kalamazoo,* in which a fourth grader in rural North Dakota writes a legendary essay entitled "Why I Would Hate to Be a Basement" (13), write a take-off on the line "Why I would hate to be a _____." (The possibilities are fun—toilet seat, cigar, dollar bill, road.)

- Write what you see when you look in the mirror. Describe the obvious first—eyes, hair, nose, lips, skin—being as objective as possible. Then move deeper. What do you see that might not be apparent to others?

When we've spent an hour or so on Tuesday morning writing to the journal exercise prompts, we return to the prose and poetry pieces assembled overnight. This will be our first extended sharing session, and I know in advance that it will be a transformational moment. Over the next sixty or seventy minutes, as we read our long-dormant stories of childhood, dozens of invisible spiders will spin tiny, interconnecting webs of familiarity and friendship. By the end of the morning we'll be a team—or more precisely, an orchestra. We'll have the piccolo and oboe, the muted horn, the timpani and cello. We'll hear each other's distinct voices, and we'll learn to care about what each person says. The rules for this are simple. After one of us reads, we'll snap our fingers, commending the effort with a round of snaps.

Then we'll talk about what worked. We're not simply noticing. We're selectively noticing *only* what is good—idea, language, structure, syntax, irony, detail. The writer listens as we touch on the merits of her piece. At no point does she apologize.

We don't follow any set order. When a writer wants to read, she does. We're just a small circle of listeners and noticers, like some ancient civilization telling its stories under the stars. During that hour we'll laugh often. We might cry, too. And when the last writer finishes, we'll look at one another in a new way.

When we've finished reading, we might have forty minutes left. I want to build upon the just-forged sense of community by pushing everyone into a new round of self-entertainment. I assign a lie poem— twenty minutes, no more—to be written on a quarter-sheet of paper I've provided. I use the simple rules set forth in Jesse Hise's article, "Writing Poetry":

A. Tell a series of lies about yourself.

B. Begin with the line, "I wish I were not so . . ."

C. End the poem with an "If" section.

I'll read an example of a completed poem and set them to work. Twenty minutes later I call time. We don't sign the lie poems. Instead, we fold them and throw them into a hat. Then we redistribute them among the group and start reading. One writer will lament that she is too tall and thin, another that she is too organized, another that she is overly endowed. Other writers regret their blondeness, creativity, or talent. We chuckle at the improbabilities and absurdities. And we enjoy the twists we've added this time around: the writer gets to hear her work read by another voice, giving her words a far more "finished" sound than the writer thinks possible for a piece written in haste only minutes before. Also, after all of the lies have been read, we get to guess who wrote them, leading us to new recognitions about the personalities and voices in the group.

Practices That Invite Success

The lie poem marks the end of the session, but I want to make sure that workshoppers have an overnight assignment. I expect them to continue working on other pieces that have surfaced, but I also want to keep new stuff coming at them. I might, for example, give them a generating frame that specifies a structure and asks them to build content into it. In the familiar "Jack and Jill" nursery rhyme, for example, the essential structure goes this way: This person and this person went to this place to do this thing, something happened to the first person with this result, and then the same thing happened to the second person. A generating frame is something like a paint-by-numbers exercise, except that the writer can choose whatever paints he wishes. So I give them a frame of some kind and send them off for the day.

When students arrive on Wednesday morning, our third day together, we're so anxious to talk that it's hard to prod everyone back to writing. The community is squarely in place, to the point that we could easily become chatterers instead of writers. For the remainder of our time together—Wednesday morning, Thursday morning, and the hour or so on Friday before the big group read-around marking the conclusion of the week—we're a solid team. Everything is in place and we continue in much the same way as we have been, with writers putting out as much text as possible and sharing it in a supportive atmosphere, and I pull from a variety of prompts to get different kinds of writing started in between rounds of working on writing already in progress. (The prompts come from the list of ideas that appear in the article "Going Where the Lightning Is," elsewhere in this book.)

As we continue to work together, we count on certain fundamental practices to invite success:

Prolific Writing: Good things happen when you don't try so hard. I try to get the writers in my charge to write speedily, fill pages quickly and uncritically, and reduce their expectations.

Prompts: Rather than let students choose what they want to write about (essential at a later point but not for starting out), I let them roam freely within prescribed boundaries by giving them easily-completed tasks which have the capacity to surprise.

Community: Writers need readers—or listeners, anyway. A writer who never shares—or shares only with the teacher—never grows. It is important for the writer to put her words, read in her own voice, in front of other people and to listen to the words of others.

Acceptance: The proper attitude of the community is one of attentive acceptance. They listen carefully to the writer. Afterwards they comment in detail about what they heard, being careful to keep their remarks positive. All writers, including the best ones, need support; the less experienced they are and the less confident they are of the value of their writing, the more support they need at the outset of their writing lives.

In my classroom, as well as in this workshop, I find these practices are effective ways to engage writers in their own writing. Students and workshoppers alike find them easy to generate rewarding results from, giving them the chance to begin at a place where writing pays off for them. Once they have a sense that writing can reward them, once they have a sense that their mastery of language is sufficient to produce both pleasing and potent results, they feel more willing to make further demands on themselves rather than expect the teacher-evaluator to do it. They can accomplish far more than they ever expected once they become engaged, and writer engagement comes more readily when the writing classroom invites success.

Imagine that the Writer Engagement Index is painted on one of those classic tests of strength on a carnival midway, the metal tower with the bell on the top and gradations painted on the shaft from "Weakling" near the bottom to "He-Man" near the bell. Substitute on the Writer Engagement tower terms near the bottom like "Bored," "Detached," "Disenfranchised," "Going Through the Motions," then follow the phases upward through "Alert," "Attentive," and "Involved" to "Committed," "Absorbed," and "Excited" until, just below the bell, you reach (in workshopper Karen Lulich Horwath's happy phrase) "Drunken Wordlove." That's the level to aim for, the sledgehammer force of engaged writing that drives the clapper to the top and sets the bell clanging. As teachers of writing, we have an obligation to teach structure, order, logic, clarity, correctness, and precision. But before we do any of that, or while we're doing it, we need to pour the melted butter of sun into their pens and give them freedom.

References

DeVries, Peter. *Slouching Towards Kalamazoo.* Boston: Little, Brown, 1965.

Hise, Jesse. "Writing Poetry: More Than a Frill." *English Journal* 69.8 (1980): 19–22.

Applications in the Classroom

Do five minutes each

Inviting Success: Ways into Writer Engagement

Writing Prompts to Get Started

relate to earlier child piece

- Provide a verbal photograph of yourself at a certain age.

- Write about a fence or boundary.

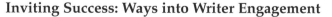

- Write about a garden or flowerbed, a time you grew something or helped something grow.

- Write about a basement, attic, or outbuilding.

- Write about sounds at night outside your bedroom.

- Write about a spot to hide.

- Write about something your family did together.

- Write about a TV program you saw early in your life.

- In two minutes, list all the neighbors you can think of. Write about your neighborhood.

- Write about a job for which you earned money.

Philosophical Prompts

- How were you innocent? How were you shielded? How were you sheltered or protected?

- What are the laws of the universe? Try to formulate the laws of the universe from your perspective, the viewpoint of your unique history.

- What would you do differently if you had the chance?

- Imagine a conversation between yourself in childhood and yourself now.

- What was the biggest adjustment you had to make?

Log Entry

Today's morning workshop was difficult. We were working with different types of prompts for poetry and I was struggling with the emotions from last night's funeral. Writing, as I have always known, when approached with the heart, brings out so many things that would otherwise go unheeded. As always, another lesson in all of this, not only for me as a hurting individual but for me as a teacher of young writers who must plumb the depths of their seventeen years to write with clarity and openness. The trust that must be brought out in a classroom of this sort is paramount. If the writers cannot trust one another, then they begin to write in a vacuum or cannot write at all.

This observation comes from the same process happening to me this morning. As I sat off from the group trying to generate ideas, I felt isolated and hurting. When, in sharing my first piece, I also shared that I was dealing with the loss of a very important friend, I gave myself permission to write precisely and openly. Then the poetry began to flow from the heart and soul. May I be able to support my students with the same genuine concern and sensitivity that was shown to me.

—Maryalice Stoneback

WRITING FAIR

Small Talk
Maryalice Stoneback

It's a
    nice day
      nasty day
        muggy day
          crappy day
            helluva storm last night now it's clear day

No we don't need extra milk just the usual today
Did I tell you what those goddam neighbor kids did to
    my yard
      my car
        my bushes
          my sidewalk
            my trees yesterday?
Damn near destroyed them with their traipsing through.
        No damn respect for anyone anymore.
He pulled himself deeper into his threadbare sweater
Still in control of his neighborhood perch.

I
  won't
    can't
      shouldn't
        wouldn't
          couldn't
            DON'T care if
              no one comes to visit anymore.

▶

Final Amen
Maryalice Stoneback

Lines
Lines
Everything
in
lines.
First class first, second class next,
Lines,
More lines.
   Alphabetical
   Academic
   Boy–girl
   Girl–boy
Ssh . . . SSH! Quiet, please!
To the "caf,"
To the gym,
To confession . . .
To confession?
Kneeling, kneeling,
One after another
Quick headshift left, headshift right
Anybody listening?
"Bless me, Father, for I have sinned . . ."
(I can't believe Mary french-kissed!)
" . . these are my sins . . ."
What do I say?
How much do I tell?
Will he be shocked?
My God, he's a priest!

The ordeal is over; Obligation fulfilled.
Penance assigned
"Three Hail Marys, one Our Father, and a Glory be"
Genuflect
Cross myself
Return to
Lines
Lines
Whispering,
Chattering,
"Sins forgotten" lines

Dreaming Places
Jan Andre

Aunt Minnie's dressing table,
Left to me—
Her gift.

Its curved front
opened,
Revealing a shallow
drawer for hidden
treasures.

An eyelet skirt
hung gracefully
to the floor,
The top protected
by glass.

Mirror framed
above,
provided a
Dreaming Place.

How would I change?
Do braces really
straighten teeth?
Do freckles fade?
Will my nose
always be so big?
Can hair
thicken?

Sitting on the
padded stool
Gazing at the present
Hoping for the future.

Answering Questions

Linda Dinan

My mother's favorite:
white, pink, ruby
peonies
floating delicately
in the back of an
elegant, swan
flower bowl—
full, ruffled,
fragrant.

Please don't tell.
I brushed aside an ant,
plucked a
golfball-sized
bud,
and opened it
prematurely,
carefully,
petal
by
petal,
looking for an answer
to how
all those layers
snuggle into
such
a small space.

The answer
wasn't there.

II The Writing Center: Being and Becoming Writers

Introduction

John S. Dinan
Central Michigan University

Michael Bacon
Kentwood High School, Michigan

The experience of being and becoming a writer is at the center of the Traverse Bay workshop, and for many participants the Writing Center is an important part of that experience. We chose the room that houses the Writing Center because it is open and comfortable—qualities we hope to encourage in the people who come there. For two hours every afternoon Monday through Thursday, the Center provides workshop participants with assistance on the writing projects they have been working on during their morning sessions. The two of us who supervise the Center have one overriding goal: to provide a positive experience for those who come to us to share their writing. We are helped in achieving this objective by other workshop staff members who volunteer to help out at least one afternoon a week.

We consult with a very diverse group of teacher-writers in the Writing Center. Some already see themselves as writers; they write poetry or fiction or essays on their own and tend to confidently set their own agendas in the Center. More often, however, workshop participants have done little writing in their lives except for occasional functional pieces (memos, reports, and the like)—or if they *have* done more "creative" pieces along the way, they have generally done so in the safety of solitude. These participants do not yet look upon themselves as "real writers," and they often share a great deal with the young students they teach in their own classrooms—uncertainty, fitfulness, and an unfocused desire to "get better at writing."

As we deal with this varied group in the Writing Center, we try to operate with goals and methods that apply to successful writing classrooms and workshops wherever they may occur. Our central goal is to confirm the positive self-perceptions of those participants who see themselves as real writers and, probably more importantly, to help those who still feel like outsiders to "join the club." We also try to keep in mind two objectives that derive from the very structure of the Traverse Bay workshop as a whole:

1. to help participants create a piece of writing that they can proudly share during the Friday morning assembly;
2. to model teaching and tutoring behavior that will give them some ideas to take back to their classrooms.

To achieve our goals, we provide workshop participants with two different kinds of responses to their writing. During each Writing Center session we ask the large group to divide themselves into two sub-groups. One group meets with Mike to engage in a group peer-response process. The remaining participants meet for one-to-one conferences with John. At some point, either halfway through a session or the next day, the sub-groups switch places so that they can experience a second and substantially different kind of response to their writing. What happens in each kind of session is described below by the person who conducts it.

9 The Individual Conference in the Writing Center

John S. Dinan

As writing students do in general, Traverse Bay workshop participants come to the Writing Center looking for expert responses to their writing. When I am working with them in one-to-one conferences in the Writing Center, therefore, I am guided by two related "expert" models for interacting with writers: the Writing Teacher model and the Professional Editor model. When guided by the Writing Teacher model, I try to be *developmental* in my assumptions and approach, looking at the participants I work with as *in the process* of becoming writers (and eventually accepting that they *are* writers)— uneven in their growth, but nonetheless moving forward over a period of time. When taking the role of Professional Editor, I am more *product*-oriented, tacitly accepting participants' sense of their own "writerliness" by concentrating on assisting the evolution of a quality product that must be produced in a timely fashion. As the week in the Writing Center unfolds, I move back and forth between these models; which role dominates depends upon the day of the week we are conferencing and the experience and self-concept of the writer I happen to be working with at any given moment.

Just as I do in my own writing courses, I try for a while to keep the writing products being created in the Writing Center subordinate to the attitudes and growth of the writers themselves. As the week progresses, however, the written products take center stage, just as they generally do in regular writing classes. This shift occurs not just because of the Friday deadline, but because by that time the attitudes and growth of the writers have become closely tied to the quality of their written products: by that point they'll feel a lot better if they are producing good stuff. In effect, I gradually shift the tenor of my role and become more of a Professional Editor than a Writing Teacher, focusing more on the writing itself than on the writers.

A week in the Writing Center, then, tends to mirror what goes on in a regular "writing workshop" classroom. It usually goes something like this. Monday is a "take the long view" day. It is a day to be patient and encourage risks, just as good writing teachers do when first working with a class of young writers. On this first day of the Writing Center, participants are just trying to decide what writing project to devote themselves to for the rest of the week. As quietly as I can, I encourage them to select topics to which they feel drawn but which also make them anxious. Such topics have proven to be various: Susan's brassy, thoughtless, yet compelling best friend upon whom she took easygoing revenge in a narrative essay; Tom's bemused frustration with his unrequited love for nature, dealt with in a sardonic descriptive essay that had its readers laughing aloud; Kathie's confrontation through metaphor with her hospitalized father's mortality—each piece of writing different in tone and genre, yet each a *working out* of something, each an act of growth. Topics such as these, whether in a summer writing workshop or in our classrooms, do wonders for the writers' sense of *being* writers.

On Tuesday the drafting has usually begun in earnest, but I can still afford to delay the inevitable shift to their texts in order to take the long, teacherly view of the process the participants are going through. Our conversations, therefore, are still about content, for the most part. I ignore error, awkwardness, and even disorganization, because these disturbances are signs that significant writing is going on and that a "real writer" is at work. Because of this orientation, I am far more likely at this stage to say "The lake you describe is a lot spookier to me than it was yesterday" or "I still don't see the meanness in the guy," rather than "I don't get the connection between these two paragraphs."

By Wednesday, however, we've reached the point of no return, and we have all become acutely aware of the Friday deadline and the piece of writing that will be shared with all workshop members. At this point I become more of a Professional Editor than a Writing Teacher (or perhaps it is more accurate to say that I put into action more fully the "professional editor" aspect *of* the writing teacher). I'm apt at this point to criticize more and suggest more—often a *lot* more—so that the demands of publication can be met. I am not worried about taking ownership of their work. They have fully established their claim in the first two days; I am only their editor, albeit an active one. I recall, for example, that Cheryl's narrative about a frightening moonlight chase was by Wednesday still too thin and slow-paced to be very effective in engaging and keeping a reader's attention. More than anything, Cheryl needed to do some successful writing so that she could draw energy from it as well as build upon it, so I worked intensively and exclusively on helping her develop two tense, evocative paragraphs that could set the tone and style for her next revision. Susan's piece about her "sorta" best friend also wasn't working well when she came into the Writing Center on Wednesday, largely because she wanted to put in *everything*. I told her so (kindly, I hope), then together we listed the stuff that could be eliminated in the next draft. With both Cheryl and Susan, I felt compelled to shift somewhat into the Professional Editor role, creating an emphasis on the finished product that continued with them, as it does with nearly all Writing Center participants, on Thursday, the last day the Writing Center is in session.

As this pattern unfolds in the Writing Center during the week, I try to negotiate a good working relationship with each teacher-writer. How I do so depends on the confidence and self-perception of the individual participants. If a writer is unsure and inexperienced, the tenor of my approach is more that of a student-oriented Writing Teacher than that of a product-oriented Professional Editor. My first step, familiar to writing teachers everywhere, is to ask these writers to describe as fully as possible the writing project they are working on and what their purposes and plans are for completing it. My questions are casual ("Where are you at right now?" "Are you getting a sense of what you'd like to have happen here?" "Have you thought of some people you'd like to have read this when it's done?"). Negative answers to such questions lead easily to further questions. It is questions that get them talking, and having *them* do the talking at this point does more than provide me with information I need to respond purposefully to the text they create; it also helps them "own" their work, both process and product—something inexperienced writers are not used to doing.

I then ask the participants how they would like me to read their text this first time around. Do they, for example, want me to look to see if certain themes are emerging or if certain emotions are coming through? Or would they prefer me to read the draft without any further briefing and tell them what I see trying to go on or what I see as the most promising material? This second alternative is a popular option with those who don't have much to say during our initial conversation. Indeed, more often than not, these participants short-circuit that conversation by thrusting their writing at me and saying, "Here, just read it and let me know what you think." So I do. I recall one very unsure writer, Diana, who early on was so nervous about her writing that she regretted coming to the workshop at all. On Monday Diana brought two things to the Writing Center—some scattered notes taken while thinking about her encounters with nature and a timorous hope that she could somehow make it add up to something the way a real writer would. Through our relaxed, almost theoretical conversations during the first two days, Diana's notes became "video clips," the video clips became "scenes," the world of dramaturgy was evoked, and she discovered the handle with which to deal with her material. From there, largely on her own and feeling very much "like a writer," Diana constructed her "play of nature," not only using imagery to elicit the comedies and tragedies outside our windows, but also bringing onstage the ambiguities faced by those of us who want to be both actor and audience as we experience nature's drama. By the time the process was completed, Diana had taken complete ownership of her writing—the way real writers do.

As was the case with Diana, early in the week I find that the participants have often been writing on a topic but haven't yet developed an angle or purpose; they have been "zero drafting" their essays, as Donald Murray calls it. Writers such as Diana need encouragement, but I can be *selective* in that encouragement, because they are not yet so committed to their text that they'll refuse to let go portions of it. I rarely do a line-by-line running commentary when I read this kind of material, for such a procedure implies that the text being read is likely to be a part of the final product. Instead, I save my commentary until I am finished reading. Then I talk about what I think the writer is *starting* to drive at and where I think the emotional center of the piece might be.

These conversations are deliberately personal. I want our relatively inexperienced, unsure "non-writers" to find themselves being responded to *as humans* and *in human terms*. I want them to start understanding that *they*, not their texts, are at the center of this process. When Kathie came to the workshop, for example, she had a wonderful essay to write but did not yet fully realize it, and she had the skills to do a fine piece but did not yet believe it. A casual, oblique approach seemed best, as it often is with anxious, uncertain writers. It helped that when Kathie arrived in the Writing Center on Monday she seemed distracted and sad. I didn't ask her what was wrong; I didn't know her well enough to do that. Instead, we chatted about how things were going in the morning workshop. Things were going okay, she said, but she had just come from visiting her father in the hospital, so she was having trouble concentrating. He wasn't the sort of person to get seriously ill, and she didn't like the way he looked. I told Kathie about my own hospital visits to my ailing father several years earlier, and how someday, when I felt ready, I planned to use the workshop as an occasion for writing both about him and about the shocking recognition of mortality that came with his illness. Perhaps she'd do the same someday. Then I read the unfinished draft she had brought with her. Kathie was in the "Nature Writing" group, so she had jotted down a page and a half about a garden across the road from the house where she grew up—a garden she used to dig, plant, weed, and harvest with her father. Kathie's father was in that initial draft, but only peripherally, a piece of historical data. Constrained for the time being by the title of her morning workshop, she was trying to write about nature, not a personal relationship.

As do many unsure writers who are working in a defined context (writing classrooms being the most familiar example), Kathie needed to understand that her best move toward "becoming a writer" would be to write about an important subject even if it did not fit exactly into the genre (as she had narrowly defined it) being used by her classmates. But telling her this straight out would be less enabling than using conversation to help her discover the connections between her nature notes and the things she wanted to say about her father. From making such connections comes the energy that feeds real writers.

Since I was a gardener too, I decided to put Kathie's piece aside and just talk with her about gardening for a while, especially about how the *manner* in which the three of us—Kathie, her father, and myself—did our garden chores more often than not was a manifestation of who we were. This conversation, like the earlier one about our fathers' illnesses, was at first personal, but before long shifted to the possibility of increasing the presence of her father in her essay. And out of these personal conversations came a moving and evocative essay about Kathie, the garden across the road, and a father whose spirit permeated both.

With writers such as Kathie, I try to remain personal even when specific sections of their text is clearly the focus of my comments. The best way for me to do that is to use (as I did in this case with Kathie) phrasing such as "I see you looking for a connection between your dad's gardening and the way he dealt with you as a kid," rather than "The piece could be centered around a metaphor comparing your dad as a gardener with your dad as a father." Such personal language reminds writers of their connection with the text—something anxious writers, including those in our writing classrooms, often try to subvert. The message of such comments is clear: *They* are the ones doing the writing here. My role is merely that of someone observing the process and commenting upon it.

Another option I give to less experienced writers in the Writing Center is to have me do a general, holistic reading, during which I just try to see if and when the goals they have described to me are being accomplished. This is obviously a good choice for those who are at a stage where they are drafting purposefully but not always effectively. During this reading I usually make comments as I go along, rather than wait until the end of what could become a lengthy silent reading.

I tend to do a lot of what I loosely call "reader-response" when reacting aloud to these texts. "I'm really getting a sense of anger here," I might say, or perhaps "God, that's a riot!" or "I'm expecting something awful to happen real soon." That is, I let them know what happens to me when I am reading their work. Occasionally, to be sure, I break from this mode to comment on how well I see them accomplishing the goals they set up for themselves ("Yeah, the sheer scariness of the forest really comes through there"), but basically I give them *an oral account of my reconstruction of their text.*

I use this kind of response with both the "non-writers" and the confident writers in the Writing Center. With the less-than-self-assured participants, however, I once again stress the *writer's* creative processes rather than the text per se. Letting the Writing Teacher role dominate, I am less interested at this point in the quality of their products than in whether they are starting to see themselves as "real writers." As a result, my comments range from "Right now I'm seeing you setting me up for something—but I'm not sure yet what it is" to "As I go along in this paragraph, I'm not sure whether you are trying to push the balloon metaphor or starting to introduce a new one."

I like how they respond to this kind of reading. Though they do not see themselves as being "real writers," these participants generally *do* operate with goals and with a purpose, and they make many of their writing moves consciously. For such writers, attending to a reader's reconstruction of their text amounts to a reliving of their experience of writing it. In the Writing Center, then, they follow along, attending to my experience of reading their texts and saying such things as "Yes, I was really trying to show my fear there and I'm glad it worked," or "I was messing around with a connection between the garden and our relationship, but I can see that I need to work on the details more if you're going to really get it." When workshop participants talk like this, they are laying claim to their identities as writers and asserting their rights to their own text.

The workshop participants who don't see themselves as writers are gratifying and often easy to work with, for their needs are very clear and they take so much pleasure in their emergence as writers. Those who feel quite confident of their status as writers are also a pleasure to work with, but my relationship with them is usually less emotional and more "professional." Most of the self-confirmed "real writers" who come to the Writing Center are mature adults who are willing to subject their egos to some wounds for the sake of improving their craft. In fact, they will often take control of the conversation and are more likely to ask "Is this working?" than "What do you think I should try to do with this?" As a result, I generally treat them the same way I treat writers when I am operating as a Professional Editor. That is, I am more consistently "product-oriented" in these cases, focusing earlier in the week on matters of technique and style.

With such writers, the *text itself* becomes the central focus. We examine the piece of writing before us as a developing artifact that does not need to be validated, but which, we all agree, still needs some work. I use few second-person pronouns. Instead, I am likely to say such things as "The images here work together nicely, except maybe for the sagebrush one, which made me think of old cowboy movies instead of desolation," or "The transition here threw me off." I still try to give the writer a sense of my experience of his or her text, but now the emphasis is on what seasoned writers prefer to focus on—the text itself, not the writing process. I don't worry about appropriating the text of such writers. They wouldn't let me even if I tried.

When I think of the self-confirmed writers I have worked with in the Writing Center, I always think first of Mary Ellen, a woman in her sixties who came to the workshop as an accomplished poet who was finally ready to use her poetry to deal with her husband's death two years before. A quiet woman, Mary Ellen did not want to use her time in the Writing Center talking with me about the strength of her late husband, about the calm richness of their life together, or about the pain of losing him. Instead, she wanted me to read her poems the way an experienced editor might read them, looking in particular for moments when her attempts to objectify her feelings through images became too confusing or too contrived. Even when dealing with this most sensitive of subjects (or perhaps because it was such a poignant subject), Mary Ellen's craft came first, and my role was to help her keep her artistry focused and under control. My work with her, as it is with most of those workshop participants who already see themselves as real writers, was the kind of interaction which goes on between two professionals who are both good at what they do and who share a common goal—creating a high-quality written product.

As I've noted earlier, there is a point late in the week when my playing of the Professional Editor role becomes dominant with "non-writers" and "real writers" alike. By then, however, I hope that the gap between the two groups will not be nearly as large as it was when the week began. By the end of the workshop week, all of the participants will have had what is for them a great luxury—the time to "be a writer." Creating an environment where "being a writer" is possible, both in one-to-one conferences I have just detailed and in the response groups Mike describes in the next chapter, is at the heart of the Writing Center experience.

Log Entry

John (the slasher) helped me with my paper this afternoon. Such affirmation I have not experienced in relation to my writing since I was published in that magazine years ago. I certainly hope that the powers that be continue to run the writing center in future years. I was so confused and apprehensive about what I was writing. John read it and immediately sensed a structure and a message that I was unaware of. Not that he told me how to change it . . . it was always the question and response type exchange. Alan Weber's session on conferencing was exemplified by John today. It was so good to have someone understand what I was writing and *encourage* me in the manner he did. I simply can't wait to get at rewriting the material. Another of the all-too-famous "I have to remember this next fall when I am working with students." The excitement that I feel about writing this is partly because of the paper I am creating and partly a result of the confidence and acceptance that I experienced with John.

—Kathie Johnson

WRITING FAIR

Gardens
Kathie Johnson

Together we perform the traditional evening ritual of touring the garden. Dad moves carefully using the walking stick that I chose primarily for its name, unwilling to admit my father needed a cane. Down the rows of meticulously tended vegetables and flowers we wander, discussing the relative worth of Glamour tomatoes as opposed to Rutgers or Jet Stars. This year for amusement Dad has planted a half row of pink tomatoes. "Can you imagine?" He chuckles, "Someone is sitting around breeding tomatoes in different colors. Seems like they would have something better to do, doesn't it?"

"Think I planted enough potatoes?" Dad laughs again. "There's two rows of Onaways. Those are white ones." Always the teacher, he reminds me of lessons long forgotten as he points out another two rows of Russets and six long rows of Pontiac Reds.

"Who's he planning on feeding?" I wonder, for no longer are there six children crowded around his dinner table. There is little doubt, however, that those same children were the primary cause forcing the abandonment of his dreams of farming. Instead of rich fields of crops, an assembly line filled his days, leaving only summer evenings for his garden.

Across the dusty country road from this garden stretches the tangles of an abandoned farmstead. It was there I spent the long peaceful evenings of childhood, after my chores in Dad's garden were complete. Never pruned, the apple orchard bordering the wreck grew wild in its private interpretation of fruition. The apples collected as a child were small, sour, pockmarked, and mine, gathered for private picnics on my verandah. The fences of my garden had already sagged to the ground, boundaries long since abandoned as futile.

I, too, abandoned the orchard for years but as a teen I returned across the road seeking a place to write in my first journal. Already caught in the frantic life of a resort waitress, I retreated to the comfort of this familiar home. It was there, in a stand of aspens that were rapidly replacing the original gnarled apple trees, that I jumped two deer. I remember the fragility of their legs as they sprang up—inches from me. Leaping from their beds with fluid grace they cleared the fence row and were gone. Kneeling I touched the warmth of the trampled grass where they had slept. Stretching full length in their bed, I lay, usurping another's home, until the moment cooled.

Caught in the strength of my memories I turn impulsively. "Dad, let's go across the road and walk through the orchard."

"No, not tonight. I'm bushed. But you go on ahead." Dad's eyes twinkle up. "After spending another day in that classroom of yours, you could use some time to yourself. Walk quiet though," he warns. "There's a deer run towards the back of the orchard and you might scare one up if you're careful."

With another satisfied chuckle and his instructions complete he walks back deliberately toward the house as I make my way across the road, leaving the garden empty.

10 Response Groups in the Writing Center

Michael Bacon

The Rationale

Teachers come to the Traverse Bay workshops to rub shoulders with compatriots, learn more about writing, and practice more of their own writing. They are professionals who keep current on the latest research in their field, and they keep in touch with other professionals who do the same thing.

A peer response group is an ideal structure for allowing teacher-writers to learn for themselves that writing is fun, writing is valuable, and writing can be learned. The response group offers participants a chance to look at writing as it works. Plus, the response group is a useful activity for teaching writing. For these reasons, the Writing Center makes the peer response group method available to the workshop participants. By learning the specific strategies involved in this method, participants can take proven group techniques back to their classrooms and introduce their student-writers to the process and to the group experience.

The premise for the group is that every member and every member's work is worthy of the attention the group gives. This premise produces results. The structured sharing and focused responses provide direct and meaningful views of each member's writings, so much so that even a reluctant writer can experience a change in his or her attitude towards writing, exclaiming after a few sessions that "I really am a writer!"

Another aspect of the group situation which drives its success is that writing is a social activity, and the group is a social structure devoted to writing. Dealing with writing in a social context, giving meaning and importance to the act and the product and the author, all give credibility to the notion that writing is an important teaching and learning tool.

Besides, where else can teacher-writers receive fifteen minutes of undivided attention from a group of their peers, sharing with them some of their most personal and important ideas and skills? Writing ceases to become a threat and becomes instead a vehicle for communicating among friends.

It's true that many English teachers do not teach writing because they do not know how to write. Response groups can give these teachers the guidance and the support they need to take the risk and begin teaching writing to their students. I have seen it happen time and time again.

Getting Started

When the first Writing Center session meets on Monday afternoon, John and I explain to the participants their opportunity to engage in both one-to-one conferences and group-response meetings throughout the week. We have found that the participants arrive that first day in different stages of writing and have different levels of confidence. Their needs vary. Some have brought with them pieces—or at least ideas—that are already partially developed; they want to begin one-on-one sessions right away. Joan, for example, may have a memory piece about her first night at summer camp and the competition she entered with her best friend to see who could pull off the most outlandish prank. She has worked on it for three months and has with her a version that is a fourth draft. Others, on the other hand, are just beginning to work on a piece that is developing out of their first morning session; these people quite often will choose to begin immediately with the response group. Bill might have written the first five paragraphs of what is developing into a commentary on the ecology of the Great Lakes.

If the weather is nice, and it usually is, the response group will go outside. In the warm air, and under the pines, they quickly circle the chairs. Then, I review the rules and structure which provide the response group with its effectiveness: size of ideal group, kind of writing to bring, time-keepers, disclaimers, procedure for sharing, listening to comments, commenting techniques, and thank-yous.

Size of Group

Fifteen minutes is an ideal amount of time for the group to devote to a single writer and a single piece of writing. And two hours is about the maximum amount of time a group can function before it becomes exhausted. Obviously, then, the group should number no more than seven or eight people.

(For a class which meets for less than an hour, the teachers are reminded that the student groups need to be smaller, and the amount of time per writer needs to be reduced. For high school, four members to a group with eight minutes allotted to each will work very well.)

Writing to Bring

It is important to establish that in the first growing stages of a response group, the writers should bring rough draft, first version, and garbage or throw-away pieces. A writer's investment in his composition can be intense and personal. To avoid hurt feelings and until they learn to trust their group, writers can offer pieces in which they have very little invested.

One important rule that keeps beginning groups working well is to restrict the pieces of writing to one page each, or one poem if it is complete and not longer than one to two pages. Participants in response groups learn that when close scrutiny of writing is in play, longer pieces don't receive the proper attention.

Timekeeper

The group chooses a timekeeper whose job it is to ensure that all writers receive exactly the same amount of time, no more and no less. The timekeeper confirms with each author how much time he or she desires at the end of the fifteen-minute block for a response or "rebuttal" to the group's comments. One minute is usually sufficient.

I find it helpful when serving as watch-watcher to record on note paper the time each speaker begins. I then mark next to it the time at which the group needs to be reminded that the author has asked for a minute or so to respond to the responses.

When the timekeeper calls "Time," whoever is speaking should stop immediately, even in the middle of a sentence. If the timekeeper is not forceful, speakers will continue offering their "insightful and brilliant" comments, and before you know it, one member has received several minutes of somebody else's time. The result: the other members of the group receive the message that either their pieces were not as interesting and worthy of attention or that the current piece of writing "really needs more help" than their own. In either case, the group members can develop feelings of jealousy, a natural human reaction.

The timekeeper's job is important to making certain that the group remains a collaborative, effective effort. Comments not voiced during the group meeting can be shared in later, private discussions. Just because the group session ends, the work on the piece of writing needn't.

Disclaimers

There are two kinds of disclaimers: one is inappropriate to the group effort and one is necessarily appropriate.

We learn early in education to hedge our bets. You will hear from every teacher-writer comments such as, "This is something I just dashed off on the way over here. It isn't very good. It wasn't what I wanted to work on at all. Tomorrow I'll have something better." I tell the group not to make such statements.

If the group's work is to be effective, the writers must believe they can learn about their pieces of writing as they *exist*. Our goal is to take a piece of writing and make it better once we discover what it needs. If the writer makes inappropriate disclaimers, the writer is telling the group, "I know what's wrong and I don't need your help, nor do I trust you to help me." These kinds of comments cause the group to limit its comments and to reduce the amount of help it can offer.

Without any limiting comments, the group should feel free to comment about all elements in the piece. Sometimes, though, a piece has been worked over thoroughly and it just needs sharing again and maybe a final proofreading. In that case, the author should say, "Just let me read it to you, and would you please help me with a final proofreading for spelling and punctuation only?"

My worst experience in a group occurred when an author offered a poem and we worked with it as if it were a rough draft, only to find out later that she considered this her best and most polished piece, and she actually only wanted the group to praise it. At our next meeting, she offered her piece of writing which detailed her frustrations with our insensitivity, and we all learned a lesson about how to set up a response so it meets the author's expectations.

Procedure for Sharing: The Process Begins

After the preliminary work has been done and the rules established, we choose a person who will begin the group response process. I remind the rest of the group that each will follow in a clockwise rotation around the circle of writers.

The writers read their work out loud first. This allows them to hear what they have said. (They may make immediate mental changes to their draft as they read.) Also, the audience hears the original voice in the piece. Quite often, if the work is a poem, a writer is requested to read the work a second time. Marcia reads her narrative quickly, so the audience of writers gets the impression that time must pass quickly in the piece; so we begin listening for words which can be eliminated to help the reading pass as quickly, too.

(Ideally, each member of the group should have a written copy of the piece to follow and to mark on, but it is not always possible in a group that has never met before.)

Listening to Comments

After each reading, the author then lowers his or her eyes to the piece of writing and avoids making eye contact with the group. This is very difficult to accomplish, but it is what must happen for the response group to work its magic.

The group will discuss the piece, talking among its other members about the piece of writing, as if the author were not present. This technique allows writers to become eavesdroppers on the group's comments, and it allows them to hear how their piece of writing is working solely as a piece of writing.

The other group members *do not* engage in a conversation directly with the author, except to make inquiries about textual matters. Why not? Because the purpose of the exercise is to allow the author to hear how the piece of writing works as a piece of writing, not as a handout which accompanies a speech or discussion.

If Jack hears that the conversation between his grandmother and his father doesn't sound real or is confusing, he is more apt to pay attention to what his writing needs. If an audience member just looks Jack in the eye and says, "You need to work on this," he is less likely to think about changes he can make than he is to feel defensive and to wonder what the commenter means. This procedure obviously makes the audience work harder at talking about the piece of writing, the importance of which is discussed in the following section.

Commenting Techniques

I urge that the first comments about the piece include a reference to the whole piece, and might best be worded as something like, "I notice this is a narrative poem about watching Disney movies with young children." Another response might follow with a comment such as, "Yes, and I notice that the metaphor of animation is carried through each stanza." The group needs to work at this, because many teachers have the tendency to zero in immediately on a specific error such as a misspelled word and to overlook the piece as a whole.

Remember, most of this initial work is first draft, throw-away stuff. It isn't yet ready for the final, proofreading stage.

The best comments the group can make have to do with what they notice about each piece of writing. My most enlightening group experience resulted from a fifteen-minute discussion about a four-line poem. The total word count probably didn't exceed twenty, yet the group noticed the number of syllables, the repetition of sounds and letters, the smooth rhythm, the use of simple words in context, the use of vowels, and many other things as well. We even had time to explore a completely different interpretation based on the very same elements noticed for the first interpretation. An added benefit was that the audience received a practical lesson in close reading.

After a few minutes, responders will want to say something about specific parts of the piece under consideration. Moving from the whole to parts of the whole during the group conversation gives the writer excellent feedback. Positive comments are just as valuable as other kinds. One comment might be, "This essay ranges over a lot of ground. Repeating the same phrase at intervals, here in paragraph one and again in paragraph three, keeps me focused on the topic." Or a group member might say, "Look how color dominates the imagery of the poem, yet not one color is mentioned. I just automatically see black when I hear *raven* and I naturally think of red when I think about a bullfighter's cape. And here, *parakeet* makes me see light green."

I can just hear the author saying, "Yes!"

Quite often, the remarks discuss sections that need work. Instead of saying, "Hey, this line sucks swamp water!", I encourage the commentator to offer a solution to the writing problem. He could say instead something such as "What if this line were replaced with one that says . . ." or "What if this character was a woman instead of a man?" I've found from others who have been in groups that this helping effort also pays off in giving them practice at seeing and correcting weak parts in their own writing.

Another unproductive commenting device that I emphasize avoiding is saying "I like . . . ," or "I don't like . . ." I reinforce the comment by adding, usually, "If you like something, buy a copy of it; if you don't like it, don't buy a copy. In the meantime, make your comment helpful, such as, 'This word brings the right feel to the scene.' Let the writer know what's working or which part needs a what-if."

Thank-Yous

When "time" has been called, and before the writer offers any response to the peer group's comments, he should say, "Thank you." This reinforces the positive, helpful, effective group procedure.

Then it is time for the next author to read.

Ending the Session

At the end of each session, I try to hold a short debriefing episode just to review what happened. We might discuss such ideas as how Jack felt when the group noticed his conversation, and then we might discuss how the commenter felt noticing the color imagery of a poem. Usually, the group's comments reveal that each piece of writing deserved attention, and each writer succeeded in pursuing his or her topic. Every writer and commenter claim they have never experienced this feeling about their writing before. Many even distrust the good feelings because they are so new and foreign to their experiences. But when a group member says, "I want to hear more about your story, and I really want to know what you thought Uncle Fred would do with the insurance money," the writer knows something is working and he needs to continue.

Then, I invite them back tomorrow.

Final Thoughts

Because they deal with their work as both author and audience, nearly all participants feel very good about their pieces of writing by the time a session is over. One member or two may not. A group can have a bad day, or a writer may have a piece that doesn't work one hot August afternoon. Expectations can be off base as well. Three sessions will work out the bugs, however, and the value of a response group should be clear. I suggest that writers meet for three group sessions before making any decisions about a group's worthiness. Besides, it takes time and effort to learn the process.

The peer response group experience as well as the one-to-one conferencing in the Writing Center give participants understanding and skill to support their professional development as teachers and as writers. By the week's end, each participant leaves the Traverse Bay workshop with the feeling that he or she is now a practicing writer as well as a practicing teacher. The intensity and variety of their Writing Center experiences play a role in that emergence.

Log Entry

Today I was in the writing center for the first time and participated in small group response as done by Peninsula Writers group. This is a workable response process for the classroom. Modeling would have to be done, maybe John, Lissa, Nancy, and I, so students would see and hear process. This would serve to model the process as well as the writing. I can see this working in all classes where writing is going on. Mike Bacon said it can take a great deal of responsibility off the teacher's shoulders and put it onto the author's and audience's. This I like.

My students' weakest skills are in revision. Not surprising, as I know they all have lots of things to say. How, though, do I get them to take it seriously and talk about the writing? Does this mean the assignments have to be revised so they are more valuable to the students? Probably; since I will have a student teacher, maybe we can work on this together in Advanced Composition as well as Modern American Lit. They have to share what they're doing—give them a real audience. The audience, the rest of the class, needs to think of themselves as writers, people who make meaning out of their lives or at least attempt to. The process is simple; it just requires listening (something they can and need to work on) and talking in a constructive climate.

—Laurie Kavanagh

WRITING FAIR

"She is a trooper. . ."
Laurie C. Kavanagh

She is a trooper,
tolerates the injections,
daily blood work,
filled bladder, like
a water balloon about to burst.

She lays on the gurney,
morphine-induced smiles,
as the doctor pulls follicles from sore overripe ovaries.

▶

She waits and is brave,
learns new words and procedures
like some young med student.

And when none of it works,
she cries as expected
but inside a little girl
rages,
tries to understand a world
that builds fairytales on lies.

"The world narrows . . ."
Mary Ellen Kinkead

The world narrows
I'm going home again
where wind chimes
            never know the breath to birth
Where chink of china cup to fit its rim of earth
            speaks to empty space
Where a cat's incessant need for conversation
            is the fault line grating
A world erupting into widowhood.

III ... And Gladly Teach

11 Creating Our Own: Writing about Literature in Expressive and Imaginative Forms

Michael Steinberg

The English classroom is the place . . . wherein the chief matters of concern are particulars of humanness—individual human feeling, human response, and human time, as these can be known through the written expression (at many literary levels) of men and women living and dead, and as they can be discovered by student writers seeking through words to name and compose and grasp their experience.

—Benjamin DeMott

Log Entry

In the afternoon session, we all tried our hands at defining what we mean by "literature," and why we teach it. I defined it this way:

> Literature is reading material that enables the readers to see themselves, their circumstances, and/or their environment in a new way. Like a gem being cut, readers use literature to hone new facets of their own being that will allow greater depth, reflection, and brilliance. I teach literature because I believe approaching life with a multifaceted philosophy is valuable.

. . . After teaching students that our profession terms "basic writers" for about fifteen years, I've come to the conclusion that Mike is right. Many of the "problems" these students have in their reading and writing ability will not be remediated in ten weeks or a semester or sometimes even in a year. What I attempt to do is to encourage the ability that they do have and try to move them one step further down the road of reading and writing for pleasure.

—Janet Swenson

Most English teachers I know grew up loving books. As William
Sloane observes in *The Craft of Writing:*

> Watch a child's body when he is reading if you want to see the
> real reader. He wants to get on with the 'story,' to be caught up
> in it and to take it into himself. In the process, he may find
> much more, but he does so through that delight that is the
> highest form of entertainment. . . . For me that 'delight' means a
> kind of inner celebration, joyful in a deep sense; an act of
> receiving from the outside a gift, which by the nature of its
> reception, makes me more human. . . . It means also participat-
> ing in the experience that the work of art is . . . something good
> coming out of myself, and an element of growth, of becoming.
> The whole experience is pleasurable . . . (45)

Many of us became English teachers because we wanted to share that
same passion for literature Sloane writes about. Why is it, then, that
we seem to have so much difficulty getting our students to value literature? Why is it that most of our students don't gain some of the satisfaction from reading literature that we do?

The easy answers are the ones we always hear: too much T.V.,
print media overload, standardized testing in the schools. All of these
certainly contribute to the problem, but there are other factors we
need to pay attention to. Let me illustrate.

In my Traverse Bay teaching workshop, Responding
Expressively to Literature, I start off with two handouts. The first is a
copy of an episode from Jeff MacNelly's comic strip, *Shoe*. In this strip,
Skyler, a sixth grader, is in his room reading over his English assignment. The assignment asks, "Write a 200-word book report comparing
the themes of *Tom Sawyer* and *Treasure Island*." Skyler has not read
either book, yet without thinking or hesitating, he hunches over his
paper and writes:

> Comparing the themes of *Treasure Island*, which is Robert Louis
> Stevenson's most famous work of fiction, and the theme of the
> novel *Tom Sawyer*, by the beloved and very well known
> American author and writer, Samuel Clemens (otherwise known
> by his nom de plume, or pen name, Mark Twain), is a very hard
> and difficult job indeed, and requires a lot of careful study.
>   The first thing that one must do when one is asked to com-
> pare the theme of *Tom Sawyer* to the theme of *Treasure Island* is
> to find out where the two books are the same, if indeed they
> are. But also, however, be that as it may, the fact remains that
> while we want to find out the points where the two books are
> the same when we compare the two themes, we want to also
> find out, if we can, where the two books are different, if indeed
> they are different at all.

> In fact, such a question as comparing the themes of *Treasure
> Island* and *Tom Sawyer* is so difficult and complex a question that
> it certainly can't be properly discussed in a book report of two
> hundred words, of which this is the two hundredth. (74–75)

In the discussion that follows, we all agree that Skyler is neither
an uninformed nor unintelligent student-crow. He knows what "nom
de plume" means, he recognizes this is "a complex and difficult"
question, he writes grammatically correct standard English, he's constructed a clear beginning, development, and ending, and he's able to
come up with the required 200 words. As a matter of fact, he hits 200
on the nose. If you don't believe me, count the words.

Jeff MacNelly, the strip's creator, knows this territory all too
well. Skyler has solved the prescribed format; he knows how to write
the two-hundred word book report (on two books he hasn't even
read). And in the process, he's managed to say nothing concrete, give
no specific examples, and make no discoveries. In short, he's done no
serious thinking or reflecting about the books.

I know a lot of English teachers, like myself, who'd be angry
and frustrated to receive a batch of those themes. We'd say to our students, "You're missing the beauty, the ideas, the fun; you're not getting the meaning of all this." Once the anger subsides, though, we
soon realize that we're reading this kind of gobbledygook because it's
exactly what the assignment asks for. Skyler, I'd say, is a pretty smart
sixth-grader: he's learned how to give the teacher just what he or she
has asked for, a "200-word book report comparing the themes of *Tom
Sawyer* and *Treasure Island*."

The second handout is a Sandra Boynton comic/broadside entitled "The Turkey as English Professor." The turkey (a college literature professor), in a tweed sports jacket holding a pipe, lectures a dog
(his student) on why the dog's paper is remiss. The turkey/prof says
to the mutt/student:

> In your essay, you failed to consider the <u>human</u> elements of the
> novel, the dynamic flux between innocence and pathos. You
> did not adequately deal with the work's central themes: the
> tyranny of blind hypocrisy, the visionary eloquence of silence.
> You failed to fully appreciate the essential and ultimate value
> of compassion. You flunk.

I cite those two examples with tongue in cheek; yet it is largely
because of prescriptions like the 200-word book report and five-paragraph theme—and because of teachers who make literature into a
private, inaccessible language—that too many young students view

literature either as a fixed body of facts to be memorized and tested, or as having some pre-existing meaning that only their English teachers can decipher. It's a self-fulfilling prophecy: asking students to write exclusively in prescribed forms gives them the wrong message about what literature is. Ultimately, it dehumanizes the subject and distances readers from the "felt life" of all literary writing.

If we want our students to view literature as a dynamic, participatory form of human expression and as a vehicle for self-exploration and discovery, we need to get them back in touch with what William Sloane calls "that delight which is the highest form of entertainment." One way of encouraging that delight is to have students create their own "literature" in response to the literature they read; in other words, to read and write from the inside out. In my freshman classes, when we read poetry, fiction, drama, and personal essays for the first time—before we analyze, synthesize, or even discuss the works—we write prequels, sequels, and letters to authors and characters, and we compose our own poems, stories, and dialogues.

Using this approach I'm often delighted, but not surprised, that the results are so positive. Over time, my students' writing becomes more imaginative and original, literature discussions are richer and more energetic, their insights are incisive and authentic, and when I finally ask them to write in any of the required, prescribed forms, my students are more adept and capable than those who have written exclusively in required academic forms.

Since creating their own literature seems to animate even my first-year college business majors, and since so many teachers now seem to need to rediscover their own love of literature, I designed my afternoon teaching session at the Traverse Bay workshop to allow us first to read some literature, and then to write expressively—that is, to play, and have some fun.

After we discuss the two handouts, we talk about what literature is and what roles it has played in our lives. Then I hand out a simple narrative poem by Portia Nelson, entitled "Autobiography in Five Short Chapters." To break the ice, I ask twenty people in the group to each read one line of the poem aloud to the rest of us. The piece goes like this:

> Chapter One.
> I walk down the street
>   There is a deep hole in the sidewalk
>   I fall in.
>   I am lost . . . I am hopeless
>   It isn't my fault.
>   It takes me forever to find a way out.

Chapter Two.
I walk down the same street.
There is a deep hole in the sidewalk.
I pretend I don't see it.
I fall in again.
I can't believe I'm in the same place
But, it isn't my fault.
It still takes a long time to get out.

Chapter Three:
I walk down the same street.
There is a deep hole in the sidewalk.
I see it is there.
I still fall in . . . it's a habit.
My eyes are open
I know where I am.
It is my fault.
I get out immediately.

Chapter Four:
I walk down the same street.
There is a deep hole in the sidewalk.
I walk around it.

Chapter Five:
I walk down another street. (Nelson 2–3)

I chose this piece because it's simple and accessible, and because teachers can identify with its theme. After the read-around, we talk about how the writer uses the metaphor of the hole as a way of suggesting the ruts and habits we are all subject to, and how the poet uses meter, line breaks, etc. In this informal yet analytical mode, everyone feels relaxed and safe. We're modeling, after all, what English teachers are trained to do.

Next, I announce that we will brainstorm some ideas for responding to this piece—in writing. The only ground rule is that we will write expressively rather than critically. As soon as I mention "writing," the room falls silent; people nervously shift in their seats, many lower their eyes. I try to relax them by explaining that anything they write is okay. No one exhales, though.

We begin to brainstorm. Tentative at first, the teachers soon come up with suggestions. The first ones are poems, stories, and dialogues, the expected forms. Then someone calls out, "How about a drawing?" I hear another person yell, "Try a mime," then another says, "Song lyrics," and we're on a roll. We quickly list other forms such as news stories, personal essays, editorials, feature stories, satirical sketches, mock psychological profiles and case studies, prequels, sequels, invented endings, letters, and so on. I like the spontaneous energy that's building, so I tell them it's time to write. Silence again, accompanied by rustling of papers and clearing of throats. A few people get up to go to the bathroom; the rest pick up their pens and tentatively begin to scribble some words on the paper.

I know they need a nudge, so I quickly explain how to do a copychange, a generating form to help get writing started. To write a copychange, you follow the existing form of the piece and fill in your own subject, language, images, etc. For example, I begin my own copychange like this:

> I step into my first classroom.
> A group of students stare at me.
> I try to speak.
> I am lost . . . I am hopeless.
> It will take me forever to become good at this . . . etc.

Once we get going I write along with them, keeping one eye on my watch. After about fifteen minutes, I sense this group is warming. And when I announce that it's time to break into small groups and share our writing, several teachers groan and ask for more time. Surprise number one.

Within minutes after they begin sharing, another piece of magic occurs: people in the small groups are crying, laughing, and spontaneously volunteering to read their pieces aloud. The full-group sharing session is just as lively. We hear from a man who creates a satiric narrative written from the point of view of the hole: "Why do all these people keep dropping in?" he begins. A woman displays an abstract drawing of the hole, embellished, in calligraphy, by the poem's text. We listen to a mock angry letter written by a citizen to the negligent construction company. And we share some poems, a psychologist's report, a few song lyrics and dialogues, and so on.

I'm elated by the energy that's been unleashed, so I decide to nudge us a little further and see what happens. I ask for volunteers to talk about what surprised them in the writing, what discoveries they made, what problems they did and didn't solve. One woman says she was surprised to find that her piece wanted to be a newspaper article instead of her pre-planned narrative. Even more of a surprise was that she went with the newspaper article. A man tells us that, in inventing a made-up dialogue, he found the poem's meaning. Another woman says the poem reminded her of her early teaching days, so she wrote her own teaching poem. I ask her to read it, then I chip in and explain how reading the poem also prompted me to write my own teaching poem.

I do this for two reasons: to make the reading-to-writing process more visible; and to let teachers know that connecting their experience with the literature they read can yield unexpected discoveries. The full-group sharing also helps us see the diversity of responses; it shows us that when we're engaged in making meaning we're always analyzing, synthesizing, clarifying, connecting, predicting, speculating, reflecting, inquiring—all the things students are asked to do when they're required to write in the prescribed forms. In short, the session dramatizes the original premise of the workshop: that students who can write expressively about literature do have a critical and analytical understanding of what they are reading.

Finally, we talk about where we might go from here. Writing expressively about the poem has taught us how to use literature as a catalyst for critical thought and inquiry as well as how to make connections between our own experiences and what the text is telling us. In fact, most of us agree that we are in fact exploring, interpreting, and analyzing the poem in more original and incisive ways than we would have done if we'd written a "critical analysis" of it. Finally, by making our own metaphors, we are teaching ourselves how a poet uses metaphor to express and convey his or her meaning. In short, we are discovering, from the inside out, how writing our own "literature" leads us to a critical awareness of how a piece of literature works.

For the last ten to fifteen minutes we brainstorm lists of activities we might find useful in our own classrooms: a unit on narrative poetry which builds from expressive journal entries and meditations to more fully developed poems; a thematic unit on "the sense of self," which includes a variety of alternative forms and modes of response—debates, group writing, role playing, panel and game shows, etc., as well as fiction, drama, and poetry; a research unit where students chose an influential person from history, literature, or the popular culture and then develop their pieces in a multi-genre approach, mixing autobiography, poetry, visual arts, media, fiction, narrative, dialogues, etc.

We agree that by responding in these diverse, open-ended ways we're addressing an imbalance that has existed for far too long in our public school English/Language Arts curriculum. But equally important, we know we are helping ourselves—and in turn our students—to engage with literature more readily; in the process we are finding ways to make writing about literature more accessible and meaningful. Moreover, we are reinforcing the notion that if we want young readers and writers to see literature as a dynamic, human medium and as a catalyst for self-exploration and discovery, we need to provide them with more opportunities to compose in the diverse forms which reflect their own inner and outer worlds.

My hope is that the teachers in this workshop will bring those messages back to their schools—that they will encourage their students to see that literature and writing are not simply artifacts to be memorized and given back on a standardized test or rehashed in a canned term paper. And finally I hope they will continue to do what James Moffett suggests when he writes, "Learning literature is not learning about literature, but learning to use literature as a source of experience and as a resource for personal growth."

References

DeMott, Benjamin. *Supergrow: Essays and Reports on Imagination in America.* New York: E.P. Dutton, 1969.

McNelly, Jeff. *The New Shoe.* New York: Avon, 1981.

Moffett, James. *Teaching the Universe of Discourse.* Boston: Houghton Mifflin, 1968.

Nelson, Portia. *There's a Hole in My Sidewalk: The Romance of Self Discovery.* Hillsboro, OR: Beyond Words Publishing, 1993.

Sloane, William. *The Craft of Writing.* Ed. Julia H. Sloane. New York: W. W. Norton, 1983.

Tchudi, Stephen N., and Diana Mitchell. *Explorations in the Teaching of English*, 3rd Edition. New York: Harper & Row, 1989.

Applications in the Classroom

Writing about Literature in Expressive/Imaginative Forms

■ Rewrite the Story/Poem in another form: Fairy tale, music video, fable, sci-fi, adventure story, romance, Western, T.V. show, movie, children's story, poem to story, story to poem, story to script or play, dialogue, talk show, interview, song, Reader's Theatre, etc. Make any changes in characters, point of view, setting, etc. that you wish.

■ Write a Prequel to the story—your own imagined account of what happens before the story opens.

■ Write a sequel.

■ Write a letter from one character to another.

■ Write a letter to the author telling him or her what your thoughts, feelings, responses were. Ask him or her any questions you like. Then write a letter of response from the author to you.

- Write a letter of advice, praise, criticism, complaint, etc. to one of the characters.

- Put one of the characters on trial and write the script.

- Write a character profile of any of the story's characters.

- Assuming the point of view of one of the characters, write a memoir or personal reminiscence.

- Write a book review (not a book report) of the story for a self-selected magazine or other publication. Read some book reviews before you do this one.

- Write an editorial point of view or commentary for a specific publication or radio/T.V. show supporting whatever views of the story/poem you'd like to discuss.

- In a Personal/Analytical Narrative, compare this story/poem with another piece of writing you've read.

- Write an article for a magazine specifying how you'd teach this poem/story to children or young adults—or senior citizens.

- Write a satire or parody of the story/poem.

EXTENSIONS

Becoming Another Person Theme
Wilma Romatz

Write a theme in which you step into the shoes of a person from another place and time, and relate in the first person point of view an afternoon's events that show significant aspects of his or her life.

Objectives

1. Use research materials in a new way—the third person approach of the encyclopedia must be changed to the personal point of view, related in what you think the words of the character would be.

2. Expand your understanding of another time and person by thinking about what that life would have been like.

3. Focus on one critical moment which can demonstrate specific aspects about the person. For example, if you want to show Marilyn Monroe as a promiscuous sex symbol, you would choose one set of details, one situation, but if you want to show her as a misunderstood intelligent woman, your emphasis would be much different.

▶

Steps

1. Brainstorm people: Make a list of at least ten people who interest you, famous, infamous, or common. Choose one.

2. Dialogue study: Eavesdrop on a conversation and write it down in dialogue form, trying to capture the personalities of the speakers by the words you choose for them to speak.

3. Check encyclopedias for information that will be useful. Bring to class brainstorming on these bits of information. Write a summary of significant details from an encyclopedia article related to your subject in your own words.

   Facts to consider and look for:

   - political climate when he or she lived, famous people he or she would have known
   - significant situations in the life—crisis points
   - home life, occupation, interests
   - country and time in which the person lived
   - significant events of the day

4. Write the formal paper, 300–500 words, using dialogue as one way of revealing character. Make sure you use first person—actually become the other person in your mind. Consider what kind of conflict would reveal the character, and what other persons the conflict would involve. Reveal the setting quickly in the first paragraph. Then let the events develop the points of character you wish to reveal.

Character Sketch
Nanci Tobey

Purpose:

- To provide a prompt for creating a fictional character
- To apply understanding of elements of fiction studied in short stories to their own writing
- To help students learn how writers make discriminating choices about describing their characters
- To help students write more vividly

When I have freshman students for one half of the year and the focus is literature, I don't have a lot of time for lengthy creative writing assign-

▷

ments, so (adapting an idea from Linda Robinson at Harrison [Michigan] High School) I have developed a way to help students create a character sketch. Because of the nature of the assignment, I can easily check the students' progress after each step, and the assignment takes no more than three days. In the process, they review and apply various elements of the short story which we have previously discussed to their own work.

I find that students generally prefer a writing prompt and require some help getting started, so I begin with a picture to help them visualize their character. First I have them search for a couple of advertisement pages from magazines featuring a human subject. I specify that they choose unknown subjects rather than celebrities because I don't want them to have any preconceived notions about the personalities in the photographs.

Next, I have them observe the pictures and imagine what each subject is like (physically and personality-wise) based on the visual information they have before them. I ask them to write brief but vivid descriptive phrases in the categories of *Face, Body, Movement, Voice, Props/Costumes,* and *Attitude* as if they were describing this person to a friend. Sometimes they have to extrapolate ideas from scanty clues a picture suggests. We review simile, metaphor, and the use of vivid language at this point. Students then share their work with a partner for suggestions about making their descriptions more realistic and for getting rid of anything that doesn't "ring true" to the picture.

Finally, I require the students to pick out one of their photo subjects and imagine him or her as a character in a fictional setting. They may imagine an expository scene or a scene of conflict with another character. I have them write their idea in two to three paragraphs, directing them to choose only the characteristics from their list that help make the point of the conflict or that help define the attitude of the character in the exposition of a story excerpt. We look at short story cuttings for ideas of how to begin the writing. After the rough draft is completed, students may work together in groups or in pairs suggesting additions to the characterization or deletions of unnecessary physical description. We work at getting away from the kind of "police report" description that some students feel compelled to make.

After students revise their work, I post the papers around the room with the magazine photos attached. This always invites students from other classes to read the work, and the writers are usually pleased to see their work displayed.

12 "Well, I Was Born in a Small Town": Popular Media in the Language Arts Classroom

Robert L. Root, Jr.

Log Entry

I got this idea after Root's class on visual literacy this afternoon. I'd do this unit with my class of gifted eighth graders. Using examples of TV sitcoms about American families from the 60s, 70s, 80s, and 90s, we could discover how the view of the family has changed in our culture. I would like to end the series with *The Simpsons*. I'd like to incorporate cooperative learning strategies, writing assignments, discussions, role playing, and perhaps the production of their own video which they have written and produced.

—**Mary Jo Converse**

Our students are steeped in popular media. They provide the chief sources of both entertainment and information for our culture at large. For people whose business is the teaching of language and literature, they are also pervasive, ubiquitous models of rhetoric, poetry, drama, and narrative—not so much the antithesis of traditional literature and rhetoric as alternative resources. The following unit draws upon popular media to focus on the home town experience, but although it involves some critical analysis of song lyrics and music videos, popular media serves not as a focal point but rather as a way of initiating a series of opportunities for students to explore in and about the English language arts, examine their own backgrounds and life experiences, and express their feelings and insights about their lives, their feelings, their reading, listening, and viewing in both expressive and transactional ways. The unit was devised for students in the rural schools and small town school districts of central Michigan, where I live and whose classes I visit, but it is readily adaptable to surburban and urban students as well, because it is essentially a unit about where students live and how they they think about it.

Popular Songs about Hometowns

When I have taught this unit to groups as varied as fifth graders, eighth graders, and twelfth graders, I have used three songs in particular which provide a range of responses useful for class discussion: "My Hometown" by Bruce Springsteen (available on the album *Born in the USA*), "My Little Town" by Paul Simon (on *Still Crazy After All These Years*), and "Small Town" by John Cougar Mellencamp (on *Scarecrow*"). Students will be familiar with these artists— Mellencamp's video for "Small Town," in particular, has been a staple of both MTV and VH1 music channels—but my selection of these three songs is based chiefly on the parallels in theme and subject matter and the clear contrasts in attitude and perspective of the first-person speakers in the songs.

The Springsteen song is useful for establishing typical elements of a popular song: lyrics, melody, arrangement, and the structure of stanza/refrain, stanza/refrain, bridge, stanza/refrain. The first stanza recounts the narrator's memory of being eight years old and sitting on his father's lap behind the wheel of a "big old Buick"; as they drive, the father tells him, "Son, take a good look around // This is your hometown." In the second stanza, racial tensions in the singer's high school years have changed the character of the town; the bridge brings us to the present: "Now Main Street's white-washed windows and vacant stores" and economic hard times have closed the mill and left the narrator unemployed. In the final stanza he is now thirty-five, discussing with his wife "heading south" in hopes of employment and sitting his own son on his lap for a final tour of the town. The refrain, "This is your hometown," usually repeated four times at the end of each stanza, is sung only once here, then played instrumentally, as if the singer has gone. The use of parallel images to serve as the frame of the song, the chronological shifts and changes in the connotation of the refrain, the way the bridge signals a change in direction both lyrically and musically—all of this is clear to students and prepares the way for discussions of structure and attitude in the other songs.

These three songs establish a range of responses to the hometown experience. Springsteen's narrator recounts a history of social and economic changes forcing a family to leave the town in which they grew up ("foreman says these jobs are leaving and they ain't coming back"). Simon's narrator rages against the emptiness and boredom of the town where "when it rains there's a rainbow // and all of the colors are black // It's not that the colors aren't there— // it's just imagination they lack"—there, he says, "I never was nothing, just my father's son" and there is "nothing but the dead and dying back in my little town"; Mellencamp's narrator celebrates the simple pleasures of growing up and living in a small town, with nary a word of criticism—"I cannot forget where it is I come from, // cannot forget the people who love me. // I can be myself in a small town // and people let me be just who I want to be."

Students find it easy to identify with at least one of these viewpoints, to find the expression of their own feelings about their hometown in one of these lyrics. Having discussed and analyzed these lyrics, I give students the following informal writing prompt:

Thinking about Your Own Lyrics

We've just been talking about three songs about hometowns. Just for a moment, think about your hometown and the ways that hometowns have been represented in the words (lyrics) of these songs. Which of these songs makes you think of your hometown? Why? What would you have to change about that song to make it more appropriate as a song about your hometown? What would you take out? What would you put in? How would you write your own song about your hometown?

For the next ten to fifteen minutes, record in writing any thoughts you have about these songs and your hometown. When you've done that, we'll talk about some of your ideas.

Then, having used this writing occasion to prepare the students, we discuss their reactions to the songs in terms of personal responses rather than as literary artifacts. The discussion gives them an opportunity to begin thinking about themselves and their own feelings about their community. One student who identified with Simon's "My Little Town" observed that

[I]n a small town you are too sheltered and don't really get to know different kinds of people. Everyone in the small town is exactly the same. I would like to move to a bigger city so I could meet those different people.

Another liked Mellencamp's "Small Town" because

[I]t doesn't make living in a small town sound rough. . . . Sometimes it is nice to know everyone. Sometimes you wish that you couldn't be picked from a crowd.

A third student wondered,

> Is there something about how we're originally raised that creates a need to return, a need to keep the small town in us no matter where we go—can we be in a big city but essentially still see it as a small town?

Both complaints and compliments about their hometowns generate discussion—students generally will fall in a range from positive to negative, with many variations in between. The discussion also gives them a chance to hear other ideas which will begin to make them more balanced and more concrete about their views; the writing gives them images and language of their own concerning the community.

While the small town is the focus here, songs about urban environments can also be compared. On the theme of neighborhood, for example, there are a large number of songs to choose from, such as "In My Neighborhood" by the JB Horns, "In the Neighborhood" by Spice 1, "In My Neighborhood" by Jennyanykind, "Living in My Neighborhood" by Magic Slim, "The Neighborhood" by Los Lobos, and "Neighborhood" from the Original Broadway Cast recording of *Smokey Joe's Cafe*. Record stores often have a computerized customer-operated consulting service which can identify song titles, artists, and music formats; students can also be resources for tracking down these songs. With all recordings and videos, teachers should preview the material before playing it for a class, since some selections can have problematically graphic language and content.

Depending on time constraints and the overall length of the unit, I would here allow students to either revise the lyrics of the song they find most appropriate until it fits their own response, find lyric sheets and tapes of other songs on this subject that they identify with more, or compose their own songs by putting new lyrics to an established melody or creating both lyrics and melody. If this were as far as you wanted to take the unit, this would be a good culminating project. Final writings could be shared selectively on the bulletin board or universally in an anthology published by the class; oral readings of the projects could substitute for or supplement these publications.

Music Videos

We begin by talking about the conceptual and the narrative forms of video by watching a couple. John Cougar Mellencamp's music video for "Small Town," which draws heavily on family photographs and home movies interspersed with new illustrative footage of particular images or ideas, is a good one to use, because it draws upon so many personal items that students immediately see the potential for adaptation. When the song speaks of work, a montage of small town laborers provides a background; when it speaks of marriage and family, actual snapshots and yearbook pictures of Mellencamp himself, his wedding, and his relatives make up the visuals. These are the stuff of everyone's visual montage. Compared to his video for "Rain on the Scarecrow," a protest song in defense of the family farmer, with images of farm work and rural families intercut with images of a farm auction and delapidated barns, or the video for "Pink Houses," with its images of a trailer park bedecked with American flags beneath which a biker deals drugs, its sense of lost hopes, and its ironic refrain ("Ain't that America? Little pink houses for you and me"), the "Small Town" video can be seen as a particularly positive production, matching pleasant images to optimistic lyrics.

With "Small Town" we have the chance to note how music videos work, the ways scenes either illustrate or ironically subvert lyrics. We also have the opportunity to see a video that enhances the lyrics of the song by giving specificity of image to generality of expression. After analyzing the video we conjecture about the images necessary for similar videos of the songs by Springsteen and Simon (only a concert version exists for "My Home Town" and none exists for "My Little Town"); if time allows, we can examine script format and allow students working in small groups to come up with a shotlist or series of images for a conceptual or narrative video for either song.

As with the song lyrics, when we have examined the music video as a literary form, I again begin to turn the students inward by giving them the following:

Thinking about Your Own Images

We've just been looking at videos about hometowns. Just for a moment, think about your hometown and the ways that hometowns have been represented in the words (lyrics) and images of these songs. Which of these videos makes you think of your hometown? Why? What would you have to change about that video to make it more appropriate as a song about your hometown? What would you take out? What would you put in? How would you film your own video about your hometown?

For the next fifteen minutes or so record in writing any thoughts you have about these songs and your hometown. When you've done that, we'll talk about some of your ideas.

The discussion which follows this piece of workaday writing should get the students thinking in terms of images and sequences of images about their home town. In St. Louis, Michigan, students brainstorming their own videos immediately saw possibilities all around them. "You'd have to show the 7–11," someone said, "and everyone hanging out there. That's really the social center of town." Someone else picked up on the economic decay in Springsteen's song and applied it to his own circumstances; he proposed, "You could have a whole bunch of pictures of the chemical plant, starting when everyone was working there and showing them tearing it down and then ending it with a picture of the empty lot where it used to be." Other students immediately chimed in with suggestions for where to get still pictures and postcards and news footage. They have a great deal of information about life in their community; comparing their concept of hometown life with that in the video(s) they've seen, they immediately begin to visualize the kinds of videos they could create.

Given a script format and some basic camera terminology and methods (illustrated in specific videos), students can readily begin to write video scripts. An assignment should entail every student writing a video script about a song of the student's choice (including those students themselves compose); it should invite them to explore that assignment at first informally, in journal entries, peer group discussion, or class brainstorming sessions, and then provide them with workshop occasions in which they can plan, draft, and revise. Those who find the musical nature of the assignment too daunting could attempt a non-music video script about their feelings, experiences, and ideas of their hometown.

A good many variations and alternative extensions are equally possible. The unit is adaptable to almost any grade level: after presenting the workshop to eighth graders in St. Louis, I was invited to also present it to fifth graders, who also reacted enthusiastically to this chance to think about popular media *and* to talk about their familiar community. To further discussion of songs and videos, students might be invited to bring in further examples of either or both. I have found that a presentation to virtually any group of students leads to follow-up questions and comments about an additional range of resources, some of which have particular power in the classroom because the students have already connected to them in some way; after a presentation discussing songs and videos on the larger theme of American life, in which I drew chiefly on Woody Guthrie, Jackson Browne, Springsteen, Simon, and Mellencamp, high school students suggested a wide range of other titles—Metallica's "And Justice For All," "Which Way to America?" by Living Color, "Color Code" by Steve Taylor, "America" by Neil Diamond, "Livin' in America" by James Brown, "Allentown" by Billy Joel—only a few of which I was familiar with.

Moreover, the extensions needn't be confined to popular media. Discussions of song lyrics lead naturally to drawing upon similar themes in poetry (for example, in the works of Edward Arlington Robinson, Robert Frost, and Edgar Lee Masters) and reinforce the relationship between song lyrics and traditional poetry. By the same token, other literary forms can extend the analysis of small-town life with fiction (i.e., works by Willa Cather, Eudora Welty, Booth Tarkington, Sinclair Lewis, Sherwood Anderson) or drama ("Our Town" by Thornton Wilder). Music videos extend easily into visual forms such as television or film.

Just as the reading and viewing moves out into other forms, so the writing could move out as well, inviting poetry, short fiction, and essays. Students might turn to an intimate examination of their own pasts by reading copies of newspaper columns which print reader submissions on local and family history, and by composing their own column to submit about parents, grandparents, family recollections in their hometowns. Even if the columns never were published by the local papers, such a series of essays, carried out thoroughly and carefully prepared for publication, would make an interesting class anthology to publish and distribute among class members and possibly their families, the school, or the community.

In schools where the facilities were available, students could make their own videos, either individually over an extended period of time or as group projects, several students to a group, several projects to a class, or as a class project to brainstorm, script, research, photograph, act out, tape, edit, and finalize for the school or the community. In one of the communities where I presented these popular media explorations of hometown experience, two fifth-grade teachers combined their classes to produce a hometown video to be presented to the town council, reflecting their feelings about their hometown.

Such projects allow students to connect popular media with traditional literary and rhetorical forms, to link professional artistic creation with their own creativity, to use their reading and writing to foster their understanding of themselves and their communities as well as of literary forms; they engage them in collaboration, whole language situations, a range of learning opportunities and styles, all the language arts.

References

Mellencamp, John. "Small Town." *Scarecrow.* John Cougar Mellencamp. Riva Recording. 824865.

Simon, Paul. "My Little Town." *Still Crazy After All These Years.* Paul Simon. Columbia Recording. PC33540.

Springsteen, Bruce. "My Hometown." *Born in the USA.* Bruce Springsteen and the E Street Band. Columbia Recording. AL 38653.

Applications in the Classroom

"Well, I Was Born in a Small Town": Popular Media in the Language Arts Classroom

■ Play "My Hometown" by Bruce Springsteen (*Born in the USA*), "My Little Town" by Paul Simon (*Still Crazy After All These Years*), and "Small Town" by John Cougar Mellencamp (*Scarecrow*) one at a time and discuss the lyrics and the music.

{*Extensions:* Explore the poetic dimension of this subject by turning to such figures as Edward Arlington Robinson, Robert Frost, and Edgar Lee Masters, among others.}

■ Provide students with a writing-to-learn activity in which they think about which songs they identify with most and how they would change lyrics to match their feelings about their own hometown.

{*Extensions:* Invite students to revise the lyrics of the song they find most appropriate until it fits their own response, bring in lyric sheets and tapes of other songs on this subject that they identify with more, or compose their own songs, either being wholly original or putting new lyrics to an established melody. Final writings could be shared on the bulletin board, in an anthology published by the class, or through oral readings.}

■ Show students other videos which are either conceptual or narrative, and discuss the ways music, lyrics, and images go together.

{*Extensions:* Examine the video as an art form, showing several examples of each subgenre, and invite students to search for images to go with lyrics by being brought back to songs for which no video exists, working in small groups to come up with a shotlist or series of images for the video.}

■ Give students a writing-to-learn activity, asking them to revise the "Small Town" video to incorporate images that reflect their feelings about their hometown as well as reflect its individual personality.

{*Extensions:* Extend the analysis of small-town life into other examples, such as short stories ("Paul's Case" by Willa Cather, "Why I Live at the P.O." by Eudora Welty), novels (especially by Booth Tarkington, Willa Cather, Sinclair Lewis, Sherwood Anderson), drama ("Our Town" by Thornton Wilder), television ("Mayberry, RFD," "Leave It to Beaver," even current daytime and prime-time soap operas) or film.}

■ Assign students to write video scripts on a song of the student's choice (including self-composed material) or about their feelings, experiences, ideas of their hometown.

{*Extensions:* Where the facilities are available, students could make their own videos, either individually or as group projects.}

Using Popular Media in English

Analyzing

■ Replay specific commercials to compare images with words.

■ Play scenes from film adaptations of literary works to focus analysis of literary scenes and characters.

■ Ask students to predict the nature of adaptations based on their reading of original literary texts.

■ Ask students to react to the visual components of documentaries and newscasts as they relate to the verbal components.

■ Compare printed lyrics with visual interpretations in music videos.

■ Compare literary texts with cinematic or video adaptations.

■ Compare remakes of original screenplays with earlier versions.

■ Compare items in genres and subgenres (e.g., sitcoms, black family sitcoms, detective shows, etc.; commercials for food, cars, etc.)

■ Compare newscasts from different channels reporting the same stories.

■ Compare print and video reporting of the same story.

■ Compare thematically related music videos.

■ Read scenes in fiction aloud to compare description, characterization, and dialogue with film scenes.

Creating

■ Write scripts for music videos of original or recorded songs or original or published poems.

■ Write commercials for real or imaginary products, including those inspired by literature assignments (Macbeth action figures).

■ Write public service commercials for the community.

■ Write newscripts.

■ Write commercials based on literary texts in the same way some are based on contemporary films.

■ Write scripts of scenes in literary works.

■ Write scripts of parodies or remakes of literary works (Oliver Twist in Detroit; Julius Caesar in Washington; Huck Finn in California).

■ Videotape any or all of the above, with student casts and crews.

■ Write fiction or drama based on scenes in film scripts.

■ Write poetry in response to visuals in music videos or commercials shown with the sound off.

■ Write dialogue for silent films.

■ Propose popular music for silent (or silenced) film scenes (a la *Metropolis* with the Giorgio Moroder soundtrack).

■ Write a newscript after viewing silent footage from a newscast and reading a newspaper version of the story.

EXTENSIONS

Writing on Location
Kathie A. Johnson

Purpose: to write a journal to establish narrative voice.

Materials: paper, pencil, a firm surface for students to write on (another book) and permission to leave the classroom.

In helping my students begin to write freely and explore different voices in their writing, I have found that taking the class to an actual location for the writing experience and allowing them to recreate the situation from a variety of viewpoints helps them understand the concept as well as providing stimulation for writing.

One of the first expeditions in the fall is to the football field. Because many students are involved in football (player, band, spectator, cheerleader) and because of the appeal of extracurricular events, this is a good place to start.

I divide the class into different groups: home players, visiting team, band, parents, bench sitters, etc. If my class includes actual players, I allow them to choose specific positions and to explain those positions to the class. Each group is then given a short introduction explaining their specific situation. For example: You are a bench sitter. You have played only once in an actual game, and that was the last two minutes of a game your team was losing badly. Record your feelings as you sit watching your teammates play. Start with "I."

▶

The groups are seated in corresponding places according to their roles—on benches, in the middle of the field, in the end zone, on bleachers, in the stands. Throughout the writing experience, I move from group to group, providing guided imagery to encourage their writing. The only requirement is that they write—spelling, sentences, etc. are not a concern. After approximately 15 minutes, the students change groups for a new perspective.

These writings are then placed in the students' folders for ideas for short stories, first-person narratives, poetry, essays.

Hometown Video, or Not by the Chamber of Commerce
Patricia Stedman

After finishing my first year of teaching a low-level ninth-grade English Skills class, I firmly believe that one more year reviewing the same seventh- and eighth-grade material is not working for these kids. My only two successes all year were a simulated news broadcast, which was video taped, and a fairly relaxed "exposure only" treatment of "Macbeth" in which the students wore crowns and capes, carried swords, and re-enacted only the most violent of scenes before watching Orson Welles' version of the play. These students like to actively participate, to move. These two notions, heavily influenced by Bob Root, have produced the following idea for a writing unit.

In this project each student will write, design, and produce their own segment of a hometown video. The project will use the music video format to motivate students to write; supply a subject area in which all have something to say; explore the sensory nature of writing by matching visual and sound images to the text; and provide the students with an occasion to be physically active in class.

My hope for this unit is that it will provide the students with the chance to connect emotionally with their pasts and surroundings and develop the desire to write about their thoughts and experiences.

Pre-writing

What do we already know about Harbor Springs, Michigan? Some research on the teacher's part will be required here to prime the pump. Brainstorming will lead to anecdotes which tell about Harbor Springs by focusing on events in the students' lives. By using a mix of stories, songs, and videos, see how other authors have dealt with the same topic. This step could take several days and should include a wide

▶

range of viewpoints from Truman Capote to Bruce Springsteen to Patrick McManus. Follow each selection with a search for similar emotions and situations in our own lives. Give each student a large piece of newsprint and a felt tip pen to create a graphic organizer of Harbor Springs. Dialog, diagrams, pictures, character ideas—all are encouraged at this stage. These subconscious blueprints should be shared. Look for the connections. Is there a story to tell?

Writing

At this point each student should have something to say. Plenty of time should be provided in class for writing, revising, and also for technical instruction when and where necessary. I plan to keep a daily log of each student's progress. The unit could end at this point with the publication of their final drafts in the local weekly paper.

Video Production

Give the students newsprint and have them draw a cartoon strip of their video. Draw pictures to correspond to numbered segments of their final draft. Show them what a real script looks like with the visual and auditory directions coordinated to the text. Only when the video scripts have been written will the actual taping begin. Pay attention to the time it takes to read each passage. Use a stop watch so there is enough footage. Actual taping and dubbing will be time consuming. Count on out-of-class time being necessary. Although contracts could be used to assure completion, I'm betting the students will be self-motivated, because they have their own story to tell. And besides, this is the hands-on, fun part of the project.

13 Talking to Yourself in the Car Is Okay: A Workshop about Writing Monologues and Dialogues

Anne-Marie Oomen

Log Entry

Anne Marie Oomen's afternoon session on monologues was hilariously entertaining. I envy her students! She presented fantastic ideas for scriptwriting that until now I would never have considered trying. She began by modeling two monologues of different types; what a wonderful actress! I was enthralled! What I liked best was the way she involved us by choosing from an array of hats and developing characters for a monologue based on our choices. She also presented how this could then be transformed into a script for more characters. It was great fun and everyone was involved. I feel much more confident now and will probably try some of these techniques with my classes.

—Tracey Thompson

I tell the teacher-writers in my workshop that I talk to myself. I tell them I talk to myself through most of life's joys, sorrows, and especially angers. I explain that I try to do this when I am alone, but that sometimes I forget to check if a room is empty. As an adult I have been caught so many times that close friends have become tolerant of my voice murmuring in the next room. To save myself the humiliation of discovery, I have tried to find more private places in which to talk to myself. So I talk to myself in the car. In a car people can see me talking to myself, but they can't hear me—which is often the more embarrassing aspect of this habit. The truth of the matter is—I whisper this to my class—it's one of those bad habits I now enjoy enormously. My class laughs, I think because they identify with me.

What does this have to do with writing scripts? After years of admitting that I talk to myself, I have realized that this behavior may be used as the basis for both the dramatic monologue and dialogue. To explain, I ask my students to imagine the following: You get into a conflict with someone but find yourself so dumbfounded by this person's stupidity, rudeness, arrogance, or bullheadedness that you can only stutter your defense. You leave the scene wordless, looking like a great wimp. Twenty minutes later the conversation replays in your head and suddenly the most brilliant responses come to you. Your words are sharp and clever and you are so articulate that you could negotiate the Middle East peace talks. You offer stunning quips, dignified argument, rational logic, and absolutely cow your conversational opponent.

One of my playwriting instructors, Arnie Johnston, says the French call this phenomenon *l'ésprit d'éscalier,* the "spirit of the stairs." In other words, the right answer is the spirit who comes to you on the way down the stairs, out the door, or down the road.

Using the Spirit of the Stairs

Almost immediately after pointing out this to my workshop, one teacher-writer observes that these conversations are not just us talking to ourselves. The great majority of the time, we are really talking to someone else. YES! Two people sit in that car. And the spirit of the stairs gives us permission to turn the invisible one into a blithering idiot. As we rehearse this kind of "talking to yourself," we make up the right answers for ourselves and the wrong answers for the one who's not there. We are writing our own drama resoundingly in our favor. My students and I laugh at our audacity.

From that point, I ask teacher-writers to brainstorm situations like this, making a list of incidents which we couldn't win because we couldn't think of the right answers in time. We share these. Typical of the noisy and vehement responses are:

"The fight with my boss about recycled paper."

"The bill collector who would not quit."

"The maintenance person who thinks she cleans my room."

"That table attendant with the crab cakes."

"Mechanics!"

"My mom."

From plumbers to political figures, we all have examples of lost fights which we could have won, had we been accompanied by the "spirit." I ask workshoppers to choose one from their list, give the main character a different name from their name in life (if that makes it easier), and then begin writing "The tirade that would have WON." Whatever the topic, most teacher-writers respond with a certain relish and sinister joy. We have the rare opportunity to rewrite bad history. Chuckles rise, then silence falls as teacher-writers produce the zero draft of a monologue.

We read them out loud and discover they are often speeches of triumph and impossible self-righteousness. One teacher-writer has finally won the long-standing argument with her mother-in-law on how to start the car on a cold day. One man has truly defended, at last, his coffee. Another teacher has convinced a student of hers not to take drugs. The phenomenon seems universal; we love to win.

And all this leads to performance, that essential ingredient of writing for theater. Once we have won that long-ago argument, we have so much fun listening to ourselves win it that we read it effortlessly, with the beginnings of performance. It's hilarious and tender until one student asks, "What makes this a monologue?" Good question.

What's a Monologue?

There are many ways of writing a monologue. However, to answer the question I list its traditional characteristics:

- The monologue clearly reveals a speaker, and usually reveals a person(s) who is spoken to, the speaker's audience.

- The speaker in the monologue usually experiences a conflict, or presents a significant event or emotion.

- The character speaking often experiences some kind of change: a realization, insight, "epiphany," a change in thinking.

- Many good monologues reveal an individual "voice." No one else could tell the story quite like the character does.

I point out that these are the traditional characteristics to a monologue, but that many monologues don't fit this pattern at all. A good example of a non-traditional monologue is Nadine Stair's letter, from the oral tradition. Monologues can be discovered in interviews, poetry, songs, and fiction as well as plays. My students recall examples from movies they like—the "Church of Baseball" monologue from *Bull Durham*. Especially good women's monologues may be found in the play *Talking With—*, by Jane Martin.

The First Move: Monologue to Dialogue

Once they've written this zero draft monologue, I ask them to cut them apart. Yes! Cut the draft into sentences or partial sentences. They grumble. We are tempted to put too much value on this draft. To ease our possessiveness, I tell teacher-writers that they can make copies before they cut them up. These will stand alone. We cut up the other copy.

I ask them to place these "cuts ups" on big sheets of newsprint, leaving a lot of space between each sentence. Then, with the freedom to move sentences around and be playful, I ask them to write "the stupid answers the other guy said." This is not always great scripting, but it quickly introduces the idea of script. I also introduce the proper format for a script, which is not at all like that used in scripts you purchase from the publishing companies. (See the format used throughout this chapter.) Then students join a partner for a quick rehearsal, and we read these zero dialogues. We are laughing again, because it becomes obvious we'd all like to play the righteous one. Then one teacher-writer asks, "Is there a problem with these monologues in the way they stereotyped us? We're perfect. The characters don't end up being very real."

Right! I ask what would create "real." The answers we eventually discover involve complexity and change. Most of us enjoy the self-indulgence of winning, but we also value truth, and truth, especially for adults, involves complexity. How do we write those qualities in script form?

Character Complexity

I use the following exercise, which I learned from Judy GeBaur at the Iowa Playwrights Workshop. I ask teacher-writers to invent a new name, any name. On a fresh sheet of paper, each of us writes the name and one characteristic of that invented character. Then we pass our sheets onto the next person and each person reads the list, writes a new characteristic, and passes it on to the next student, each person adding a new characteristic. When the list returns to the original teacher-writer, he or she has a whole range of characteristics from which to begin writing. Because the list is random, it often evokes complexity.

For example, I invented the name, Amy Mae VanDerzen. Under her name I wrote that she "hates TV." I passed it on to the next person and picked up the list which was handed to me. After all the lists had circulated, mine came back to me with the following characteristics: Hates TV, loves the radio, loves all serious music, sings all the time, sings operas badly, sings but can't carry a tune, tries every new diet, is a practicing Methodist, wishes she was married, bleaches her hair, can't make bread rise, raises minks for fun and profit, has a green thumb, has no children, would love to have children, comes from a big family, likes words. With a list like that, crazy as it is, most people can begin writing a more complex character, at least externally. In addition, since the characteristics don't fit perfectly, we create a good deal of freshness in our characters. I tell them the wilder the list, the more fun the monologue. From my list, I invented the following character and situation. Amy Mae has suddenly and tragically become responsible for her nieces and nephews. Here's a monologue to the children at her breakfast table.

Amy Mae

Look at this morning. You can take it in like a bird, like a big bird. I know I'm not your mom and dad but I'm what you got and I'm telling you, you may not watch any more sit-com, re-run, electromutated pablum today. The TV is off.

Sarah, next to you on the floor is an unbelievable machine. Called a radio, its finer points are a broad range of selections, called stations, reflecting the taste of the brilliant and the insane. You just grab that little dial and you twist all hell out of it but stop at eighty-eight because, yes folks, it's opera.

You're hungry? I'm on a diet; therefore you're on a diet. Take a lettuce leaf and wrap it around a grape and pretend it's a pop-tart. Breakfast is not a democracy. You eat what I eat. Oh, there is bread but it fell. Health bread. You'd hate it.

Listen, kids, I hate this too. But we got to find some way of moving on. Let's sing. While we sing, we'll water the plants. Just take these big buckets and go around. About forty different plants live around this house and they all have to be watered to live. I love plants because they are not afraid. They feel pain, just like we do, but they can't know fear. So they don't have to work so hard at avoiding. They don't know what could happen. It just happens. Hey, not so much water. Even though they are succulent you can baptize the life out of a Begonia. Then we'll go feed the minks.

That's as far as I got. Not great writing but a beginning. Eventually someone notes, "It's all character. We can't go any further because we don't know how the person thinks." This comment addresses the need to move into internal motivations. Characters have an inside too.

Monologue Two: Discovering the Inner Character

Change often stems from tension or a discrepancy between what a character appears to be and what they actually are, or what they say they want, and what they really want. When we look back at the earlier monologues and dialogues, even in these zero drafts, we find characters whose words foreshadow change and resonate with more than surface meaning. To give an example I retell a bit of dialogue which I learned from playwright Arnie Johnston. A couple are sitting in an airport and the wife is telling the husband that she is going to leave him. His response?

HUSBAND

You can't leave me. If you leave me, I'm going to take the car, drive out to the middle of the Golden Gate Bridge, and drive off.

WIFE

(after a pause)

You don't understand. I'm taking the car.

The exchange reveals their relationship, especially the impending changes. Following is one teacher-writer's dialogue which reveals internal motivation as well as foreshadowing change.

MARSHA

Do you have anything you want to say before I start reading the paper?

HARRY

Nope. I'll wait until you're in the middle of it—just to keep the peace.

Sarcastic, yes, but as one student observed, "Good dialogue is slippery, because you can't tell where it's going, but you know it's going somewhere it's not." Many of the teacher-writer monologues automatically involve change, because someone started out losing and ended up winning. But only a few maintain complexity of character, tension, and the resonance caused by change. To tap into that need, I introduce a new monologue starter. In this one, teacher-writers may begin by speaking in their own voice again or in an invented voice. Either way, I write the following starter sentences on the board and ask them to finish each sentence with one or two or several sentences, and if, at any point, they feel like expanding, they should follow that urge. The sentences are:

- I am hopelessly . . .
- I remember . . .
- I have to have . . .
- I really need . . .
- I want . . .
- Once, I dreamed . . .

Teacher-writers write as much or as little as they want about each sentence, but they are encouraged to write something in response to each. We write seven to ten minutes. I share and encourage each person to read what he or she has written, introducing their character each time. Here is Clara's.

Clara

I really need something in this world to be real, more real than snipers and war and hunger and living in a small room with a spotted mattress and pigeons on the sill. Why do I keep expecting that happy thing? I know now the most important thing is to be fed. To eat. I want to eat something real. Tasty. Pastrami sandwich. Kentucky Fried Chicken. A windfall apple. Once, I dreamed this was over and I loved reality. Isn't that funny?

Intriguing? These monologues are speaking of deeply personal things. We are, in some concrete way, discovering the inner workings of character. Now, writing that character's dialogue becomes easier because we have learned some of the character's motivations or fears. We may combine these with the external characteristics that the earlier exercise tends to produce.

The next exercise is a subtle extension into dialogue, and begins to evolve when someone finally says, "Good dialogue is *not* always the way people really talk but the way the character thinks." Ah. I ask them to do the following. Again, we copy our most recent pieces, cutting one copy apart until we are holding a collection of sentences. I ask them to place one sentence on a big sheet of newsprint. Their partner follows with a sentence of his or her choice which may or may not respond to the one given. They play this game, putting down one sentence after another, free associating from the deck of sentences they have written and cut, letting their partner's sentence trigger their selection. Sometimes they discover they need to stop and write a few lines of new dialogue, or reorder the ones they have, but they keep going until they have used the sentences.

Their reaction is immediate. Students find this dialogue strained, often weird, sometimes contrived, and they note characters are often not listening to each other. And yet, after they have read it together two or three times, they can often make up the story, or at least part of the story, for these two people. Through read-arounds they get closer to the tension which reveals meaning. They also find this dialogue more attractive than their previous dialogue which, by contrast, may now appear predictable. They begin to ask more good questions. How did these two end up talking? Why don't they listen to each other? What happened between them? And then the statement I wait to hear: "We could, if we revised this dialogue, create a story for them." Plot?

Where the Action Is

A good plot involves action as well as some of the other elements of playwriting: setting, theme, mood. But essentially, it's what happens. I cut up a bunch of three-by-five cards and generate as many as I can in the following four categories:

1a. a list of professions, hobbies, leisure—doctor, lawyer, skier, homeless person, college student

1b. a bunch of character types (optional)—cynical, sweet, stupid, brilliant, friendly, weak

2. a bunch of activities which infer a setting—flying, teaching, babysitting, mowing the lawn, playing tennis, doing dishes

3. a bunch of moods—anger, grief, happiness, revenge

4. an incident—an accident, an argument, a date, someone is killed, someone falls asleep, something is stolen, etc.

I put these into labeled coffee cans and we choose one from each, mixing and matching randomly. This exercise tends to produce more plotted situations because it focuses on incident rather than on character. It often generates conflict. Here's an excerpt about an old woodworker named Joe, talking to his ten-year-old grandson Matt in his workshop. (Joe was invented from the list exercise.) They are alone and the man is building wooden ducks in his workshop. As you read, can you feel the plot beginning to form?

JOE

Here, drink this.

MATT

What is it?

JOE

Whiskey. Don't tell your mother.

MATT

Why not? She drinks.

JOE

She does? But she doesn't know you do.

MATT

I don't, grandpa.

JOE

Now you do. It's a rite of passage.

MATT

What's a rite of passage?

JOE

Doing something stupid so you can do something else stupid.

MATT

That's stupid.

JOE

Go ahead. Just so you know what it tastes like.

A great deal is set up in this one page. We can see story forming from character. We want to know what Joe's intentions are and what happens to the boy. After we read this, the class brainstorms potential follow-up scenes. Teaching the formal elements of plot may be less important if the writer can develop it from character, complexity, and situation. My teacher-writers are nodding. But what happens next?

From Scene to Play

Even though we often follow our baby scripts right out of the workshop into revision, the workshop is designed to be an introduction, not a full course. The last exercise is merely a final challenge to teacher-writers to write more than one scene in a sequence and to play with different kinds of scenes. Even if a published script feels seamless, plays are made up of different kinds of scenes: memory scenes, ritual scenes, crucial scenes, confrontation scenes, pay-off scenes, information scenes. I suggest they leave with this assignment, which I was given by Judy Gebaur at Iowa. Write four scenes. They may use characters they have already invented or new ones. They can write the scenes as related or unrelated. But the idea is to view these unrelated monologues and dialogues as potential pre-writing for a whole play. To get them started, however, I give them a fairly contrived list of conditions. For each scene, they must include an object, an action, an emotion, and a specific line. For example, what happens if you have to use glass? These conditions force them outside the predictable, and keep them away from the clichés. Here is the list I gave to my students:

> Scene 1
>
>> object—jagged piece of glass
>> action—to take control
>> emotion—authoritative
>> line—I'm beginning to notice I'm forgetting things.
>
> Scene 2
>
>> object—spectacles
>> action—revenge
>> emotion—bitter
>> line—This pain won't quit.
>
> Scene 3
>
>> object—hammer
>> action—threat
>> emotion—anxiety
>> line—I guess it's hell over there.
>
> Scene 4
>
>> object—cantaloupe
>> action—approval
>> emotion—fear
>> line—I don't mind talking but I can't argue.

I hear a student say, "Boy, this is gonna have to move." And that sums up how this exercise works. The playwright and his characters can't sit for too long. The writer must force her characters into change in order to discover the transition which will lead them to the next requirement. Of course, after the zero draft, these conditions can be cut from the script. But the real purpose is to help new playwrights begin to think of the whole script.

I started out with talking to myself. And all of these characters are ways each of us talk to ourselves. Only better. It's a way of getting out of the car, and saying it all out loud, in front of everyone.

References

Martin, Jane. *Talking With—*. New York: S. French, 1983.

"Nadine Stair's Letter." In *Poets of the Stone Circle.* Dir. David Seeman and Susan Schneider. Paradigm Video, Inc., 1985.

Applications in the Classroom

Talking to Yourself in the Car Is Okay: Monologues and Dialogues

Literature

■ Write a monologue in which you choose a minor character from one of your literature texts, and have that character tell part of the story from a different point of view.

■ Write a scene that's not written out in the text but which happened.

■ Dramatize an essay, a newspaper article, a poem, a fable, or fairy tale where the characters don't speak much. Write a monologue, dialogue, or an entire scene for it.

■ Improvise conversations between characters. Assume the character, tape it, and then adapt a revision.

Writing

■ Write a monologue in which you win a longstanding argument with someone.

■ Build a character by passing around a sheet of paper and have each person add a characteristic until it comes back to the original person. Write a monologue based on the character.

■ Improvise a scene by having two or three of these characters get together and converse. Tape the conversation and use it as the basis for a scene, changing it to make a story, if possible.

■ Use these sentence starters to build a monologue: I am hopelessly . . . I remember . . . I have to have . . . I really need . . . I want . . . Once, I dreamed. . . .

■ Create dialogue by asking two students to cut apart their monologues and put them back together, alternating sentences. Adjust and revise, but keep in mind, this will be an unusual dialogue.

■ Create an incident as described in the chapter. Fill four coffee cans with slips of paper on which are written careers, an activity or incident, and a predominant mood. Ask students to draw a slip from each one and build a scene, dialogue, or monologue from that information.

EXTENSIONS

Mapping a Memory Trip

Barbara J. Rebbeck

A very effective way to help young writers find vivid material for writing prose or poetry is to lead them through visualization on a memory trip. I use this technique with students after they have explored left brain/right brain theories. I also have them dabble in Betty Edwards' work on drawing upside down using their right brains. With this background we have loosened up and are ready to begin our trip.

I begin the trip with my students by talking about visualization. I compare it to running a movie through your mind, all the time being aware of the senses. We talk about the idea that if you can't visualize something, you can't do it. I give them examples of practical uses of visualization such as the Olympic downhill racers who concentrate and visualize the entire course before a race. Next we talk about the importance of visualization for writers, and then we begin:

> Close your eyes. Relax. Block out all noises except my voice. Breathe deeply. Now concentrate, with your eyes closed, on what you are wearing now. Picture you. Move back in time now to your first day at middle school. You're excited but a little scared. You have new clothes on. You enter the school for the first time. Who do you see? Where do you go first? Now you are in second grade. You are outside at recess. What are you playing? With whom? What do you look like? What season is it? How can you tell? Kindergarten—you are five years old. Walk around your classroom. Notice all the details. All the people. Now you're out the door and moving home. You play outside at your favorite place. Look all around at places, buildings, trees, people, animals. Now you move into your house to your bedroom. Look around again. You pull out your favorite toy and play until dinner. Be aware of everything—voices from downstairs, the color of your bedroom walls, smells of dinner cooking. Is it your

▶

favorite meal? Now open your eyes and take your sheet of paper. You are going to draw a map of your bedroom (other options: classroom or neighborhood) from an eagle's view. Fill in at least ten objects. [This could be a homework assignment.]

The next step:

You are now going to take your map and with my help make a key for it. Place a #1 on your map at a spot where you are playing with your best friend. Below your map or on a separate sheet of paper, place a #1 and give three sentences which tell us more about this item. Who are you playing with? What are you playing? (Ex. I was playing with Patty with my Barbie doll. I thought Patty was my friend until she left and my favorite Barbie skirt left too. From then on I called her *Bratty*, not Patty.) Place a #2 where someone has entered the room to give you a serious message. Explain below. (Encourage kids to use imaginations and make up responses) #3: a secret you've never told anyone. Explain below. #4: something you are afraid of in your room. Explain below. #5: an object you'd love to bring for show and tell. Explain below. Continue on as desired.

Have students add their own items after discussion. Students mark two favorite items with stars. Students then meet in groups of four and share maps and two items. One member of each group reports back best ideas.

Psychology Journals
Christa Siegel

Purpose:

- to have students explore their thoughts and feelings in writing
- to have students use new terminology in their writing
- to have students apply newly learned concepts to their own experiences

Although my psychology class is basically an information-oriented, lecture-based course, the current emphasis on writing across the curriculum has led me to add some additional writing to the course, without doing it in the form of reports or research.

▶

At the beginning of the semester, students start writing in journals several times a week, both in and out of class. They are encouraged to write about anything of interest, but once a week I also give them a topic, question, or current event to discuss which is related to our current unit.

After several weeks, I ask the students to read through their journals again, listing some of the most important and interesting topics they have written about. From the list, they then share ideas and journal entries as a reflective work-in-progress in groups of threes and fours, make revisions, and share a second time. Third drafts are then shared with the entire class, anonymously if desired, and discussions follow in which students are asked to respond to the essay using psychological concepts they have learned.

A second writing activity spawned from the journal writing is the "Dear Ann Landers" letters. Students once again go through their journals and look for problems they can write to "Ann Landers" about. They compose letters and then work in small groups to critique them before submitting them to a letter box to be answered. Each student randomly selects a letter and is expected to answer the letter seriously, looking up information in the textbook or in the library if necessary, thus combining the subject matter with the writing. Answers are critiqued and rewritten before discussion about the "writing" aspect and about the problems and their proposed solutions. Obviously, the discussion periods are time-consuming, and I usually use the essays and letters to fill in at the end of an hour when the assignment has been short, or if attention is waning and there needs to be a change of activity.

14 Going Where the Lightning Is: Fifteen Ways to Start Writing

Paul Wolbrink

Log Entry

Although we know that, ideally, we should always try to get the students to use "self-selected" topics, sometimes we might feel the need to offer some prompting. In his handout, Paul provides an excellent list that offers ideas for expressive writing as well as a list of journal topics. The *entire* handout that he provided will be used over and over in my classrooms. He offers suggestions from copy-change to diction-change, all of which will be helpful.

A few comments that he made that made a lasting impression on me are:

- If you want to produce literacy, you have to practice, practice, practice!

- Mapping something positions you in the moment.

- Invite success as often as you can by making sure the materials are appropriate for grade levels.

- When kids have instant success they lend themselves to being "risky" writers.

—Jan Hagland

Writers are always casting about for fresh ideas. One method of getting ideas is to wait for them to strike. Periodically they do, usually when the writer is performing a routine activity such as driving the car, mowing the lawn, cooking, or shaving. For some reason, mild distraction seems essential to the process known as inspiration. We often speak of the way an idea or solution to a difficult problem comes in like a bolt from the blue.

The problem with waiting for ideas is that it is possible to go a long time between lightning strikes. Experienced writers resort more frequently than is generally known to idea-generating devices. Rather than wait for lightning to strike, the writer goes where the lightning is—climbs to the top of a barren peak, stretches to full height, and raises a copper antenna overhead.

Here, then, are fifteen different ways of trying to electrify student writers—to get them where the lightning is:

1. *Spontaneous Generation.* Choose at random a noun beginning with V, a verb beginning with E, an adjective beginning with R, an adverb beginning with B, any word beginning with S, any word with L, and any word with B. Work them into a piece of writing.

2. *The Given Sentence.* Use the first line of a short story or a line of interest from any text as a launching point for your own writing. These first lines come from the Summer 1991 issue of *Story:*

   "This time Virginia knows exactly what is happening, and she knows there is nothing she can do to stop it." (Wickersham 38)

   "Harter had expected the affair to end badly, but he had not expected it to end as badly as it did." (Millhauser 58)

   "On the first night, this was the dream." (deBuys 26)

   "All day long, on that day in the sixth grade when my life changed forever and the world became a better place, everything had been smelling and tasting like overcooked eggs." (Allen 30)

   In *What If? Writing Exercises for Fiction Writers* (HarperCollins 1990), Anne Bernays and Pamela Painter suggest this opening line: "Where were you last night?"

3. *The Core Sentence.* Write dozens of variations on a basic core sentence, continuing to compose variations until you feel the tug of an engaging subject. These examples of core sentences come from *Beat Not the Poor Desk* by Marie Ponsot and Rosemary Dean.

   a. Once/Now. "Once I was _____ ; now I am _____ ."

   b. Opposing Voice. "They say _____ , but my experience tells me _____ ."

   c. Two Voices. "You can do it another way, but you can also do it this way."

   d. Hindsight. "That _____ is the way it was, and that made this _____ difference."

   e. Foresight. "When I saw that fork in the road just ahead in my life, I chose this _____ instead of that _____ ."

    f.   Insight. "In this dilemma or crisis, I turned to this tradition or principle."

Or construct your own core sentence by varying well-known lines: "I went to (*the woods*) because I wished to (*live deliberately*)."

4. *The Generating Frame.* Construct a generating frame (that is, a "recipe," which provides broad directions) of your own, or have a writing partner make one for you from an existing piece of writing. The following structure is borrowed from Beth Nugent's "Cocktail Hour":

> This person (A) performs this action and it has this immediate effect. "_____," A says, and does this. "_____." Then A makes this gesture and says, "_____."
>
> "_____," B says. " _____." [B reacts to A's comment, perhaps agreeing, perhaps being combative.] "_____?" [B continues, asking a question.] There is no immediate answer, so B does this in the silence. Meanwhile, A does this.
>
> "_____," B says finally in this way, answering his/her/its own question. "_____." B makes this facial expression while A reacts this way, facially or by performing some trivial but revealing action.
>
> "_____?" A inquires. B stops what he/she/it is doing and does this instead, perhaps approaching A, perhaps performing some action that heightens the confrontation or furthers the agreement.

5. *The Pattern Poem.* A pattern poem also uses a recipe structure. There are dozens of pattern poems floating around writers' groups. Here are two simple ones that work well with young people and adults (from Jesse Hise, "Writing Poetry").

> I Do Not Understand
>
> A. Begin the poem with "I do not understand . . ."
>
> B. List three things you do not understand about the world or people.
>
> C. Name the thing you do not understand most of all.
>
> D. End with an example of something you *do* understand.
>
> Mood Poem
>
> A. State a mood.
>
> B. Write three things the mood is *not* (two stated briefly, one stated as a comparison).
>
> C. State three more descriptions of the mood.

6. *The Given Structure.* Write within an established structure. In poetry, this might involve choosing an established form (haiku, sonnet, villanelle, among a zillion others). In an essay, it might involve employing the familiar assertion-evidence-recapitulation model. Or it might involve choosing any of the familiar structures of the oral tradition, including "the fable, the parable, the curse, the complaint, the riddle, the song of praise or aversion, the myth, the romance, the cautionary tale, [and] the catalogue" (Ponsot, *Beat,* 13). Working within a familiar structure makes it possible to focus exclusively on content. For poets, Barbara Drake's *Writing Poetry* is indispensable.

7. *The Copychange.* Find a piece of writing you enjoy or admire. Perform an exact content change, retaining the grammatical structure of the original but changing the words. If the sentence has this arrangement, "Prepositional phrase/noun/verb/adjective/noun/conjunction/adjective/noun/verb/participial phrase," try to duplicate the structure precisely, but with entirely different words.

> Original: "Half an hour later you pull into the parking lot of the K & B Pharmacy. Inside you look at red jumper cables, a jigsaw puzzle of some TV actor's face, the tooled-leather cowboy belts, a case of cameras and calculators, the pebble-surfaced tumblers on the housewares aisle. At the medical supplies you try on several different finger splints, then stare at a drawing on a box containing some kind of shoulder harness designed to improve the posture. You look at toolboxes, opening the fatigue-green plastic ones, then the cardinal-red metal ones. You pick up a plumber's helper and try it out on the floor, surprised when it pops loose by itself—it reminds you of a camel getting off its knees. Near the stationery, you face a shelf of ceramic coin banks shaped and painted like trays of big crinkle French fries smothered in ketchup" (Barthelme 61–62).
>
> Copychange: "Two minutes earlier you've laced up your Reeboks with the white leather uppers. Now you gaze at pink leg warmers, a trendy leotard with some reptilian jungle scene, Paula's hand-held exercise weights, a collection of tights and headbands, the lean-buttocked occupants of the front row. During the warm-up routine you ease into several different slow stretches, then massage the muscles of your back, seeking some sort of quick relief intended to aid flexibility. You respond to commands, executing a leg-dragging hip slide, then an up-tempo windmill series. You check your pulse rate and count it against the clock, astonished as blood cascades wildly

through you—it reminds you of the Missouri churning through a turbine. At the end, you become a puddle of slick warm perspiration, exhausted and drowsy, like an armada of goosedown pillows floating in space."

8. *Assorted other changes.* You can often get ideas by performing other types of alterations on an existing piece of writing. You can create a time change, a sex change, or a number change, from singular to plural. You can also experiment with voice by performing a diction change (or register change), changing formal diction to informal and vice versa, as high school senior Sean Allen did with the opening of the Constitution: "Us guys in the U.S., to do this place some good, make things fair, keep everyone chilled out, stop us from getting whomped by another country, do good for people all over, and help get rights for us and our kids, put together this bunch of rules for the U.S.A."

9. *Hale Chatfield's Double Telephone Number Personalized Syllabic Acrostic.* Down the left margin of your paper write your phone number twice. This gives you fourteen lines. Now print your name vertically next to the digits of your phone number (if it's a short name, begin again). The digit at the beginning of each line tells you how many syllables that line must have; the letter following the digit is the first letter of the line. Zero counts as ten. Okay, it's a pattern poem, but anything this capricious deserves its own spot.

10. *Snaphorisms.* A snaphorism is an aphorism that snaps out of your pen. It begins with an association of incongruous elements and leads to some observation or truth, often comic. In the film *Shirley Valentine* one hears the line, "Sex is like a supermarket—you know, overrated—just a lot of pushin' and shovin' and you still come out with very little in the end." Later in the film Shirley says, "Marriage is like the Middle East—there's no solution." Go down the row at the local card shop and you'll see set-up lines like these: "A birthday is like a cold toilet seat—," "A true friend is like moldy bread—," or "Honey, my love for you is like a flat tire—." A good snaphorism compresses a lot of punch into a small package. Sometimes they can function as core sentences, leading into an essay, short story, or poem.

   With a group of writers, it's fun to throw out the first part of the line, "Writing is—," for example, and have the group generate the comparisons. When I did this with a group, we chose the associations "underwear," "a balloon," and "a dead fish." In three minutes we wrote some truly amazing lines.

11. *Empathetic Voices.* After reading a novel, a short story, or a moving poem such as Robert Frost's "Out, Out—", become another person in the scene, perhaps one not even mentioned, and write from that perspective. You can even become an animal or an inanimate object. Write rapidly in the first person in the voice of the character you've chosen.

12. *Headlines.* Find a newspaper headline that has possibilities and then, without reading the article, begin writing. You can write about human drama stuff, if you want, or you can do as Nancy Willard does and find interesting juxtapositions on the sports pages. She has a whole series of poems with titles like "Buffalo Emerges from Cellar" and "Dolphins Thrash Broncos." From the papers of June 24, 1991, I plucked these possibilities: "Angels Rock Tigers" and "Belcher Stops Bucs Again" (referring to Dodger player Tim Belcher).

13. *Absurd Impositions.* Some writers impose absurd conditions on themselves, devising seemingly impossible tasks that force deep concentration. Richard Hugo, poet and teacher, found much success with the following assignment, which can be varied to produce less or greater rigor.

Nouns	*Verbs*	*Adjectives*
tamarack	to kiss	blue
throat	to curve	hot
belief	to swing	soft
rock	to ruin	tough
frog	to bite	important
dog	to cut	wavering
slag	to surprise	sharp
eye	to bruise	cool
cloud	to hug	red
mud	to say	leather

Use five nouns, verbs, and adjectives from the above lists and write a poem as follows:

1. Four beats to the line (can vary)

2. Six lines to the stanza

3. Three stanzas

4. At least two internal and one external slant rhyme per stanza (full rhymes acceptable but not encouraged)

5.   Maximum of two end stops per stanza

6.   Clear English grammatical sentences (no tricks) that make sense

7.   The poem must be meaningless

14. *Specific Encounters.* This idea, too, comes from *What If?* (28). The authors suggest composing a list over a week or so of ten things that make you angry and ten things that please you. Each item must be sufficiently specific to be applicable uniquely to you—not "I felt good when I woke up on Wednesday morning" but "I ran into Ms. Butler, my third-grade teacher, in the Star Market and she said hello to me by my right name." Lists of positive and negative experiences give the writer specific situations to draw upon.

15. *Outrageous Premise.* Begin with a bizarre line, something surreal, dreamlike, or improbable. Look at your own straight sentences and tilt, corrupt, or pervert them in some way. Another way is to think of a common, everyday situation and twist it. The poet Russell Edson is a master of devising such lines. Here are a few first lines from Edson's *The Clam Theater.*

   - "In a back room a man is performing an autopsy on an old raincoat."

   - "A rat owns a man, which it operates with apron strings from its rathole in the wall."

   - "A husband and wife who are without child adopt a wheel."

   - "A gravy boat had run aground, and now gravy was spilling through the landscape."

   - "The rich hire orchestras, and have the musicians climb into trees to sit in the branches among the leaves, playing Happy Birthday to their dogs."

   - "The car won't start. He wonders if he shouldn't just allow it."

   - "After Cinderella married the prince she turned her attention to minutiae, using her glass slipper as a magnifying lens."

   - "The book was blank, all the words had fallen out."

These are only a few of the ways writers go about getting ideas. Students, who often worry unduly about having something to say, can gain from experiences in which they are put in the path of inspiration and made to plunge into writing without worrying about how to start. Development, new beginnings, revisions can all follow once something has begun, but as several of Shakespeare's characters say, "Nothing will come from nothing." These ways of getting writing started are simply ways of getting students to go where the lightning is; we can begin to tap and channel the electricity only after it's been generated.

References

Allen, Edward. "Burt Osborne Rules the World." *Story.* Summer 1991: 30–37.

Barthelme, Frederick. "Moon Deluxe." *Moon Deluxe.* New York: Viking Penguin, 1984. 61–72.

Bernays, Anne, and Pamela Painter. *What If? Writing Exercises for Fiction Writers.* New York: HarperCollins, 1990.

deBuys, William. "Dreaming Geronimo." *Story.* Summer 1991: 26–29.

Drake, Barbara. *Writing Poetry.* New York: Harcourt Brace Jovanovich, 1983.

Edson, Russell. *The Clam Theater.* Middletown, CT: Wesleyan University Press, 1973.

Hise, Jesse. "Writing Poetry: More Than a Frill." *English Journal* 68.8 (1980): 19–22.

Hugo, Richard. *The Triggering Town: Lectures and Essays on Poetry and Writing.* New York: W. W. Norton, 1979.

Millhauser, Steven. "The Way Out." *Story.* Summer 1991: 58–71.

Nugent, Beth. "Cocktail Hour." *The New Yorker* 66.11 (30 April 1990): 40–50.

Ponsot, Marie, and Rosemary Deen. *Beat Not the Poor Desk—Writing: What to Teach, How to Teach It, and Why.* Upper Montclair, NJ: Boynton/Cook, 1982.

———. *The Common Sense: What to Write, How to Write It, and Why.* Upper Montclair, NJ: Boynton/Cook, 1985.

Wickersham, Joan. "Lena." *Story.* Summer 1991: 38–45.

Willard, Nancy. *Water Walker.* New York: Alfred A. Knopf, 1989.

EXTENSIONS

Life Lines

Mary Beth Looby

Example:

| | | | | | | | | | | | |

yr./born   (significant high points and low points) yr./death

Purpose:

- to help students focus on their goals
- to provide students with a visual means of reference for biographic writing

Materials: newspapers, magazines, booklets, brochures, tape or glue stick, lined paper, and folder

Early in the semester, to help my students focus on their goals, as well as to provide them a visual means of reference to draw on for their writing, I ask them to construct a life line. We begin with the year they were born, and I even ask them to project the year they might die. At first, students are afraid to write down a year when they might die, but you assure them this is not voodoo and it won't come true. Once we have established a beginning and end, we mark our time line in ten-year segments, and proceed to plot in significant high and low points which have happened in our lives. I find it helpful to model this on the blackboard with my own life line. We also move on to project future goals—to fill in those years which lie ahead of us. This sometimes requires a bit of soul searching; we begin in class but students finish at home.

Once students have their graphic life line in hand, we can draw from this for many writing assignments. In early weeks, we think, write, examine, and discuss goals. This, we know, is a necessary first step in accomplishing those goals. This map also provides a good springboard for an autobiographical piece, and for students who have trouble getting started, or generating much print, this visual stimulus often guides them along. As writing and thinking proceeds regarding careers, students often move on to research individual careers, and write about their findings.

In addition, any of the significant events on the life line can provide topics for expressive writing. Many times, these are experiences students will have in common, such as births, promotions,

▶

graduations, moves, deaths, etc. This can lead to valuable sharing and discussions, and yes, better writing for those involved. In short, the construction of a life line can lead to valuable self-examination for the student, and, through writing, important discoveries. This, after all, is what the teacher is after.

Developing Specific Imagery: The Obituary Poem
Jan Mekula

Student writing often embraces the abstract, no matter how often we scrawl "be specific!" and "vague!" in the margins. Poetry expounds upon "love," "life," and "eternity"; characterization stops at "lazy," "sloppy," "sentimental." The goals of this assignment are to show students the effectiveness of specific imagery in revealing personality, and to have them characterize a real or imaginary person by writing a "list poem" of things that person would leave behind. The poem I modeled, "Obituary" (in *forum*), was written by Reginald Page, so I credit him although I've since lost the original.

I begin by presenting poems written by students in imitation of mine. We identify how the poems differ from newspaper obituaries, and what each item reveals about its owner's personality. Why, for example, is a book "thumb-worn" or a record "scratched?" How would the character's personality be different if the book were described as "uncreased?"

The students then picture a character: It might be themselves, a living or dead person, an imagined character, even an animal. As they begin their list of items that character would leave behind, I circulate to point out personality characteristics suggested by the items and ask for more details. After their lists are complete, we write some of them on the board and discuss indentation of parallel-structured lines, punctuation between items, and other questions of format. The finished poems can be posted, read aloud, or published in a *Spoon River* type of class anthology.

OBITUARY

(after Reginald Page)

The deceased is survived by:
    a thumb-worn copy of *Birds of America,*
    a little white-button quail and all the birds
      of the Clinton River woods
      whose songs are sadder now,

▷

a blue-eyed Himalayan cat
    who wonders where the soft lap went,
a chorale a little thinner in the alto section,
students who learned more than volleyball
    watching her lose the Game like a winner,
the tears of those
    who loved her more than she ever loved herself,
       and these lines.

Jan Mekula

OBITUARY

The deceased is survived by:
    A full-length black mink coat,
    gold and diamonds
       that will all be pawned off,
    a husband
       not quite sure how he feels,
    credit card bills
       that her husband will have to pay anyway,
    Emery boards, nail polish,
    exquisite wardrobe
       to be given to the "needy poor,"
    friends who only knew her
       as the President of the Social Club,
    a diary
       where she hid so much.
    a heart
       that showed so little.

Jena McCausey

OBITUARY

    The deceased is survived by:
Four Andreas Vollenweider albums
    scratched from overuse,
a fifty-dollar phone bill
    in calls "Just to say hi,"
a car that never seemed to work
and a pen that never stopped working,
rejection letters from the finest academic institutions,
a Monet calendar filled with the birthdays
    she always forgot
    of people she always remembered,
nightmares of cancer,
a video library of Hepburn/Tracy films,

subscriptions to *Connoisseur, Opus, Books 100,*
    and *Twilight Zone Magazine,*
and an ocean
    to hold the ashen remains of
    a girl who laughed
        at all the wrong things
    and cried
        at all the right ones.

Kelly Beehler

OBITUARY

The deceased is survived by:
a bright, newly painted red bench
    now occupied by pigeons,
shoes that look like they have been run over
    by a steam roller,
a pair of gloves with holes on every finger,
an old bottle of whiskey he had been sipping
    and saving,
and bones
    covered by skin.

Jenn Chudnof

15 Writing and Grammar: Bridging the Controversy

Alan Weber

Log Entry

Parents and most teachers think that writing is spelling, punctuation, and handwriting and that you have to teach these first in isolation before kids can write. All of these skills are necessary components of transcription. These skills can be addressed during the editing step of the writing process.

I have found that my students expect for the writing to be right the first time. With them it's "Now I've done it and I'm finished." It's hard to demonstrate to them that writing often requires many revisions. One way that I can demonstrate this to them is by using my own writing as an example, perhaps taking the same piece and revising and editing it throughout the year so that they can see the change over time. Another way to teach them that writing can evolve over time is to allow them to use the same piece but rework it for a different audience. There is a definite advantage to allowing kids to work together while writing as we did at the conference.

—**Mary Jo Converse**

While working with hundreds of K–College English and language arts teachers, I have found the one issue that ignites heated passion, sparks intense debate, and fuels verbal assault is the relationship of grammar and writing. While some teachers accept the research claiming the relationship is negligible, others feel that it is virtually impossible to talk about writing in the classroom without explicit knowledge of grammar.

In order to help teachers resolve their conflicts about the role of grammar in the teaching of writing, I devised an afternoon pedagogy workshop that attempts to convey five major ideas:

1. that what a person says and how it is structured is what makes good writing,

2. that there is a difference between language usage, mechanics, and grammar,

3. that mechanics and usage are important reader considerations but have little to do with good writing,

4. that grammar study has little value in the writing process, and

5. that sentence combining strategies are a practical alternative to teach students about sentence completeness and correctness.

Characteristics of Good Writing

Before confronting the issue of grammar, the workshop participants reflect about what they think is good writing. We individually jot down what we believe are the characteristics of effective writing. These lists include a wide range of responses: Creativity, good ideas, sentence variety, spelling, use of detail, humor, punctuation, organization, voice, and grammar. Many of the lists contain the same qualities of good writing that Donald Murray mentions in *Write to Learn,* such as clarity, design (structure, focus, and coherence), and meaningful content.

After this short sharing session, we find a partner and categorize our lists according to three criteria: Surface Elements, Organizational Elements, and Content. Surface Elements include any qualities that determine the "correctness" of writing or its presentation. Sample responses that people fit under these criteria are margins, spelling, usage, grammar, legibility, and spacing.

The second criteria, Organizational Elements, includes any elements that relate to the structure of a piece of writing or the way it is put together. Elements such as sentence order, style, development, format, unity, and "easy to follow" usually fall into this group.

Content is the third category and consists of elements that relate to the author's ideas. In most cases when participants finish classifying their lists, the Content category contains the most items. Creativity, meaning, clarity, details, realism, honesty, word choice, humor, and imagery are the terms which people most often list.

In reading those back, the groups discover that a few elements fall into more than one category and are difficult to classify under one heading. For example, some view word choice as a Content Element because words denote ideas; others see it as an Organizational Element because some transitional words, such as moreover and likewise, help structure writing. One group argues that paragraphing is a Structural Element because it blocks ideas into some organizational pattern; another group sees paragraphing as a Surface Element because it is a format consideration. One participant concluded that "style" is a melding of Organization and Content and likened it to McCluhan's idea of "the medium being the message."

Though some elements cross two categories, the terms under Content and Structure far outnumber those listed under Surface Elements. In other words, most people feel that good writing mainly consists of Content and Structural Elements.

The Surface Elements of Writing

Having agreed about the characteristics of good writing, we discuss in detail the role of Surface Elements. We share our views about the idea that Surface Elements have little to do with good writing. Yet, it is ironic because spelling, punctuation, usage, and grammar are the backbone of many writing programs. Some people feel that these qualities, though not as important as those listed under Content and Organization, are still essential for good writing.

In order to understand Surface Elements more clearly, we subdivide them into three components: Physical Appearance, Mechanics, and Usage. People have little difficulty identifying the terms that relate to the physical appearance of a piece of writing—things like legibility, margins, footnote formats, and quality of paper. We discuss how audiences balk at reading good or bad writing if the print is too small, the margins too slim, or the paper too creased. When we view a film at a theater, we get annoyed if the picture is out of focus or the sound is inaudible. These cinematic surface elements aid the presentation but have nothing to do with whether the film is good or bad. Likewise, we agree that a political diatribe full of jargon and gobbledygook and a short selection from *The Adventures of Huckleberry Finn* are examples of bad and good writing even if each is crumpled into a ball. While both are difficult to read, *The Adventures of Huckleberry Finn* remains well written.

Participants next attempt to identify the terms related to Mechanics and Usage. We first create a definition for Mechanics as transcription conventions, such as punctuation, spelling, and capitalization. These elements make it possible for a person to read someone else's writing. The following sentence demonstrates why readers need mechanical aids:

thissentencebecauseitlacks,mechanicsisdifficulttoread.

Mechanics are standardized conventions which, as Toby Fulwiler states, "are akin to good manners." I show the group a copy of F. Scott Fitzgerald's *The Great Gatsby* and ask them if they would consider this book good writing even if it contained 5,500 spelling errors. After lengthy discussion most agree, although they admit publishers would be put off by Fitzgerald's ill manners and teachers would probably grade it very low. I then relate that Fitzgerald's final draft of *Gatsby* did indeed contain 5,500 spelling mistakes.

Next, we define usage as the customary or relative manner of using words in language. It consists of a range of language choices within the grammar of a language. "I ain't got no money" and "He be looking good tonight" are statements that are grammatical but not considered standard English. The uses of who-whom, to-two, and I-me are other examples of usage choices that can be technically deemed "correct" or "incorrect" although proper usage varies for speakers from ethnically or culturally diverse settings.

I then share a paper written in English by an Asian student in my college writing class. The paper contains many usage problems such as subject-verb and pronoun agreement. Again participants agree that the writing is exceptional, but is not user-friendly. Below is the final paragraph of the paper:

> But really the whole situation is my falt, I think my writing has improve over the past year, but still I lacked a basic under-standing. The knowledge is available, it is the want to learn it which I must master.

By this time the participants feel that the Surface Elements of mechanics, usage, and physical appearance are important because they assist readers in dealing with the writing. Technically, they are skills that help polish writing into acceptable and correct form, so readers have easier access to the writing.

The Gremlin of Grammar

Our discussion of Surface Elements provides the background knowledge for the group to tackle the unpopular notion that grammar and usage are not the same beast. We describe grammar as the knowledge of the components of language and the ways they fit together. Grammar is not the rules of usage, but the configuration of the language. The group distinguishes grammar and usage by looking at some sentence patterns. We decide that "Him and me went wading in the brook" is grammatical because it follows the basic patterns of English; its syntax is recognizable, though not acceptable to many, because it lacks "standard" usage. "Who is the phone call for?" (For who is the phone call?) is another example of a grammatically correct sentence that contains improper usage. We concur that the sentence pattern, "Walked he and I the store to," is not grammatical because no meaning is possible with the unfamiliar syntax. As Jean Sanborn states, "Grammar is an abstract set of rules describing what we do with the elements of language to make *meaningful* utterances, not necessarily correct utterances" (74).

The participants begin to realize that grammar, and its accompanying activities of identifying parts of speech, diagramming, and parsing sentences, has little if any relationship to the writing process. They agree that grammar has no connection with the Content or Organizational Elements of writing. And, unlike mechanics and usage skills, grammar does not provide writers with skills to proofread and polish their writing. The reason that grammar study has no effect on writing performance is that "grammars are simply not meant to change usage habits" (Judy 36).

Our discussion about grammar does not alleviate many apprehensions about teaching writing. Many participants ask in unison, "How do we teach our students about subject-verb agreement, run-on sentences, and fragments without the labels and language of grammar?" The group brainstorms a couple of ways to address this concern. For middle school students, teachers might create a brief unit introducing the basic terms and definitions of grammar. A second idea was to develop an elective course in grammar (traditional, generative, and transformational) for high school students intending to go to college.

While these two suggestions are legitimate options, they are divorced from the teaching of writing. A third alternative, sentence combining, helps students gain insights about the structure of language during the writing process without burdening them with meaningless labels and grammar exercises.

Sentence Combining

Sentence combining is a method for talking about language structure. It doesn't use excessive amounts of class time and, more importantly, is taught in conjunction with the students' own writing.

In order to expose the participants to sentence combining, groups of three people are asked to combine clusters of sentences, fragments, and run-ons into one coherent sentence. Their task is to create a sentence that conveys the original intent of the individual statements without leaving out any ideas. I ask the group to combine the statements, so they "sound" right. Below are the sentence clusters, adapted from William Strong's book, *Sentence Combining*, that the group combined:

1. She relaxed under the noise.
2. Was unable to think about anything.

1. Her consciousness was focused.
2. She focused on the spray.
3. And was prickly.

1. The beef patties are pink, They are grainy.
2. They sit on a griddle.
3. Beginning to sizzle in the grease.

One group combined the first cluster by adding a comma after noise: "She relaxed under the noise, unable to think about anything." After some deliberation, they discovered that the noise wasn't unable to think, it was the girl. So, they revised the sentence to: "She relaxed under the noise and was unable to think about anything." Another group combined the same cluster in the following way: "Relaxing under the noise, she was unable to think about anything." In both cases, the groups manipulated sentence structure without knowing or referring to the definitions of a dangling modifier or a participle. The group that combined the cluster, "The beef patties which sit on a griddle are pink and grainy," didn't have to study subordinate clauses for three weeks. Teachers might waste an entire semester of writing attempting to explain the grammatical logic for the combination, "Her consciousness was focused on the spray."

Before applying this strategy to a student piece of writing, we talk about the three most common ways that statements can be combined. The first way is by using a coordinate word (and, or, for, nor, yet, so): "She focused on the spray, and it was prickly." The second way is by inserting a subordinate word such as "which," "although," "because," or "when": "Because the patties sit on a griddle, they begin to sizzle in the grease." The third way is by embedding ideas from one statement into another one: "She focused on the prickly spray." We discuss how these three strategies can be useful in showing student writers different possibilities to consider when revising their ideas.

Classroom Applications

After sharing our sentence combinations, I model one way I use this technique in my own writing classes. I give them a copy of an actual student draft from a freshman writing course (see Example 1), and ask them, as I do with my students, to improve the sentence structure by combining ideas.

EXAMPLE 1

Student Writing Sample

Five key pieces of equipment are needed before you can tube. First, you will need a boat. There are no specifics in the way of size. The engine must be able to tow a water skier without any problems. The minimum would be between 45 and 60 horsepower. Second, you have to have a tow rope. The best thing to use is a ski rope. Ski ropes were made for towing people and objects across the water. A nylon rope will do if you don't have a ski rope. Make sure the rope is fifty feet long. Thirdly, you must have an inner tube. An old inner tube from a semi-truck. The tube should not have a diameter bigger than three feet. Fourthly, you need a life preserver. This is a safety must. A ski belt will work best because it will inhibit your movement the least. Lastly, you will need a briddle. A briddle is a piece of nylon rope four feet long with a pulley. The briddle gives the inner tube lateral motion.

Again, they may use any of the four sentence combining strategies for assistance, but are asked to revise the sample so it "reads" more clearly. Thus, they also have the option to change words and de-combine sentences that are too long or convoluted.

The participants enjoy manipulating the ideas in this student sample and have little difficulty talking about language structure without the use of grammatical terms. The reason for their success is that sentence combining focuses on meaning rather than the knowledge and analysis of sentence parts. For example, the fragment "An old inner tube from a semi-truck," is most often combined with the previous sentence to read "Thirdly, you must have an inner tube, preferably one from a semi-truck." or "Thirdly, you must have an old inner tube from a semi-truck." While a knowledge of subject-verb is helpful in correcting fragments, many students can't apply this grammatical relationship to their own writing; and it can take weeks, if not months, to acquire.

We share our versions of the revised student sample and marvel at the diversity of style from each group. At this point the groups list their reasons for making a decision to combine the statements. What clues prompted them to make a change? We discover that there are five indicators or reasons that combining sentences might improve the writing:

1. redundant words or phrases
2. presence of "to be" verbs

3. pronouns without referents, especially the "naked this." Example: " . . . to secure the camera to your body while taking a picture. *This* is done to prevent any movement while taking the picture."

4. use of passive voice

5. series of short sentences with repetition of words

In order to see whether these clues might be helpful to students when combining sentences in their own papers, we apply these criteria to a second student example (Example 2), a letter that analyzes the poem "Mariana" by Tennyson.

EXAMPLE 2

Mariana Student Sample

Dear Dave:

I heard that you needed help with your English paper. I'll try and help but I'm not promising much.

Mariana is put in a very dreary setting. The dreary surroundings are old and falling apart. For example, the crusted-over flower pots, and the broken sheds. This shows that she really doesn't feel like keeping the place kept.

The cold winds display the fear she possesses. She fears that the man she is waiting for may never come home. The cold wind is like her cold or numb emotions on life. The way she faces each day.

After we revise the piece in consort, the group is surprised at how these clues, not grammatical labels, detect ways of improving syntactic fluency so the writing is clearer and more controlled. Example 3 is the workshop revision of the Mariana letter.

EXAMPLE 3

Group Revision of Mariana

Dear Dave:

I heard that you needed help with your English paper. I'll try and help but I'm not making any promises.

Mariana is put in very dreary surroundings which are old and falling apart. For example, the crusted-over flower pots and the broken sheds show that she really doesn't feel like keeping the place neat.

The cold winds display her fear that the man she is waiting for may never come home. The cold wind is like her numb emotions on life and the way she faces each day.

We end the workshop by talking about how sentence combining can be misused if students are relegated to complete pages of exercises. Sentence combining, like usage and mechanics, is only beneficial when incorporated into the students' own writing.

This workshop is the first step in helping people digest the subtle but important distinctions between grammar, usage, and mechanics. It temporarily douses the concerns that continue to simmer in people's minds about grammar's proper role. How students prepare for standardized exams which test knowledge of grammar and how teachers convince parents that grammar is unimportant in the writing process are two concerns waiting to be rekindled.

References

Judy, Stephen N. *Explorations in the Teaching of English.* New York: Dodd, Mead, 1974.

Murray, Donald M. *Write to Learn.* 3rd ed. Fort Worth: Holt, Rinehart, Winston, 1990.

Sanborn, Jean. "Grammar: Good Wine Before Its Time." *English Journal* 75.3 (1986): 72–80.

Strong, William. *Sentence Combining: A Composing Book.* New York: Random House, 1973.

Applications in the Classroom

Writing and Grammar: Bridging the Controversy

Mechanics and Usage

- Develop editing sheets which distinguish between surface, organizational, and content elements.

- Ask students to keep an editing log which tracks their improvement in writing mechanics and usage.

- Ask students to compile lists of words they have difficulty spelling on the inside covers of their writing folders.

- Focus your correction of papers to no more than three types of mechanical or usage mistakes per assignment.

- Have students work in cooperative editing groups where each student is responsible for locating errors in others' papers but allowing the writer to correct them.

- Develop editing groups that help authors proofread a paper before you do.

■ Identify student errors in mechanics and usage, but refrain from correcting them for the student.

■ Conduct ten-minute mini-lessons on usage and mechanics problems that a majority of the students are experiencing.

Grammar

■ Have students analyze a paragraph comprised of short, choppy sentences before and after sentence combining takes place.

■ Model sentence combining on an overhead projector with your own writing.

■ Provide students with opportunities to develop conference questions which inquire about how writers organize their ideas.

■ Give students copies of Lewis Carroll's *Jabberwocky* and have them speculate about the meaning of the nonsense words by how they are positioned in the text.

■ Have students combine short, choppy sentences found in their own writing in more than one way.

■ Have students copy-change a character sketch by substituting words and phrases in order to create a different personality or character. (If the original sketch is about a nurse, have the students copy-change the piece so it tells about a bag lady.)

■ Demonstrate how you add and rearrange ideas in your own writing by actually cutting and pasting a piece written on butcher paper or flip chart paper.

■ Conduct mini-lessons that depict the style and craft of professional writers.

EXTENSIONS

Within the Family of English
Mary Beth Handeyside

Young people often are unaware of the right linguistic variations within the family of English. This teaching idea might help them to understand:

■ that they often make value judgments based on how a person speaks,

■ that the language is enriched by the variant forms,

■ that those forms can be controlled by individuals who may wish to keep, eliminate, diversify their personal language patterns.

▶

I would like them to grasp, inductively, the value of learning Standard English while appreciating and respecting the variant forms.

First, I would solicit ideas from students' own life experiences by asking them to write for a few minutes in their journals about someone in their own lives who speaks differently from them. Then, as they share some of these with the class, I would record a list on the board. The list might include regional dialects, urban and rural vernaculars, ethnic, occupational, generational variations, etc. But the labels will not be given at this point.

Next, I would play snatches of recordings of various dialects and ask students to write down what kind of speaker they think each represents and what it was about the speech patterns that tipped them off (accent, idiom, vocabulary, etc.). We would share our conjectures, and in the end I would reveal the identities or occupations of the speakers.

I would have ready a short "test" in which the students would receive a list of the people in the recordings, and they would have to rate them according to who spoke the "best" English. At the bottom, they would write a short explanation of their choices

The assignment would be a reading of Faulkner's short story "Two Soldiers," which is written from a young, rural Mississippian's point of view.

On Day 2 the goal is to help the students identify variant patterns to prepare them for their personal research projects. In class they would work in groups to identify the words, figures of speech, syntax, and grammar that don't seem "Standard" to them. Some direct instruction in the meaning of linguistic terms might be appropriate on this day. The assignment would be to interview a parent or guardian and ask how their language use has changed over time—and what might be the explanation: education, geographical moves, contact with certain individuals or groups, occupational changes, etc. Other questions might be, "What are some of the slang words he or she used in his or her youth? Does he or she feel that one way of speaking is better than another? Why?" From this information, and from further class work (perhaps a viewing of portions of the television series "The Story of English"), they would develop a short research paper of their findings.

16 English through the Open Door: Foreign Language in English Language Study

Marguerite Cotto
Northwestern Michigan College

We are always reminded to look for simple opportunities that can "make the moment" in our classrooms. However, we generally assume that these flashes of insight or of collaborative learning will take place within a certain context of familiarity. English and Social Science or English and History are easy and fruitful combinations that enhance both subjects, often initiating the "spark" of true associative learning in our students. It is harder, though, to see around the corner to those less common associations that also require us to make the "leap of the imagination" along with our students.

The "open door" I'm referring to leads into the multicultural English classroom and away from the idea of using only English for the teaching of English. The basis for this approach is not the need to address an ethnically diverse student body faced with the acquisition and mastery of English as a second language. (Unfortunately, this environment is still viewed more often as an obstacle rather than an opportunity.) The open-door classroom approaches English itself as the ongoing product of cross-cultural experience. The intention is to re-listen, re-sound, even re-play with English, and perhaps ultimately change our traditional role as *users of language* to one in which we are also *inventors and creators of language, style, and meaning.* You can think of it as using an outside language, which might be more "real" to some of your students, as another tool for exploring the beauty of English itself.

My students are mostly English speakers learning Spanish for the first time. I know that the elements of language structure, vocabulary, common expressions, and even cultural nuance will come to them in due time. But my greatest concern is that the sound structure of this new language be offered to them in such a way that they neither fear playing nor perceive that these new sounds are separate from what they already know about their own language. I don't think this concern is all that different from the way a literature teacher anticipates a class studying any particular genre for the first time. We want to give our students both a sense of security and a sense of adventure in the exploration. It's essential to establish from the very start that a new sound or word or a limited understanding does not suggest that "a sense of the meaning" isn't there. Students will wallow through material without real understanding—even though the language is English—because they've never been told that their "instinct" about meaning is a significant part of understanding. I feel that developing that "instinct" is enhanced by attuning their ears to rhythm and sound and giving them plenty of room to hear the familiar in a new way.

I go right after their ears with the poem "Danza Negra" by Puerto Rican poet Luis Palés Matos. This piece is a gem of Afro-Caribbean poetry, rarely heard in the United States. It's a description of a dance as orchestrated by the sounds of the forest. Rhythm is the meaning of the piece, and Palés Matos created this dynamic world by building on the single vowel sounds of Spanish and by inventing most of the words. I haven't run across a translation of the poem, so I'll offer my own for the opening passage:

Calabó y bambú.	Calabó and bamboo.
Bambú y calabó.	Bamboo and calabó.
El Gran Cocoroco dice: tu-cu-tú.	The Great Cocoroco says: tu-cu-tú.
La Gran Cocoroca dice: to-co-tó.	The Grand Cocoroca says: to-co-tó.

Any piece of literature in another language read with some dramatic flair could serve as a similar prompt. I don't recommend that you give your students any advance information on meaning. Have the prompt read dramatically to your class by a foreign language teacher or a student who speaks another language (generally found just around the corner from our usual collaborative haunts). Encourage your students to listen, perhaps with eyes closed, to capture their immediate impressions from the reading, and then to shape those impressions into any written form they choose. The goal is to let rhythm and sound inspire new and different associations rather than to let content limit and influence interpretation.

It isn't very far from my Spanish class to your English class. To work with English and language arts teachers in the Writing

Workshops, I looked for a way to encourage us to break away from the expectations we have about "internationalizing" curriculum, or those for creating a "cross-cultural" experience in the classroom, and to look instead at the power of phonemes and syllables as "playing blocks" across all borders, so to speak. Sometimes language has to be relieved of the burden of being complicated or too meaningful.

I use "Danza Negra" because it's a fun ice-breaker and an effective prelude to an afternoon's exploration of sound. It takes a class no more than fifteen minutes to learn the vowel sounds for Spanish. (Five fixed, short vowel sounds, and a few new consonant sounds—consult your modern language faculty member.) Once you have these sounds down, you and your students can play with cognates—words that have equal or almost equal spelling and meaning in two languages. Read lists of these words together until the new pronunciation feels natural. Without changing anything other than vowel sounds, you can explore a world in which everything is visually familiar and aurally new. It's funny at first because it sounds so different in our mouths, a bit like a hard-edged piece of candy. But within minutes the conversations are turning toward our reactions to these newly flavored words, the differences between the imagined sounds and the real, the similarities to other languages they've heard at home or perhaps studied.

In the context of familiar meanings, explore with your students sound itself. Sometimes students prefer the new sound of a familiar word, sometimes they feel that a sound has altered a favorite word too much. You can take your students through language "terra incognita," applying their observations to the changes in words and sentences, considering the way in which sound shapes meaning. This is also an experience in the way language changes, in the way we can change it, and certainly in the way that changes in language affect us. The unifier to these explorations is the idea that *the familiar is new without too much effort.* This newness sparks curiosity and adventure.

Viewing the translation process is another step that can take us through the micro view of sounds to the macro view of the meaning and context of language. Why we choose the words we do is the essence of the translator's work, and it is also in essence the daily mystery we attempt to decipher with our students in the classroom. Considering the translation of "Danza Negra," a student might look through a Spanish-English dictionary and ask how a translation can take place when some of the words don't really exist outside of the writer's imagination. What does a translator have to know about a writer before trying to understand what they write? What happens when you translate the translation back to the original? Isn't this a variation on the discussion of meaning in literature? How can we truly know what the writer wants us to think? Does it matter?

Many new dual translation books are becoming available, making it far easier to introduce students (and teachers) to some of the literary gems of other languages and cultures. I recommend exploring the work of contemporary Mexican writer Rosario Castellanos, Chilean Pablo Neruda, and turn-of-the-century Spanish poet Frederico García Lorca. In the case of Neruda and Lorca, there are several editions of dual-language collections by different translators in slightly different translations. Try a library search that includes Nathaniel Tarn, Alastair Reid and Ben Bellit as translators of Pablo Neruda. If you set one or two poems side by side and compare translations—"Ode to an Artichoke" is a fun one—you can assemble a lesson plan built to illustrate the problems and the accomplishments of interpreting poetic writing across the fence of language.

Of course the open door should work both ways. Have someone read a translation of a Langston Hughes poem in Spanish to a class that has just studied him in English. I would add that a Spanish class might enjoy your discussion of Langston Hughes; they can read it in Spanish (several of his poems appear in Spanish translation by Rosa López-Nieves in her Spanish language anthology work *La Poesía Negroide en América, [Negroid Poetry in America],* Northern Illinois University Press), and discuss the difference between their interpretation and your interpretation in the original.

Explorations of language at this level don't conclude as much as they open up possibilities. New collaborative strategies are always energizing, rethinking what we know is exciting for us and for our students. We have expectations that our students will choose to "possess" and use language with zeal. The step beyond the expected is often the most fruitful.

References

López-Nieves, Rosa. *La Poesía Negroide en América.* DeKalb, IL: Northern Illinois University Press, 1967.

Palés Matos, Luis. "Danza Negra," *Tun Tun de Pasa y Grifería.* San Juan: Biblioteca de Autores Puertorriqueños, 1937.

Tarn, Nathaniel, ed. *Pablo Neruda: Selected Poems. A Bilingual Edition.* New York: Dell Publishing, 1969.

Applications in the Classroom

English through the Open Door

■ Coordinate a series of readings by works in other languages. Have your students take notes on their perceptions of the pieces before they read the translations. Select a piece where students can write about their *perceptions of the sound* of the language. Have an additional piece read that might be more suited to the *evocation of a meaning*. How close is their perception to the literal meaning?

■ Have your students prepare a brief piece to be read out loud in a different phonetic system from English. What happens to the piece when it's read with an "accent"? What images are evoked that are different from hearing the original language?

■ Host a mini-lesson on pronunciation in another language (Spanish is an easy one), then take your class through the reading of cognate word lists. For English or Spanish: *hospital, postal, tempera,* and *auto* are examples of exact cognates; *institución, libertad, educación, tigre,* and *león* are examples of close cognates, not identical in spelling but close enough to guess meaning. Discuss how the change of sounds affects the "effect" of the word. For example, is there a difference in the animal *lion* and león?

■ Have your students keep a journal during the discussion of one or two pieces in a dual translation edition. Ask them to comment on the perceptions of different structure, length, word placement. Also, ask them to think about translation and on whether emotions and subtext translate with the words themselves.

■ Open the door both ways on classic "canonical" literature, by comparing English translations of passages in Homer, Vergil, Sappho, Sophocles, Cervantes, Dante, Chekhov, Ibsen, Tolstoy, when appropriate, to the classes you teach, or go the other way and ask students to find foreign translations of American authors such as Steinbeck, Hemingway, Cather, Alice Walker, Toni Morrison. Let students also taking foreign language classes team up to re-translate American works from the foreign language back into English without consulting the original, then compare the translation with the original.

■ Compare a scene in a foreign language film that has subtitles at the bottom of the screen with the same scene in a version that has been overdubbed with English. Do the characters say the same thing in both versions? What happens to the power of language in the overdubbed version? The books and film of *Like Water For Chocolate (Como Agua Para Chocolate)* by Laura Esquivel or the translations by Brian Hooker and Anthony Burgess of Edmond Rostand's *Cyrano de Bergerac* together with the film versions starring Jose Ferrer and Gerard Depardieu are good resources.

■ Those teaching Albert Camus's *The Stranger* in either English or French classes may profit from Alice Yaeger Kaplan's article, "The American Stranger," in *Eloquent Obsessions: Writing Cultural Criticism,* edited by Mariana Torgovnick (Durham: Duke University Press, 1994, pp. 5–28).

EXTENSIONS

Educational Fair
Mary Lou Green

Purpose:

- to provide positive interaction between the school and the community
- to provide an audience for student publishing
- to provide students with an opportunity to carry out a problem-solving activity that was beneficial to the community

One of the group writing requirements in eleventh-grade American Literature this year was to compile some kind of pamphlet, booklet, paper, etc. to be used by a specific person or group and to present the material to that audience. One group of five girls decided to organize an educational fair. This project was selected because responses on a community survey showed a high rate of interest in this kind of activity.

The girls began by getting permission from both high school and elementary offices and filling out the necessary paperwork to use school facilities. Their next step was to notify teachers that they would be coming to classrooms to suggest ideas and find out how much space and what kind of equipment each display would require. They looked for similar attempts by other schools, but were unable to find much information, so they made their own plan and turned it in for approval. They kept a log of their activities and finally wrote an outline and evaluation of the project. This included suggestions for improving the project in case someone wished to repeat the activity. For example, they explained the importance of constant communication with the participants.

The idea began slowly at first; then, as the girls interviewed each teacher, interest began to build. They drew a blueprint of how the gym would be set up, numbering each teacher's space and telling the janitors where tables needed to be set up. They coordinated the use of audio-visual equipment and computers, and checked to make sure that electrical outlets would support the equipment. They organized a program for those who wished to do oral presentations; provided a babysitting area with toys, videos, and babysitters; and persuaded the home economics department to make refreshments for the event.

Even those teachers who don't usually participate in optional activities other than sports contributed samples of student work for the

▶

display. Comments from parents were positive. People from the community who were taxpayers but no longer had children in school attended in order to see how their tax dollars were being used.

Even though I work in the school every day, I was pleasantly surprised by some of the student work. Our little school presented an impressive display of quality work.

Appendixes

Introduction

The hardest part of imagining yourself involved in the kind of workshop this book has been revealing might be to imagine yourself administering it. What happens when such a workshop takes place? What do people think of all this, once they've gone through it? These appendices give further insight into the daily reactions of workshoppers through additional writing fair examples, a synthesis of entries excerpted from learning and reading logs, and an additional cluster of teaching ideas that workshop participants contribute to a Teaching Sampler. In addition, we've provided two personal views on organizing and administrating a writing conference by teachers who are also workshop administrators. Tammy Lantz brings a researcher's eye to the results of the workshop—the reasons teachers feel a need for such a workshop, and also what such a workshop might provide in order to help its participants go away satisfied and often want to come back again. John Kelley talks about the "nuts and bolts" of putting on the workshop from the standpoint of an administrator, whose job description is part financial director, part registrar, part cashier, part *maître d'*, part social director, and all-around troubleshooter.

THE WRITING FAIR: AN ANTHOLOGY

Hammock Play
Jan Andre

Striped hammock hangs
On flaking metal frame,
Fringed edges ripple
In the breeze.

Small hands grasp
Its sides—
Swing . . . and sway.

Suddenly, she
Twists and flips,
Happily encased—
  Mummy-like

Fabric strains, unfolds,
Deposits its contents
Solidly,
On soft cool grass
  Below.
She giggles and returns.

Folding Clothes

Linda Dinan

Standing at
the dining room table,
a basketful of
freshly-dried laundry
balanced on a chair,
my mother
sorted out the pieces—
our clothes,
our lives,
cleaned up,
dusted off,
straightened,
neatly stacked
into piles
to be delivered
to our rooms.

If only she could
have kept our lives
so tidy.

Love

Suzanne Dodge

Beatrice was a wife.
Weekdays she
Mashed potatoes,
Stirred gravy.
Half past eleven
"Ready for Grandpa,"
She'd say.
Home for lunch
Exactly at noon.
"My mechanic from the
Ford dealership on
Huron Street."

Saturdays in September
She simmered
Chicken soup with
Homemade noodles,
Waited for Grandpa
Coming home
From the game.

Sundays, as Grandpa
Dressed in gaberdine
And dashing plaid
Entered kitchen warmth,
She'd pull the
Clouded mirror from
Its nesting spot
On the cupboard.
Beatrice stood before
The mirror. Her hand
Powered, dabbed pink
Hints of lip and cheek.
She stood as a reverent
Hand placed her hat,
Its simplicity
Richly browned by
Patterns of amber sequins.
Sundays, Grandpa
Gathered the Rosaries and
Prayer books,
Beatrice held a moment
Before entering
Her only other world.

Nine Came In with the Morning Light

Veronica Drenovsky

Thoughts of a crew member from the Sleeping Bear Point Life Saving Station around the turn of the century.

Nearly eleven o'clock and it's been getting colder since my beach watch began at eight. I don't remember a September night being this cold since I joined the station ten years ago. It must be 20 degrees, and that wind is bitter!

Look at those clouds rolling in. I know a storm must be brewing, but I hope it doesn't start until my watch is over in an hour.

I'm almost at the two-and-a-half-mile marker where I trade coins with Jake from the next station. His wife's time will come any day now. It will be hard for Jake to be away from his wife when the child comes.

I remember the night my daughter, Sally, was born. The mild fall night had a sky filled with stars, and there was not even a whisper of wind. I was on duty that night, too.

I had begun my watch at eight, as usual. With the weather so calm, I felt there couldn't be any trouble on my last night before the station closed for winter. Soon I'd be home with Liza again until Spring.

By ten o'clock, the wind had picked up viciously. Fury-filled clouds covered the stars while the chopping waves rose to ten feet and beyond.

I had no more than settled into bed after my shift when Lefty, my replacement, shouted, "Ship aground!" The violence of the storm made Captain Ague decide to use the beach cart.

We had practiced with the cart weekly, but this was the first time that I had helped use it for a shipwreck. I was relieved that the crew didn't need to reply on my shaking hands to aim the Lyle gun so the whip line would pass over the distressed ship.

In panic, I couldn't think what to do. All I managed was to rotely go through the steps we had practiced so often. Man the cart. Dig the hole. Attach the pulleys. Set the brace. Watch and hold the rope. Wait. It seemed like hours, though during practice we did it all in less than five minutes.

Finally, we felt a tug on the other end of the line. Slowly, we pulled the rope attached to the breeches buoy. I don't think I took a breath until I saw that first person coming through the dark.

One safe, and he told us there were eight others. Two. Three, Four. Number five was difficult because we were beginning to tire and the sailor was a big man with some injuries. Seven. Eight. Just one more. Nine came in with the morning light.

Breakfast made us whole again. Shorty was cook and he outdid himself. We feasted on eggs, bacon, thick slices of bread, and plenty of hot coffee.

As I drifted off to sleep, I remember thinking about how glad I was that Shorty was cook that day and not Pete, who could barely boil water. Even oatmeal burned for Pete.

Later, while we were salvaging the ship, my sister Jo sent word that our baby was born and sleeping peacefully in my wife's arms. All had gone well—for both of us.

I see a light; it must be Jake.

The Mound

Richard Hill

Pushing open the screen door, I gaze past the asphalted driveway at my backyard, anxiously scanning its parameters for flaws. Have any twigs or branches fallen? Might that be a paper cup lying there, partially concealed beneath the corner fire bush, sticky Coke residue clinging to the bottom, red ants pouring over its side? Has Steve Avril's Brittany made an unscheduled visit? I can't help it! I worry about these things. I am the resident grounds-keeper, warily on the prowl for weed, mold, pest, debris, and decay. Finally, but only when completely satisfied that all is well, I allow my eyes to once again pan slowly across the yard's expanse.

Bordering the black chainlink fence separating my yard from the neighbors' are lilacs, forsythia, a mulberry bush, and two mock oranges, appropriate to my white frame saltbox house. This bushy wall serves to seal off that side from prying eyes. In several spots between, tiger lilies, orange and black faces stretching upward in the sunlight, provide just the right amount of needed color. Across the yard, against the sidewalk, a carefully manicured boxwood hedge reminds passersby that the yard is meant to be admired and appreciated, not trod upon by thoughtless feet. Where driveway meets lawn, a straight narrow edge has been cut into the soil, clearly defining nature's grassy limits. A black walnut tree dominates the center of the yard, branches reaching across the fence, threatening to once again rain rotting fruit on the neighbor's patio come September. In this heavily shaded place, the grass, cut once or sometimes twice a week, grows full and green. It carpets the spread of yard, connecting its divergent elements, unifying them, completing a construct at once placid and satisfying. It's the sort of yard you want to photograph, to preserve in some way for others in need of sweet peace and serenity.

Left of the big tree, perhaps fifteen feet removed, rests a small grassy mound. It seems an anomaly, an aberration in the ground's level surface. In the late afternoon, it casts a small curved shadow on the ground, a dim half moon at variance with the time of day. There is a sense of impropriety here, of imbalance. What is this disturbance in my otherwise oh-so-perfect yard? Why is it here? Townies strolling past find it remarkable. Is that some sort of Indian mound? they wonder. Is that where the body's buried?

I know what it is, this raised place spoiling the symmetry of my yard. After all, I put it here years ago, carrying the soil shovelful by shovelful to the spot, piling it up and tamping it down, smoothing its sides and lengthening its base, making everything right. This is a place of memories. They were made here; now they lay buried underneath this gentle rise.

It's a pitcher's mound, you know. Any fool can see that! Look closely. You can just make out the tiny groove near its apex, all that remains of the deep cut where countless tennis-shoed feet sought purchase and pushed off in frantic, arm-swinging motion. As I stand here, staring off in space, seeing nothing, memory reaches out her cool hand and strips the years away. And once again, it is 1979 . . .

The high-pitched sounds of youthful voices wash over me. Suddenly, the yard is filled with children in blue jeans and shorts, t-shirts and baseball caps. Everywhere there is movement—boys, and girls, ranged around the yard, waiting for the next pitch. In left corner, just behind the tree, Maria Tracy sits sprawled on the lawn, her back to the plate, carefully studying a dandelion. Somewhere near the middle of the infield—it could be either shortstop or second base—Robbie Caron, blond forelock sticking out beneath his red baseball cap, pounds his mitt and bends his knees in anticipation. Behind the plate, Johnny Abbott, his cap turned backward, crouches and flashes the sign. He wears no chest protector, no mask, no knee pads. Still, he doesn't complain, understanding that, because he is the youngest player there, the catcher's spot is his. That's the rule.

Standing sturdily at the plate, just in front of a spreading linden tree, my son Michael, eight years old, 49 inches high, Blue Jays baseball cap pulled down tight to the forehead, digs in, his right foot cutting a perpendicular swath in the dirt, just the way he's seen it done on television countless times before. He chokes up a good three inches on this 26 ounce bat. His hands are so small that when he grips his Yogi Berra Special, his fingers and thumbs do not meet. He crouches in the classic batter's stance, weight shifting slowly back and forth, back and forth, between front and rear foot. The resulting strike zone is impossibly small. But this is neighborhood ball and Michael is excited; he will swing at anything he can see.

On the mound, ten-year-old Jeff Tetz looks in, ball cradled behind his back as he leans forward. Slowly, he straightens up, bringing his hands carefully to the set position. His face is a study in concentration. Suddenly, he raises his left foot, beginning the long stride as he pushes off hard with his right. Wrist cocked, his arm sweeps up through the dappled sunlight, starting its blinding spiral descent toward the plate. His father's oversized first baseman's mitt dangles loosely from his left hand, slapping against his thigh.

Michael sees the ball coming and lunges at it, dragging his bat slowly around toward the plate. His swing is a mathematical marvel, a perfect parabolic arc that, carried to its logical conclusion, will continue up and around his head, descending rapidly to strike his left heel. His eyes are tightly closed. Still, miraculously, incredibly, the linear movement of the ball and the trajectory of the bat intersect at a point approximately eighteen inches directly in front of and slightly higher than Michael's right ear.

Contact!

As the battered rubber ball leaps off the bat, scooting toward the fence, he takes off, touching the miniature crabapple tree as he rounds first, slapping the Walnut's gigantic trunk (second), and coming to rest on a plywood plank. A triple. He looks over toward the driveway, sees me watching, grins, and waves. The game continues.

The yard, of course, is a shambles. Four relatively straight paths of packed earth from what might loosely be described as a square, a visible map to the bases. On the crabapple tree, small hands, grabbing wildly as runners make the turn, have methodically ripped away a ring of bark approximately five inches wide. Home plate is a small hole, surrounded by scuff marks, pea gravel, and dusty footprints. There is a worn path of beaten grass linking the mound to the hole, testimony to numerous animated conferences between pitcher and catcher. In left field, my sorry attempt at rose bushes has been defeated by the stomping assault of future hall-of-famers, who, crashing through my Martha Washingtons, dream of scaling Fenway's Green Monster. Yes, the yard is most certainly a shambles.

But who cares! There is something alive here, something vibrant, resonant, magnetic, something that compels the afternoon walkers to pause and watch for awhile, and the drivers, stopped momentarily at the corner, to crane their necks toward this oasis of noise and fun. The children, oblivious to all this attention, stand laughing, screaming, encouragement, derision.

"Get it over, will ya!"

"C'mon, Charley, keep it alive!"

"Can a' corn!"

"Nothing up there!"

Around us, the homes stand quiet and empty, gleaming pristinely in the sunshine. They generate no noise. No children race about them, cutting through bushes and leaping hedges. These homes, manicured and immaculate, seem somehow withdrawn, lonely, forlorn. Seeing them at this moment, I can almost imagine them leaning toward our corner house, listening to the laughter, seeking the joy of youthful communion.

Suddenly, memory reaches across my vision and turns the page. It is 1982. Michael is eleven. Again he stands at the plate. His body seems leaner, more defined now. His hands are larger, his shoulders broader. Looking out toward the mound, he impatiently waves his bat at the pitcher, a confident smile playing along his lips. One of the bigger kids now, he is afforded the ultimate compliment, as the pitcher turns, waving at the outfielders to move back.

The right-hander looks in, takes the sign, winds and delivers. Michael reaches out—somewhat carelessly, it seems to me—and strokes through the ball, sending it high into the branches of the walnut. Miraculously, it emerges behind unscathed. Still rising, it clears the fence, then the neighbor's house. Michael languidly drops his 28-ounce bat and begins the trot: crabapple, walnut, plywood, home.

"That's 62," he announces. "A new record."

My mind clears, refocuses. Another page is turned. Michael is now fourteen. We've been having trouble with the neighbors. Projectiles of various colors have been ricocheting about their yards, threatening their peonies, petunias, and persons. One young housewife, a confirmed sun worshipper, has recently experienced a close encounter with a red rubber ball. She reports that it came flying into her yard, hit a patch of merion blue with a loud "Whonk," and passed screaming over her prone form, not 18 inches above her exposed navel. She seems shockingly unconcerned about the import of the momentous contest taking place just down the street. The incidents multiply. A delegation visits my home.

As a result, Michael no longer bats. When he can find the time to play, he functions as official pitcher, umpire, coach, arbiter of all disputes. A born communicator and teacher, he relishes his new role, throwing himself into it. He already evidences the sensitivity that will grow in him as he develops and matures. He pitches underhand to the younger players, sometimes forgetting the count when it reaches three strikes. He stops the game to correct a batting stance, to show the proper way to short-hop a hard smash coming at you dead center, to demonstrate how to bunt without bloodying your fingers. He announces the game's progress as he pitches:

"It's two and one on Kalush. Hill rears back, fires a high hard one. There's a long drive . . ."

The scene fades from view. Memory closes her book with a snap, and suddenly, I'm back, standing once again beside the grassy mound, staring at the teeming perfection of my yard. All is as it was. The lawn, newly mown, is unmarred by weed or blight. A sprinkler reaches out from beside the walnut tree, sending streams of water in carefully regulated spurts toward the burgeoning rose bushes at the yard's far end. Lilies wave softly in the fragrant breeze. The quiet envelopes me like a woolen blanket, muffling me in a cocoon of silence. Michael is a college junior now; neighborhood youngsters have found a new haven in which to run the bases and circle under lazy fly balls. Sometimes, fragments of their laughter filter through the bushes, shards of sound lost amid the rustling leaves.

As I wander the yard, the artifacts of change are all about me, arranged like museum pieces for casual inspection. Autumn will follow summer, walnuts will again rain down upon the grass, and I will spend another September picking them up. Leaves will fall; the roses will be cut back. Eventually, snow will cover everything, a necessary end to a new beginning. The message is clear. Time to move on. Time to build on memory. Time to begin again, to heed the insights spread before me here.

Still, I know that there will be times when I will again stand here, gazing at the mound, seeking again the patterns buried forever under the sod. The lawn spreads lush beneath my feet as I, for old time's sake, walk the covered basepaths once more. Crabapple, walnut, plywood, home.

Land of the Giants

Kathie Johnson

His children return weekend after weekend.
They towered over me as young adolescents,
These athletic duplicates of the man I love,
And now they descend again as young adults.
Taller still.
With taller yet spouses or spouses-to-be.
All gleaming athletes seeking competition
On a family scale.
"Are you sure you don't want to water ski this summer?"
"Are you sure you don't want to use your brain every third summer?"
The yearly challenges freshly issued
We settle back into summer rules.
Safe within the boundaries of our familiar game
They head for the playing fields,
I retreat to my books.
There is no athlete in me.
Isn't it enough that I tan well?

"I find a bridge . . ."

Patrick McGuire

I find a bridge that's working and drive over the canal past the taverns and body shops to Mantia's Funeral Home, where Hammond's Italians wake their dead. Dom Buongiorno, 63, of 516 Flint Street, our neighbor for the first eight years of my life, the man who taught me how to ride a bike: heart disease. I go at 7:00, right when the evening session begins, because I'm sad, and I know that if there's a line I'll shift from foot to foot and bite my lower lip and cry all over my light grey suit.

There's no line, but my eyes moisten. At the back of the parlor, Legionnaires in short sleeves are nervously adjusting their wallet-shaped caps. I buy time for signing the book. A deep breath, a wipe of the eyes, and I'm in.

The inoffensive face of Wayne, the oldest Buongiorno son, the kid who never lost a piece of his Catholic school uniform, comes clear. He moves to me, extends a hand, says, "Jack Welch."

No, Wayne, no, for Christ's sake. Jack was my dad. He's dead—you weren't at his wake. Your brother Phil over there was. At Jack Welch's wake, Phil was shaking: Big Phil, #56, on the varsity as a sophomore; my dad compared him to Sam Huff. Phil was so shook at Jack's wake that Mom and the other kids and I took him in our arms, we incorporated him, he wound up standing behind us in the receiving line, like a stepbrother.

"No . . . Jim! Jim, whaddyuh up to, guy?"

I meet Wayne's wife, learn that Wayne's moved from IBM to Honeywell and perforce from Minnesota to Georgia, and I pass on, making the long, lonely walk up to the casket. No one's up there but Mrs. Buongiorno, Bev, alone in the far corner.

Heavy on the kneeler, I sneak a look at Mr. Buongiorno. He looks pretty much as he did when we lived next to him twenty-two years ago; like he's plagued by hemorrhoids, bills, and three sons. His brow is dug into his bushy, India ink eyebrows. His frown sinks his jowls, where his swarthy stubble overcomes the mortician's makeup. He's quiet, for once. Only in memory do I hear him growl, "Phil! Jesus Christ! What the hell?! Goddamn kids! Jim, go home. Bev!"

Breaking prayers in half, my mind is heaving and hauling. Do I pray? Do I look at him again? Do I have an urge to touch him? Have I knelt long enough? Do I look like I'm praying?

I'm rescued by a sound from without, a rustle of nylon. The smell of dry-cleaning smacks the fragrance of the funeral bouquets. The warmth of another's body joins my humidity. Mrs. Buongiorno is hugging me. "Jiiiimmm, how are you?" A kiss. "Your buddy, Jim. I know, I know, I know, hon, I know you do hon. He suffered this last month, with water and the swelling. He was miserable."

I stand, lace my arm through hers, and we stare at her dead husband. We loosen, Mrs. Buongiorno squeezing my hand. "Thanks for coming, Jim, good to see you. I'll see your Mom in the morning then, huh?"

Halfway back in the parlor, Big Phil is in conversation with his back to me. I circle him. I've many reasons to expect that Phil and I will hug and sob: the way he acted at my dad's wake, the moist ache I feel over his dad's death, the vault of memories I presume we share by having grown up the same age in homes just six feet apart—all the baseball, all the mud, all the lightning bugs, all the birthday parties, all the times we saw each other scared, lying, carried in asleep from a car, jumping off a bed, with wet pants, yelled at—and also because of the phone call I made to Big Phil, years after we ceased to be neighbors but days after a semester of cheap wine, good dope, and Led Zeppelin at Indiana State—to tell him of our roommate's wreck: "Phil . . . Robby's dead." I've never forgotten Phil's childish, wounded yelp, his instant, helpless tears.

But Phil doesn't see me now. Tall, he's leaning in to talk to others. Further back I see Tony, the middle son. In the years since my family moved from Flint Street, I've seen Tony in person only once, at least ten years ago. But I've seen his picture, balding, bearded, and grinning, like Mr. Natural, three or four times recently in the Chicago newspapers. When we were little, Tony was always either too chubby or too smart to fight—I never knew which. But he'd snarl like his old man to keep us away from his precious comic books. Comic books in plastic wrappers! Under his bed, up in his closet, in his drawers of the dresser, tight in his hands when his dad took him, special, to the comics and candy store in the shopping center where Kennedy campaigned. He was all the time reading and sorting those things, often kicking Philip and me out of their room because Tony and some strange-acting kid from across town were reading and trading.

Tony's a comics mogul now. Three stores in the affluent suburbs beyond O'Hare. I'm happy whenever I see him in the paper. He speaks well, he's always smiling, he's obviously a favorite of reporters. I read the last story about him to one of my classes, because in it Tony made strong points about popular culture and reading. I pumped up the class, asking them, "And what got Tony Buongiorno started taking comics seriously? Why has he made collecting them his life's work? Listen to this, teens, listen to this, it's comin' from the heart: 'My dad drew his own comics, and he was pretty good at it,' Buongiorno explained, 'but he couldn't support a family with his art, so he wound up working six days a week in a foundry. I've got him to thank for getting me started. He enjoys my stores; I'm proud of that.'"

I walk toward Tony and hook his eye.

"Jim!"

"Sorry about your dad, Ton."

"Yeah . . . Thanks, Jim. It's tough, yeah, it's tough . . . jeez, you know that, Jim. Hey, how's your mom? Dennis still around? What's Meg doing? What about the little kids, everybody alright?"

"They're all here, they're alright." I attempt the *bonhomie* I despise at wakes: "We read about you in the *Trib* and the *Sun-Times*, Tony. I'm teaching high school, over in Munster, English, and I read that last piece in the *Sun-Times*, the one about Batman, I read that to my classes. The kids think I'm a big deal 'cause I grew up next to Tony Buongiorno.

"What you said in the paper that last time about your dad, Tony, that . . . you . . . uh . . . that was good, Tony, that was good, that was important. I admire you for saying that."

Tony's eyes grow deep and powerful, even as his jaw and shoulders sag, worn by grief and ritual. Quietly, proudly, he says, "Yeah . . . yeah . . . Some things you just gotta—" Tony turns away, blows his nose. I think he's gone to talk to someone else; he turns back to me and says, full-voiced, "Hey, you seen Phil yet? Here he is."

"Hey, Jim, good to see you, man, when'd you get here?"

"Phil, Phil, sorry 'bout your dad, Phil."

We're shaking hands, like associates. Phil talks, rapidly. "You still with, what was it, Worker's Comp? Livin' here in Hammond? Ever get out to California? Dirt was just out there, him and Toes came out to see Mike Tezak and—you know Chuck Warbel, don't you? Them guys are still gettin' wasted, I rode my bike down to see 'em in San Diego, but those guys are goofy as ever, I can't take that stuff no more. Whaddyuh doin' now, I heard you tell Tony you're teachin'? Where at? Hey, you ever talk to McGraw? Is he still down in Nassau or someplace? Hey, how's your mom? What's your little brother Brian doin', still breakin' play pens? You got any kids now, Jim?"

This is not what I expected. This is not a class reunion. We have not just run into each other at an airport. Phil, you are standing with your back to your dead father and your sorrowful mother. Phil, where did you get that suit? You're dressed like Gordon Gecko. What the hell do you do out there in California? How'd you get so thin? You're tan. Your shirt collar isn't showing behind the knot of your tie—how do you do that? You look like this all the time, don't you? Do you remember how mad your dad got when watermelons grew behind your evergreens 'cause we spit the seeds there the summer before? Do you remember the time you stole Wally Staley's new catcher's mitt and I got blamed? Robby's not around, Phil, no, he's not here to jack around with the San Diego boys, remember? We've got one kid, Phil. Clare. She's a good kid—last week I took her to my dad's grave for the first time, it was her birthday and she decorated it with pine cones, she collects them, she's three.

"You live in L.A., Phil?"

"Philip, Wayne and your mom want you up by the casket. Let's go up there." Phil's new wife, stage-whispering. We've never met, and we aren't now introduced.

"Good to see you, Jim. Tell everybody I said hello, will ya? If you get to California, y'know, we're in La Jolla. Thanks for comin', man, thanks for comin'."

They're two steps from me and ten from the casket when they stop to talk to someone else.

I'm feeling confused and foolish, like the kid in Joyce's story "Araby." I don't understand why I'm sadder than two of the Buongiorno kids, nor why I act the self-appointed hometown keener. I've talked to everyone I wanted to talk to. I move to go.

I find my car keys in my suit coat pocket. I squeeze them, rub them against each other so they click, push my fingertips against the grooved, teethed metal. Power, freedom, sharpness: my escape from this soft-walled place, these softened and shallow voices, these fragile flowers, these suits and dresses, this whole damn mushy mess I've created for myself. Suddenly, Tony and I are again face to face. He looks as if he's been waiting for me. He grabs my right hand with both of his. He must be able to feel the keys, too.

"Jim, thanks."

"Tony, your dad taught me how to ride a bike, I . . ."

"Yeah . . . it's OK, brother."

I can't speak; I think I see a tear in Tony's eye. I take mine around the corner and out the door. In the bright, hard, hot parking lot, I'm sure of three things by the time I reach the car: I can't bring Dom Buongiorno back from the dead; I hope to see Tony Buongiorno again; and I can't wait to teach my own kid how to ride a bike.

Hat

Jan Mekula

Miss Matilda Detwiler
lived in the haunted house
at the end of the block, behind

climbing vines of roses gone wild.
Every Sunday, she carefully draped
a shawl of yellowed lace
across her birdboned shoulders
and settled the blue velvet pancake
precisely atop her head,
two glass-beaded antennae snaking up
from the base of her tight grey bun.
Lilac and mothballs,
she tottered sparrow-ankled to church,
past me and Lizzie who giggled
around the corner of Monstrey's
calling her The Crazy Lady from Mars
while she pretended
not to hear.

Gentle Insubordination

Jeanie Mortensen

Growing up with a mother who amalgamates the best and worst qualities of June Cleaver and General George Patton can be an exacting experience. I suppose few people in this world besides my two younger sisters can appreciate the difficulty I had forging my own mettle in the foundry of life under such a formidable role model.

It is Sunday, 11 A.M. precisely. I schlep to the phone in my frayed chenille bathrobe. With head bent sideways, I prop the receiver against my right shoulder and fish through torn pockets for the stale kleenex I need to blot the coffee stain that sloshed from my mug when the ringing startled me.

Mother always was good at sneaking up on a person and now continues to perfect her technique long-distance. My sisters and I used to imagine she had little rollers under her feet like the robot maid on the "Jetsons." We thought this enabled her to slide silently down hallways and catch us in our bedrooms perpetrating some infraction of the household rules. Lying on clean bedspreads without first removing sneakers, for instance, was definitely against regulation.

The mere memory of Mother's rigid stance in my doorway, Maybellined lips pursed in disapproval, soft coiffed curls quivering in indignation at one of my more felonious exploits, can still make me squirm with discomfort, thirty-some-odd years in retrospect . . . like the time I licked the middles from an entire package of lemon-cream sandwiches, then hid the naked cookie wafers under the bed and forgot about them. Two weeks later a relentless accusing dustmop uncovered my crime. I learned a valuable lesson: Always destroy the evidence of one's misdeeds.

"Hello? Mother?" I chirp in my cheeriest voice.

"Of course it's Mother, dear," comes the sweet but firm reply. (She always calls at eleven on Sundays.)

God. She's been up since seven. I can feel it. Six bits to a dollar her dishes are washed and the bed's made tightly enough for any drill sergeant to bounce a quarter on.

"How have you been, dear?" Mom solicitously inquires.

"Busy. Very busy," I lie. My gaze peruses the sinkful of last night's pots and pans fomenting in an orange-rimmed lasagna-scented dishwater slime. Thank God modern technology has not advanced to the point of making TV phones cost-effective for the average household. Not that I need any such apparatus, of course, to perfectly envision my mother. I visualize her now standing straight in her tailored shirt-waist, nylons, and low sensible heels. Behind her, on the bottom shelf of an immaculate G.E., some recipe clipped from a 1962 *Ladies Home Journal* burbles and slurps, sending out tantalizing aromas that sneak preview the meal to be eaten and duly appreciated by Father on the dot of twelve.

This morning I can safely bet my next year's teaching salary, plus fifty visits to the Dairy Queen, round trip, that my upcoming 25th-year class reunion will be the focus of Mother's call. After devoting a lifetime to the execution of her role as chief financial advisor, social secretary, and wardrobe consultant for the entire family, she likes to think, at the age of seventy, she can still grasp the familial reins whenever she is so inclined. *Atta girl, Mom. Keep your finger in the pie.*

A master in the art of subtle maneuver, however, Mom begins our Sunday morning chat with:

"Did I tell you about Aunt Elizabeth's gall bladder, dear?"

This titillating subject is immediately followed by another significant query. "What's on sale up there at your K-Mart? I can get a 12-ounce Oil of Olay here for $4.79." Next comes, "I had the loveliest beefroast on Wednesday. Practically no fat and so tender you could cut it with a fork." Bringing up the rear is the usual litany of family gossip, complete with update on Father's latest bouts with gastric distress. As all this funnels effortlessly into my ear, my mind disengages. I bide my time.

I know you're waiting to grill me, Mom, but I too can play it cool.

I watch the cat. She swats a left-over pizza crust from under the dinette. She leaps and instantly slaps it in the opposite direction like a feline Pele. I am captivated, once more, by her gracefulness.

I stretch the cord as far as it will reach. I want to stand in the open patio door and drink in the morning, full of dampness and birdsong. I feel like laying the phone quietly on the braided rug and tiptoeing out while Mom babbles on. I would like to spend an hour writing verse to the purple vetch and bright orange hawkweed that splashes the paler field grasses at the edge of the drive. Mother would call that "dilly-dallying." *Wouldn't you, Mom.*

From the corner of my eye I catch the movement of my class reunion party dress pinned to the clothesline as it jig-dances in the wind. I have hung it there for another day of fresh air and sunshine, hoping to dispel the musty odor that will bespeak, treasure though it is, its thrift-shop origin.

As if on cue, Mom's monologue begins to run down.

"Oh, I bought a beautiful jersey sweater and skirt on sale at Jacobson's," she throws out, as casually as a Kirby salesman gets his foot in the door.

Here it comes. Get ready.

"And, by the way, dear. Have you found a proper dress for your class reunion yet?"

Bingo! I knew it.

I can practically mouth the words that are coming next so familiar are they to me after years of matriarchal indoctrination.

"You know you can't go wrong with basic black, dear, and, for heaven's sake, keep it simple."

This poor woman, I reflect. Trapped for decades in the Ozzie and Harriet dimension, still trying to convert me to a Grace Kelly clone and getting nowhere. The frock in question, if Mother only knew, is not just a dress. It is simply the campiest item I have ever seen since Joan Baez drove Ol' Dixie down. Basic black? Simple? Ha! This is a multi-hued voluminous master-piece. It ties; it buttons; it has a life of its own. I am certain it will transform me into the avant garde Diane Keaton look-alike I have always yearned to be. If only I can find some soft-soled knee-high boots and dangly gold hoops to accessorize, I will flounce into that reunion with a fashion statement that'll knock those apple-cheeked ex-cheerleader types right out of their proverbial bobbysox.

Aloud I answer demurely, "Yes, Mother, I think I have found something nice along the lines you suggested."

"That's fine, dear," comes the expected reply of approval.

Oh, Mother. If you only knew.

I am amazed at the ease with which I can mentally squash the cockroach of niggling guilt that insidiously attempts to scuttle out at this small deception. Practice makes perfect, I guess, and that reminds me of the very best adage of all: "What she doesn't know won't hurt her." Besides, I think it was Abbie Hoffman who said, "A little anarchy is good for the soul."

Hello Again

Karen Opperman

I peered through the haze and watched the dryer relentlessly beating the moisture from yet another load of locker-room towels. The industrial-sized dryer and its companion washer hid out here in the cramped custodian's room with tired teachers seeking comfort and refuge from the academic rind. My stack of uncorrected typing papers lay in a sprawl on the paint-splattered desk—obviously a cast-off from the classroom. "God, I should grade these before seventh hour," my conscience nudged me. But my red pen didn't move. Another cigarette? No, better not.

I reflected on the change in pattern my days had taken over the past school year. I had begun fresh and eager in late August. The grueling sched-ule had still been a "challenge," my legs fit from a summer of jogging, and my lungs clear from a six-year abstinence from cigarettes. So how had I come to this—slipping off for stolen cigarettes in surroundings reminiscent of Dante's Inferno?

Carole sat propped in the corner under the small bulletin board beneath an array of work orders and hastily scrawled notes from disgruntled faculty. The smoke from her cigarette fanned out from her hand and rose lazily toward the discolored ceiling tiles. I noticed the pile of requisitions in front of her was suffering the same neglect as my typing papers. The heat, moisture, and smoke trapped in the small dingy room should have been enough to urge me toward the door and back to the business at hand. But, what the heck. "May I borrow your lighter, Carole?" I asked. "I'll have one more ciga-rette before I go back to my room."

I selected an "Ultralight Merit" from the shrinking pack and lit it, inhaling slowly, and took a sip of coffee from the borrowed mug. Not too bad today, I thought. It's always a crapshoot, the coffee in this place. Sometimes it's as good as fair but most times gritty and foreign—the kind that turns green when cream is added. Surprising that it was ever even fair considering the water source—a deep janitor's sink used for old mop water with the brownish-orange stains etched in an ancient track down its backside.

The custodian came through the narrow door and shuffled over to the dryer. With practiced motions, he scooped the dry towels into a laundry bin and slapped another load of wet towels into the waiting drum. The dryer's renewed lament filled the room and ricocheted off the walls. He collapsed into the nearest chair and lit a Camel—one of those old-fashioned non-fil-tered varieties like my long-dead Uncle Eldon used to smoke. It was May, the end of the school year, and it occurred to me that I didn't know his name yet. Too late and awkward at this late date to ask. I hadn't even seem him in the first eight months of the school year. Only this past month had I noticed him here in the custodian's room tucked into the bowels of the high school at the intersection of the Industrial Arts and Home Ec wings of the building. Lately, in fact, I'd been seeing a lot of "What's-His-Name" as my trips to the custodian's room had increased in alarming regularity.

"What's-His-Name" leaned forward to offer his latest complaint about Art, the maintenance supervisor, adding one more to a neverending litany of injustices served up by his supervisor. I watched his head bob in excitement to emphasize each irritation. I thought how I had never seen him so animat-ed before. Usually he shuffled around in leadened, well-worn brown oxfords and rumpled khaki uniform, his shoulders rounded into his chest. *How old is this guy?* I wondered. Maybe 50s or 60s, though hard to tell. Everything about him screamed OLD—the eyes small and narrowed against the smoke, faded brown hair tugged across his advancing skull, tired clothes, and petu-lant, weary manner. *I feel tired just looking at this guy,* I thought. The idea star-tled me. *Is this what happens to smokers? Will I be shuffling in here in twenty years—old, beaten, sour, and tired out?*

He reached without looking into his left shirt pocket with his right hand and fished another Camel from the crumpled pack. The lighter followed and he lit the cigarette, squinting through the smoke that erupted from the first long drag. The cigarette dangled from his mouth and bounced a bit as he held it there with loose lips and talked around it in a well-rehearsed routine.

The bell rang and the sounds of hundreds of rushing sneakers invaded the small clouded room. Cigarettes were quickly snubbed and, with hands on knees, Carole, Frank, and I rose in concert to leave. We filed past "What's-His-Name" still sitting with his worn wrinkled chin propped on the brown-stained hand, staring unseeing past the revolving dryer at the cement-block wall beyond.

Days of Skeezicks and Drunks

Ann L. Reasner

I am wide awake. Twice this week I have heard the tapping of the bare branches of the honeysuckle rapping on the window panes, but tonight when I sit up quietly listening, I hear no wind.

Bobbie sleeps, his face turned to the wall, and Mom and Dad cuddle closer together, knowing I am not disturbing them with the face-in-the-window story.

I pull the wool spread tight around my neck. It's September 25th, two days until Mom's birthday. Poor Mom, always complaining about living in the oil company's warehouse and poor Dad, always reminding her that it's 1948 and just a few years from the war.

Dad always laughs at me too when I tell him I'm afraid of living in a tin warehouse, and he laughs harder when I tell him I'm afraid of wandering bums who happen down the highway out in front of the Mammoth Producing sign.

The room looks ashy in the half light. It's still and yet I think I hear a brushing sound pushing against the steel siding. I slide the wool spread back and step down to the floor. The oak planks feel cold as the steel oil pipes piled in the backyard.

I hear nothing but the beating of the engines in the swamp a half mile behind. How lucky they are—peacefully pulsating in the shelter of the swamp willows and the scrub oaks.

The full moon streams across the window and strikes the wooden geranium planter in the corner next to the kitchen.

Bobbie sleeps, his heart beating faster than the thumping wells. Maybe he's grown too used to my ritual coughings and sneezings and bloody noses that splatter the purple columbines entwined in the papered walls. Mom is tired of me too, always faced with repapering the bloodied splatters next to my bed, always waking Bobby with my suffering.

"Bobbie, Bobbie, wake up!" I shake him and pull his hair and I hear Mom and Dad stirring in the next room separated only by the cloth Aunt Hazel sent from Boston.

"Earl, it's Ann again."

Dad's overhead lantern catches my cringing eyes and I move closer to the geraniums, the tears burning my face as they dribble down the side of my nose and into my mouth.

Dad cuddles me in his arms—his strong arms that cuddled me the day a six-foot blow snake crawled into my sandbox, all the while Mom carried on with Carrie Thompson's piano lesson—the same arms that held the little garden snake letting it wind gently around his bulging muscles, its little forked tongue darting in and out.

He wants me to like snakes, but I don't. I hate them. He wants me to know there are no bad people outside the window but tonight I know there is—someone evil is standing there quietly breathing.

"Annie," Mom says, "come on out in the kitchen. We'll drink some nice apple juice. I'll warm it on the wood stove. Would you like a little cinnamon too?"

Somehow Mom never knows how I feel. You'd think a teacher would have better sense. Last Monday at the library she insisted on choosing "Uncle Wiggly's Summer Picnic" and the Skeeze tricked Aunt Jane dressing up like a muskrat and, just like Mom, Aunt Jane Fuzzy Wuzzy never understood a thing until Uncle Wiggly solved the problem by digging a hole that he covered with leaves and twigs.

Tomorrow when Dad and I check Numbers 7, 9, and 12, I'll ask him about traps.

This time we all hear it. Bam, Bam on the back doors of the warehouse. Bam . . .

Calmly Dad snuffs out the light. "Ruby, take the kids to our bedroom" and he moves quietly in the moonlight towards the door leading to the warehouse.

In a few moments the lantern reemerges and there stands Dad with the real Skeeze, his hair hanging in long pointy strands that string down his face, his farmer trousers hanging with one strap flapping as he stumbles into the kitchen.

"Annie . . . Bobbie. This is Sunny Sidebottom. He's just passin' through on his way up to the old CCC camp in Grayling. Gonna help the forest service clear away some jack pines."

"Ruby, get out the coffee pot and the rest of that blackberry pie."

I stare straight into the Skeeze's eyes. They blink and he grins at me winking one eye and scratching his ear that hides under his greasy black hair.

"Hi, there, Annie."

"Hi!" I blurt out.

He looks and smells worse than the stink weeds out behind the turkey pen, his face full of sores and boils and his nose red and swollen like the geraniums in early bloom. I'll still have to be nice to him, for he's another one of my dad's long line of one-day buddies and I'll have to eat with him like it or not.

But for tonight I make a vow never to be afraid again.

THE LEARNING LOG: A SYNTHESIS

Sunday

I can't help but wonder just what exactly I have gotten myself into this time. It has been years since I have written anything except papers for classes and my Master's thesis. And actually there aren't very many of those that I would care to have anybody read. Give me a form and I can fill in the pieces but I'm just not sure how much honesty there is left in my writing. That's really rich—so what is it you expect from your students?—just exactly what these people want and you're not sure you have anymore.

I will have to admit that everyone is incredibly supportive. Even now in the beginning stages of getting to know the schedules and recognizing people they are really trying to encourage us to establish trust. I do wonder how many people are as apprehensive as I am about this class. I can't imagine that anyone has more fears . . . oh, come on, Kate, that's not very imaginative.

This is a really nice facility—even if someone neglected to include the map in my packet I managed to find it. I like the way it is nestled in the woods . . . the paths leading to the door . . . secluded. It reminds me of places I used to escape to write when I was living at my parents'. I quite regularly would escape to the woods or hill to do my writing. This is reminiscent of that time.

—**Kathie Johnson**

Monday

Today we practiced the process of observing. I really liked hearing observations of my paper . . . the dream essay that I had not wanted to write. I learned one major characteristic of my writing. I write in threes. I noticed that I repeated this characteristic in everything I wrote throughout the day. This is a habit. I teach my students to do this also. How horrible. (I later decided that this type of listing examples works for me. I will use a variation of this for myself, but I will let my students do what works for them.)

I notice that I write in a strict organization. Both the beginning and the end of my writing were mentioned in the observations.

Additionally, certain words that I used in the writing of the dream essay were most often mentioned in the observations. These are words that are my most informal, those that flow naturally from me, yet I always seem to try to make my words flowery so that my writing will sound as good as the writing of those whom I deem to be better writers than I. Perhaps I should just remember to keep my voice, and simple is better for me.

—**Nancy Bennett**

Writing the Outdoors: From Journals to Essays—this is it. I'm expected to write . . . expected to contribute and I am really scared. I keep saying to myself that this is going to be good for me as a teacher, that it will help me remember when I return to the classroom in the fall that my students will be just as apprehensive as I am. I can't seem to get beyond the fact that other adults are going to be reading this—that other adults are going to comment on my writing and that I am going to be present for that. I remember as a senior at CMU dropping a class because I had to read papers to them. I just couldn't do it and now—well, I took this class because I really want to start writing again . . . so do it.

I am really impressed with the openness of this section. I particularly like just being sent out to write. I think that one of the reasons I have not written is quite simply the lack of time. Being sent out to the woods around Olsen Center and told to just write (like we were this morning) is wonderful. Another tidbit to remember in the classroom . . . there are students who simply want to be given the space and time to write. The expectations from Bob seem to be reasonable too. The real trick is to figure out what my expectations are . . . perfection. Of course . . . write something profound. I like the way everyone says that and laughs.

—**Kathie Johnson**

I agree totally [with Harvey Kail in "A Writing Teacher Writes About Writing"] that I cannot teach writing unless I stay in touch with the writing process on a regular basis myself. That is like asking a Current Events teacher to teach from an outdated textbook or a Computer instructor to ignore new software or hardware. . . . I personally find it hard to believe that there are writing teachers that don't write. I don't share that out of any naive assumption that everyone should make writing the top priority. I just don't feel I would be very effective in my job if I didn't exercise my pen on paper frequently. There has to be what Kail calls "the community of writers" and that becomes of necessity a very intimate, supportive entity in the class room. I have no right to be a part of that community unless I contribute. To sit back and be a red-penned judge makes me removed from the process and frankly, if I were a student in that situation, I'd be wary of sharing much of anything with the teacher!

—Mary Alice Stoneback

Tuesday

One reason we have found it difficult to have student writing become a function of all curricula, instead of only being a weekly assignment of our English class, is that need we have to attach a grade to something concrete and complete. We have this intense desire to have something to show how we arrived at giving a student a grade. When teachers can look at writing as a means to an end, instead of the end itself, we may be able to allow students to become those "practitioners" we want, not just the "pretenders" that we have so often turned out.

—Joann Helsley

My question has always been how to get my students to be excited about their writing. Of course, I was always doomed to fail because I was less than excited about my own writing. I have confined my writing to that which others required. I write for classes or workshops that I take; I write killer recommendations and was told by a student that she was accepted on the basis of my recommendation; I write letters with the intent of entertaining, but I never write for or about myself. I always thought that I didn't have anything to say. In the essay writing workshop this week we began with family anecdotes, and I began by thinking that I didn't even have any family anecdotes. As I began to make a list, one idea seemed to grow on another, and suddenly I remembered the topic that eventually became my subject. I became so excited about doing this that I now already have three works in progress, and my husband is suggesting more. This self-discovery is exactly what Michael Steinberg is saying in his article "Personal Narratives: Teaching and Writing from the Inside Out." The best way to become an "active, engaged" writer is by starting with the personal narrative.

—Nancy Bennett

Wednesday

I was tremendously pleased when my teacher returned my essay and asked me to read it to the class. I might as well have been a junior high student again. This was a valuable lesson for me to remember. Kids feel the same way. I've said it before, but it's true; Paul models those behaviors that I admire in a teacher and want to adopt for myself. I can't completely change me, but I can be more low key and deliberate. He is also very observant, not just about what we did in class but about little things like our body language or how we might be feeling. It's a perfectly matter-of-fact way of behaving for him. Not artificial or gushy. His writing prompts have tapped more in me than I knew was there.

When I returned to the room all I wanted to do was write. I didn't even care if I ate lunch.

—Mary Jo Converse

Today we began the day with an oral reading of our rewritten parables with the introductions and the closings added. It turned out that we planned to read until the break and then learn a new essay superstructure. However, at the break we had read only three parables. We had all been so blown away by hearing the three that we had to hear the rest. We spent the day reacting and making observations. It was a day that we were either laughing out loud or crying. Initially we all agreed that we would just listen and not react because time was short, but we could not help remarking or telling what most remained with us. I think that this would be a very powerful teaching tool in the class. All of the students' work would be so important to them if they could experience a day as we had in the workshop today.

—Nancy Bennett

The first seven articles I reviewed were consciously chosen to help me in being a better writing teacher. This last article ["One Writer's Secrets" by Donald Murray] I saved as a reward for me, the emerging writer. . . . I bought a new notebook for what Murray calls a daybook. I like his list of ways and mean to use it, but I haven't. This article reminds me that I, too, need to follow the rule, "Never a day without a line." . . . In reference to Murray's section on times to write and protection of those prime times, I'm afraid the typical high school teacher doesn't have the options he suggests. It is certain, though, that the time is there—choosing to use it is the crunch. I have to be careful, like Murray, not to write too close to class time, but for a different reason. If I am writing and my class comes in, I find them to be intrusive and I often become angry with them for the invasion of my time.

—Kathie Johnson

Thursday

Today was the affirmation of what I learned in the opening sessions with Paul about making sure the students feel comfortable and from Alan about letting the students have their voices, reading their pieces. Gloria Nixon-John talked about the final step of the process being the CELEBRATION. The coffee house idea was just one that she offered as a suggestion—and I had already thought of it. Well, not too much smugness here . . . there are lots of ideas that I am getting excited about and the seasoned writing teachers smile and tell how often things have worked for them. I suppose that that is the way of seniority. I have been a writer all of my life but only a teacher of writing for a comparatively short time.

It was important for me to hear Gloria say, "Do it your way." I need to remember that because I am the writer and I am the professional, I have qualifications that make my opinions valid. Then, as the connector to that, I need to create the environment that allows my students to do it their way. I have heard the phrase "give ownership" over and over again throughout this week and it has so many implications both for myself as a writer and for my classroom. I have always asked my students to be responsible for their behavior and actions. . . . I have never really encouraged them to "own" their writing. I think that they have always been writing for some unseen "god of grammar" that has haunted them since first grade. I will use so many of the suggestions that I received in packets, especially the list for fashioning journals according to Ira Progoff, to loosen the rigidity and cast off that god!

The final note from Gloria's workshop that I felt good about was her admonition to "slow down." I have heard that from my family, my children, and my physician, but how radical to hear it from an educator! We are the ones always racing to cram in one more chapter like a Chicken Little trying to beat the end of the world. It won't be the end of the world if I ease off on the time structure, and in fact, it might just be the beginning of the creativity that is being stifled in some young people in so many ways today.

—Maryalice Stoneback

. . . We spent the rest of the time reading one another's pieces, workshopping, and continuing to write. I began another piece in the last few minutes of class, and I had an interesting interaction with a fellow student. She read the piece and began to cry and explained why the piece had warranted such a strong reaction from her. The next day she came in with a finished piece and thanked me for enabling her to write; she felt the personal material she had shared the previous day had prevented her from committing to a piece of writing. The point of all of this for me was that workshopping is not just sound pedagogically, it is also humane. It encourages student interaction—as people, not just as writers—and maybe it helps us understand and learn to respond to one another in more helpful ways. Not everything good happens according to plan—sometimes good things just happen given the right environment.

I didn't have an afternoon workshop; instead, I went to the computer center and continued working on my new piece as well as sprucing up the one I'm using in the anthology. Nancy and I opened a bottle of wine and toasted beginnings and endings, good friends and hard work. I realized how much I'm going to miss the stimulation and camaraderie of this group.

—Janet Swenson

They clapped for my piece! I still cry tonight over this morning. I wonder if they know what that meant to me. They clapped for my writing. This moment may have been worth the entire week, tuition, pain and all. And then after class to have Diana and Jeannette tell me how much they liked it. Of course cynical Kate says, what would they say? It stunk. No, it's OK. I am going to simply be happy with this and continue to finish it as much as I can this week and be proud. It's really funny that now I wish that I had signed up for the writing section and not the teaching section. Nothing like a little acceptance to make me want more. Oh God, it's another one of those. Remember this next fall when your students are in need of acceptance rather than continual criticism. Afternoon . . . spent the time in the writing center again, I needed to finish off the ending that I don't want to write.

—**Kathie Johnson**

The most important ideas that I have gleaned from the workshops and read-ings this past week are that we must make a personal connection with what we read and write, and all writers, whether students or teachers, have fears when approaching writing. I must admit that I do not write with my stu-dents. I cannot wait to begin the process so that they can see that I am going through the same frustrations, blocks, so poorly explained ideas as they are experiencing. I was interested in Michael's explaining to his workshop his own brainstorming and the birth of his basketball story, and his decision to move the story into his adulthood.

—**Nancy Bennett**

Friday

After a short practice session, and a frantic signmaking endeavor, we were ON! Our group seemed to be well received. It was the first time I had heard some group member's pieces, and I was thrilled that EVERYONE had some-thing to share. I was so proud of us and our accomplishments; I wonder if the students in my class ever experience that kind of bonding with their writ-ing group members—I really, really wanted every member of our group to feel successful, and I think they did—I know I sure did!

We have formed a writing group for the Flushing-Grand Blanc-Saginaw areas and we're hoping to meet four times before next summer's session. The sadness of the goodbyes to other class members was partially allayed by the affirmations by most that we would see one another next year.

—**Janet Swenson**

The presentations at the end of the week were wonderful. I wish that we had time to hear every word of every piece of writing. There are so many excel-lent writers. I do not know the names of all of the people, but I still recall so many examples such as the outdoor camping trip with the seven-year-old son and the mother hearing the ecstatic sexual moaning, and the pet peeve of the shopper trying to find the exact change, the poems, and the writers all doing different things after the writers' conference. I wish that I had been one of the people in that story, but instead I found myself careening down the highway holding the speedometer at 75 miles an hour so I could get to Detroit in time for my plane, which the airline had so capriciously decided should leave earlier so that it could make a stop before we got home. Somehow I found myself in a state of culture shock in leaving the writers' workshop. Next year I plan to stay a few days. I think I will be the person in the story who steps into the bay and swims out.

—Nancy Bennett

I wasn't really sure (as usual) that I wanted to put my writing on the wall. I wasn't really sure (as usual) that I wanted to put up a comment sheet. I wasn't really sure (as usual) that I wanted to read my little piece in front of the entire group.

I did it.

I loved it.

I hope to be back next year.

If my students would write this in their journals I would know as a teacher that the week (class) had been successful. Well, whoever is reading this . . . please feel the same sense of accomplishment that I would feel. The week was at times painful and at times happier then I ever expected. Most of all is the sense of beginning that I feel. I can write. I have zillions of miles of ground to cover but it is a start. A part of me has been reconnected. I am ready to be a better writing teacher and I know where to start.

—Kathie Johnson

. . . And finally, I left the workshop with the problem that Harrison talks about. Reentry. After writing, reentry back into the real world is both glorious and a bit scary. It is delicious because of the perceptive state of mind that I generate while writing here. It's almost hallucinogenic because I notice, feel, hear, and taste things in the real world more acutely after indulging in my writing at this workshop. It's scary because the world is not as complexly simple as the mind patterns generated by writing. Instead, the world is simply complex. Small wonder writers use drugs or alcohol so freely sometimes to ease the transition back into the world. My reentry was smooth yet a bit frightening. But I would miss it if I hadn't been at the workshop again.

—Tom Watson

THE TEACHING SAMPLER

Ninth-Grade Newspaper

Sharon Chapple

Incoming ninth graders often feel "lost" in the larger setting of the high school. In order to help alleviate this problem, I engage my freshman English class in organizing and producing a newspaper introducing other ninth graders to the resources and staff available at the high school.

1. First, I present the class with the following list of staff members I believe ninth graders should meet: principal and assistant principals, attendance secretary, Learning Lab teachers, Career Center aide, Special Needs teachers, Writing Lab teacher, Librarian, Athletic Director, Student Activities Director, Substance Abuse Coordinator, counselors, school social worker, school psychologist, Special Education Department Chair, and other ninth-grade teachers.

2. The students have the responsibility of choosing a guest, clearing the date with me, and sending the guest a form letter explaining the unit and encouraging the guest to bring a picture of themselves as ninth graders. Students are also responsible for reminding the guest as the date approaches, introducing the guest to the entire class, monitoring the interview, making sure each student is given a chance to question the guest, and finally sending the thank-you letter to the guest.

3. The day before the guest arrives I briefly describe the person and his or her position at the high school. I instruct each student to prepare three interview questions that would require more than a "yes" or "no" answer. I encourage the students to learn as much as possible about the job description and duties of the guest. I also encourage the students to learn as much as possible about the guest's personal history, including his or her experiences as a ninth grader. At this time I also inform them of what constitutes a good feature article so that they may be more careful in their notetaking.

4. The day of the interview, I remind the class that each one of them is required to ask a question and that they should jot down any important notes about the speaker. We then arrange the seats in a circle with the students and guest in the circle and teacher outside the circle. This gives the class full responsibility for the interview. After the departure of the guest, I ask the students to write a journal entry reacting to the guest. These journal entries and the notes they have taken during the interview are the basis of our discussion during the final minutes of the class time.

5. The culminating assignment to this unit is the writing of an article featuring the guest. (Our final guest is the teacher in charge of the newspaper, so that she can explain the process of writing a good feature article.) Students organize their notes and prepare their news articles about their particular guest. Photographs of each guest as a ninth grader are also submitted with their articles.

6. When each student has a news article written, I send them down to the Writing Lab to receive further assistance in the writing and typing of the article on Appleworks. (All of our ninth graders are in-serviced on Appleworks, so this is good practice for them.)

7. The final results are then published in a class newspaper.

Not only do the students learn about interview techniques, higher-level questioning skills, discussion skills, the writing of a feature article, the writing of a thank-you letter, and the resources available at the high school, but they also learn during the process of this unit that there are many caring staff members in our high school who were also awkward ninth-graders at one time! The students tell me that this is their favorite unit during the year.

Warhol and Other Artists in Your English Classroom

Melissa Newell

After months of admiring the wonderful student artwork displayed in our high school hallways, the idea of combining art, music, and writing started germinating. This writing idea combines imaginative creativity with a unique method of publication.

After a short conference with the art instructor, I was able to borrow ten pieces of modern/graphic art created by high school students. I chose this type of art to work with because the images and designs were abstract and open to many interpretations.

My next stop was the music director's room in search of music to accompany the art. I found that modern music with no lyrics, such as a recent movie soundtrack, worked well. I used the soundtrack to *Lethal Weapon,* but any mood tape would work.

With the preparation completed, the students were ready to begin writing. When the students entered the classroom, they reacted favorably because the room looked and sounded different. Music was playing and artwork was displayed throughout the room. I asked them to find a comfortable place to write, and then they were ready to receive the assignment.

I told the students that they were to respond to the artwork for approximately twenty minutes. I explained that this response was to explore the feelings aroused by the art piece. I wanted them to go deeper than just a physical description of the painting (blue lines crossing a yellow background, for example). Their writing could take any form; I received everything from poetry to essays to short stories. There was no minimum length, but if a student exhausted his or her reaction to one piece, he or she was to respond to another piece until the twenty minutes had passed.

When they finished writing, the students broke into small groups of four or five to share drafts and receive feedback, input, and suggestions. The students drafted the material at home and turned in a second draft the next day. Class time was used to read some of the writings and hear the many different reactions generated by a single piece of art.

After I had read the papers and graded the students for completing the assignment, I chose five to six reactions to each painting for display. The writings were mounted on construction paper that matched the border of the paintings' frames. The writings were then displayed on the hallway wall alongside the paintings.

I received a great amount of positive feedback from people at all levels in the school. Both student artists and student writers received recognition and learned to appreciate both "fine arts."

Lessons from the Advertising World

Maryalice Stoneback

There are valuable lessons in composing, writing, and thinking to be learned from the study of advertising. My high school students are media-oriented and respond faster to things they see and hear when presented in full color and condensed form. So, advertising was a natural vehicle to use within my eleventh- and twelfth-grade creative writing classroom, although it can be adapted for other levels of writing expertise.

We explored differences in advertising during the initial class session of this unit. The students weren't even aware of how affected they were by the daily bombardment. They admitted to looking for new products in the store based on what they had heard on television the night before or read in the current magazine ads. We also discussed how the products they chose measured up to the expectations they had from the advertising. More often than not, they admitted that the praise wasn't deserving.

The next step was to assign an ad journal. They were required to find, clip, and organize a certain number of magazine and newspaper ads. They also watched and briefly scripted several television ads and did the same for radio ads (which did not have the visual graphics to rely on). I developed a 0–5 rating scale that they used for each journal entry. It asked for their input on appeal, effectiveness, honesty, and graphics. There were several students who felt that they did not have the expertise to make such judgments, but through discussion they realized that advertisers appealed daily to the average citizen and selected audiences, and that they, as writers, were better equipped than most to assess the ads.

When that part of the project was complete and the students were more aware of how advertisers manipulated their audiences, we moved on to the writing of new ads. The students were given the choice of creating a new product to sell or using an established product that they wanted to take a different slant on. They struggled with the limitation they had on number of words, realizing that their choices depended on what media they had decided upon. If they chose television, they were restricted to 30- or 60-second segments, which we planned to videotape at the end of the unit. Magazine and newspaper ads allowed a little more freedom, but I reminded the students that costs of ads in different publications varied and that they too had to write to the point.

This became a cross-curriculum project, as writing students enlisted the help of the art students to make their words come alive. The final step was the display of the ads with the students themselves serving as advertising media critics. If the ad was a re-make of a real product, the student needed to display with it the ad that they felt they had improved upon.

The outcome of this project was multi-dimensional. It proved to be a wonderful training ground for students to better direct their writing to elicit response and to be concise when appropriate. They learned that more is not always better. The best result was that they saw for themselves how many different levels of meaning a single word can have and the impact it can have on the reader.

Scrawl Wall Writing Display

Susan Wolfe

Purpose: Students will work cooperatively as a group; they will take a piece of writing from rough draft to finished piece within the group. Students will use writing pieces to design a display for the Scrawl Wall.

Materials: pens, pencils, paper, markers, construction paper, paint, reference books, and Scrawl Wall

After weeks of experiencing the process of writing and peer editing, I divide my students into groups of five. I determine the groups by placing students according to personalities and abilities. There is a working variety of each in each group.

The group is then asked to pick one general topic. All pieces of writing must revolve around this topic. They may write in any form they choose and may write more than one piece. The final objective is to have enough pieces of writing to form a display under the Scrawl Wall. The Scrawl Wall is a large plastic sheet which attaches to the wall. It forms a moveable display case, approximately 4 feet by 5 feet. The writing and any artwork they wish to include will be placed under the plastic. Dry-erase markers are hung next to the Scrawl Wall so that audiences may write comments on the plastic. These comments can then be wiped off and the wall can be used over and over again.

The last group which did this project choose the topic of Education K–12. The group consisted of three girls and two boys. As a group, each student agreed to write an essay of personal narrative on why they felt a high school diploma was important. Then they each chose another way to represent Education K–12. They chose poetry, personal narratives, notes passed in class, and essays. With these other pieces of writing, they covered experiences with teachers, how boys and girls change through high school and alternative high school, and what it is like to come back to school after dropping out.

As a group they decided that the wall needed more than writing. Again they brainstormed and came up with artistic ways to represent Education K–12. They added xeroxed photos of their classmates from third, fifth, and ninth grade, collected drawings and doodles from classmates, borrowed art projects from the kindergarten classroom, and the two boys made a collage showing the differences between the traditional high school and the alternative high school.

They worked very well as a group by listening to ideas and revision comments. The final display was much more than I had expected. It was a very meaningful project to all and especially to those that were graduating. The display was up in time for our open house and graduation ceremony. The comments and compliments the group received were fabulous. The rough drafts included in the display showed the work they went through as a group.

THE WORKSHOPPER'S GUIDE

Writers, Teachers, and Learners: The Many Sides of Self

Tamara L. Lantz

I'm not a writer, I thought to myself when I first attended the Traverse Bay Teaching Workshop as a participant. In the years that followed, my role as Administrative Coordinator allowed me to observe and discover that this very thought was shared by many of the participants who attended the workshop. We all had the perception that "real writers" get it right the first time with no agony, no blood, sweat, or tears. We all entered with fears and apprehension; we all left feeling a renewed sense of confidence in ourselves as writers and teachers.

After both experiencing and observing this dramatic change from apprehension to increased confidence, I became intrigued by this process. It seemed to me, even after several years of teaching at the secondary level and even more years as a graduate student, that something happened during the workshop that was not available in any other teaching or learning situation. Why is this workshop a unique experience that changes people both personally and professionally? Why are participants more enthusiastic about writing and teaching after one week in Traverse City than they are after years of formal schooling? What happens during this week that serves to bridge the gap between the dual roles of ourselves as teachers and writers?

These questions, among others, led me to conduct a small research study during the summer of 1991. I carried a tape recorder with me throughout the week, and was able to conduct a series of informal mini-interviews with many of the participants in an effort to capture their thoughts and impressions of the process of bridging this teacher-writer gap. I also asked participants to complete pre- and post-workshop questionnaires in addition to the TBTW evaluation form. Through these interviews and written response, I was able to isolate some important features of the workshop that are key elements for the personal and professional growth of participants both as writers and as teachers. What follows is an attempt to isolate and expand on the recurring themes from the interviews and questionnaires, where participants explained the most important or significant aspects of the workshop leading to their personal and professional growth.

Respect

"The staff is wonderful—skilled, kind, thoughtful, *not pretentious.*" "We were treated as writers and people first and encouraged to think of ourselves that way." Comments similar to these were given on many of the questionnaires. On one questionnaire, a participant wrote about "faculty," placing the word in quotation marks, as if the term was ironic or facetious in this context. Her instinctive reaction to mark the word in this way struck me as an appropriate symbol which represents the flavor of the workshop. There is a lack of hierarchical distinction between staff and participants because we are *all* educators who believe that writing is valuable for learners of all ages. We are all trying to become better teachers for our students and better writers for our-selves.

Another commonality is the recognition that we all, staff and partici-pants alike, have expertise. Some people have 20 years of teaching experi-ence; others have been published. It is an important facet of this workshop that these different talents are acknowledged and given the respect that they deserve. Many participant comments indicate surprise that they are treated "as writers and people first." Perhaps the question should be, Why are par-ticipants so surprised to be treated in this way? Why is it such a unique and surprising facet that so many participants commented on it as a refreshing change? How are we treated in our school buildings and staff meetings? In graduate courses? Maybe what's really missing from TBTW—the thing that no one misses—is an administrative hierarchy and political agenda with a continual struggle for power.

Collegiality

Collegiality throughout the workshop meant different things at different times, but in the context of participant responses, it referred to the joy and excitement of being with a large group of people for an extended period of time who not only share the same interests in teaching and writing, but also share the same struggles.

On a personal level many participants wrote about their initial feelings of apprehension and inadequacy toward their writing. Perhaps the biggest hin-drance was a reluctance to share, to open oneself to that careful scrutiny which for English teachers usually means the bloody red editorial pen. Many seemed convinced that every other person in the workshop must be a "bet-ter" writer. For example, one participant wrote:

> [I had] dreadful fears and anxieties. I personally had never written anything but research papers and essay tests. I certainly had never read my work to a group of people who were so much more practiced and proficient than I. Everyone was very kind and generous—it made me want to write better.

The irony of the situation is that the participants soon discover that they all share the same fears. "I felt inferior at first because I thought most people had more experience than I did. Those false notions dissolved by the second day." This realization helps to dispel feelings of discomfort and participants begin to share their writing. It is soon evident that the focus is not on who has the better piece of writing, but on how we all work together as peer readers and editors to make everyone's piece a success. This is so important that one participant identified "the camaraderie of writers and the encouragement to keep 'forging ahead'" as the most beneficial aspect of the workshop.

Collegiality on a professional level summarizes the majority of com-ments from participants who are thrilled to have a chance to talk with other teachers for an extended amount of time. One participant came specifically for "fellowship," to share writing and to share teaching ideas. It was impor-tant for another to "meet other language arts teachers and talk about what we do." This theme of professional collegiality broke down into two categories: *getting* new ideas for teaching and *sharing* ideas with other teachers. The distinction, though subtle, is significant. Because we have a range of experience represented by our participants, from pre-service and beginning teachers to teachers with 15–20 years of experience, there is a tremendous number of possibilities for collegial interaction. Some teachers really need to gather ideas, techniques, and lesson plans to adapt for their own classrooms. As one participant put it:

> I've learned a lot of practical "stuff" this week that I can take back and use in my classroom. Most of it came from workshops, but it also came from the *people.* I expected this type of workshop to be rejuvenating and that's what it was!

Other teachers have the opportunity to share what works for them in the classroom in terms of lesson ideas, teaching techniques, or how they have solved particular problems. These types of conversations occur at a variety of times and venues such as during class discussions, at the coffee break, during meals at the dorm cafeteria, or on the beach. Having the opportunity to share lessons learned from their teaching practice is one way in which professional value and credibility is affirmed. Another affirmation of professional value occurs when participants realize that the techniques they use in their own classrooms are techniques that are also used by those whom they admire. The most meaningful aspect for one participant was the validation she felt when she realized that a lot of the information presented by staff members contained ideas that she already implemented in her classroom.

This sharing reaffirms the fact that participants are valued professionals. This validation can go a long way in renewing and re-energizing a teacher at the end of a long school year. While getting ideas from others can be invaluable for a new teacher, sharing ideas is a rewarding experience for an experienced teacher.

It seems that, for some participants, this type of collegiality is not readily available in their home contexts. As one participant stated: "It encourages me to continue pushing myself as a writer and a teacher, knowing that there are at least the Traverse Bay folks struggling with the same issues." Hopefully, upon returning home, these teachers created opportunities for these types of conversations in order to create a spirit of collegiality within their own buildings.

Growing as a Writer

The phrase "growing as a writer" came up many times throughout the questionnaires and interviews. In this context, participants used the phrase to mean an increase in self-confidence rather than mere technical growth in mechanics and grammar. As one participant shared, "I have gained the self-confidence to write, and perhaps even let others read my writing."

To share your writing with other people is to open yourself, exposed and vulnerable, to someone else's comments. This is a frightening thing for most writers. The TBTW environment is an excellent environment for risk taking.

The staff knows how to comment on the writing, to ask questions, to clarify meaning and intent without wounding the writer. Through modeling, these techniques soon spread to all participants who serve as peer readers and editors for one another. "Sharing my work with others and theirs with me has been an intensely personal experience."

Confidence grows each time a piece is created, but sharing is a success in and of itself. Given the comments from participants, it seems that it is very unusual to share work-in-progress with others. One participant wrote about "gaining confidence through the give and take of sharing work with the other people in my group." Yet another person wrote of "the satisfaction of 'cranking out' some writing that I am very proud of." It is important that sharing, seen as a big risk, in the end has such a positive impact on participants.

Sharing writing may seem like an example of personal growth, but it clearly has professional implications. Several participants commented on this connection: "The experience increased my confidence as a teacher of writing!" "It renewed my faith in my own writing ability. It gave me courage to do even more writing with my students." In this setting, participants learn what it is like to be in their students' shoes. If they are nervous about sharing their writing for fear that it will come back "bloody red" with editorial comments, how must our students feel when we do that to them? Is it really our job to scare the students away from writing by editing their work to death? How much more productive it is to create a writing environment which, through sharing, revising, and editing, can help bring a piece of writing to life!

By going through the writing process, teacher/participants learn that success builds on success. Drafting a piece and then sharing it with a peer is a success. Revising and presenting the piece is another success. Each stage of the writing process brings a success. Each success brings increased pride, self-esteem, and, ultimately, the motivation to continue writing: "I want to begin to write about my personal experiences. I've never taken much time for this and I really want to do this now." "I now plan on keeping a personal journal."

Writing as Therapy

Writing as therapy is a recurring theme. Whether poetry or essay, participants tap into their personal experiences for writing topics. Getting in touch with childhood memories, working through regrets, or capturing family history are all topics explored by participants through their writing. One participant shared, "I didn't expect to learn this much about myself through my writing." Writing becomes a form of personal therapy because, as one staff member said, "writing makes you deal with your life."

In learning how to deal with writing as a personal process, participants are able to work from the inside out because "until you experience it from the inside out, you can't really understand the theory." This staff member shared stories of participants in past years who, as a result of the initiation into personal writing, went on to apply the writing process and theories to their own classrooms and to become more active professionals as well.

Conclusion

Although the structure of the workshop is designed so that morning sessions focus on personal writing and the afternoon sessions focus on teaching ideas, the lessons learned are not defined by these boundaries. As outlined above, four main themes—respect, collegiality, growing as a writer, and writing as therapy—emerged from the data analysis of participants' interviews and questionnaires. These themes transcend the boundaries of morning and afternoon sessions, thus creating a melding of experiences—demonstrating that personal and professional growth are not separate phenomena, but rather, interdependent and reflexive processes. In other words, to be a teacher, one must be a learner; to be a teacher of writing, one must be a writer. Ultimately, what this workshop really seems to mean for participants is an opportunity to get in touch with the various sides of self—self as teacher, self as learner, and self as writer.

Putting on a Show: The Workshopper's Guide

John Kelley

In *Babes in Arms,* a Mickey Rooney–Judy Garland movie musical of long ago, someone blurts out, "Hey, I've got an idea—let's put on a show," and in a burst of enthusiasm and energy, an eager but naive group of performers set about to mount an extravaganza. From the title itself through the blunders and surprises of rehearsal and production to an exhilarating opening night and the successful run that follows, I can relate to the film.

In 1984 Mike Steinberg and I discussed putting together a workshop for English teachers, particularly those who taught writing but didn't write themselves. Like them, I had been a teacher who hadn't written since grad school, but after reading and teaching *The Writer's Way,* a textbook that Mike had co-authored, I had begun writing along with my students. The process worked for me, so I suggested that Mike do a summer writing workshop to help other teachers. We both felt that there were many teachers who lacked the time, were afraid of writing, or simply needed encouragement and the right environment in order to write, and so we set about finding a way to give them the time, the security, the support, and the atmosphere. I became administrator because I taught on the campus we intended to use and I knew local personnel and area resources; because of his textbook and his academic contacts, Mike became responsible for the workshop content and the recruitment of presenters. And that's how the first Traverse Bay Teaching Workshop began in 1986.

Once we had run the workshop for a few summers, Mike and I decided that the end of June would be the best time; then, school has usually just finished, leaving us and the participants most of the summer open. The workshop runs for six days, usually from Sunday evening to the following Friday afternoon. We are together from ten to fourteen hours a day for five days of intensive work; as one presenter put it, "Any longer and it would be therapy." The Sunday reception allows us to introduce presenters to their participants and give them time to get acquainted and receive participant folders with their sessions, room assignments, and course reading materials. This reception helps the morning sessions get under way comfortably. Monday through Thursday the workshop follows this pattern: in the morning we have six to eight thematic or generic writing groups with about eight to ten people in each, to keep the sessions small and personal; in the afternoon, we have four to six pedagogical presentations with enrollments of ten to twenty people and, for those interested only in writing, we give an option of attending the Writing Center.

Since we are located in one of the most beautiful areas in the country, we make sure people can see more than the classrooms and the dorms by providing a midweek tour of the scenic Leelanau Peninsula. On the final evening, we have a barbeque or fish broil with entertainment (usually Terry Wooten, a poet in the oral tradition) so all participants have a chance to socialize and take a break from writing. On the final morning we give participants time to prepare their pieces for the Writing Fair. The writing displayed, often imaginative and moving, delights and surprises the authors and produces a festive, celebratory finish to the workshop. Participants who elect to receive college credit for the workshop receive instructions and reminders about additional reading and writing to be accomplished independently by the end of July. By September all participants are given an anthology of writing from their own morning groups and a collection of one-page teaching ideas submitted by everyone in the teaching/writing strand.

As administrator, my preparation for the next year's workshop begins a year ahead of time, at the end of June, checking on projected costs and making reservations with the college for the conference center, supplementary classrooms, and dorm space for presenters and participants. Reservations also have to be made for a tour bus and a photocopier. It is also a good time to anticipate what potential problems might occur. We've had problems some years, many not of our own making, like high school wrestlers or basketball campers living on the floor above our teachers, or not being able to get buildings unlocked or meals served. So there has been some improvisation, such as producing a breakfast buffet in forty minutes. As each problem occurs, it is added to the list of concerns for the next year's planning. .

Because so many participants want academic credit for the workshop, each fall contact must be made with our cooperating institution, Central Michigan University, to arrange for the credit option. Even though we have had a good relationship with the university, it still takes time, because more than one department's approval is involved and our participants are both undergraduate and graduate students.

Based on the previous year's cost and projected increases, I draw up a budget. From this I arrive at the workshop fees; credit tuition fees are set by the cooperating university. We also have to decide how much money to invest or borrow to carry the workshop until revenues come in from enrollees.

Mike and Bob Root, our program coordinators, contact and hire our presenters. All of our workshop leaders are teachers who also are writers. Contracts have to be written, sent, and received. I also contact publishers' representatives to see if they want to display at the workshop or to help in publicizing it. We need the publishers because we want teachers to see something other than textbooks and to be exposed to what is current for professional development. Some of our presenters also do a tour of the exhibits, suggesting and reviewing a number of books.

With session synopses and contracts in hand, I begin the brochure which includes all pertinent information: who, what, when, where, how much, deadlines, refunds, and a participant application form. I also obtain (or renew) a bulk mailing permit and a post office box. I then purchase mailing labels from both commercial list companies and individual professional publications or organizations. Once I receive the labels, I address the brochures, bundle them by ZIP code, and deliver them to the post office, ideally by October. We need the brochures for professional conventions in the fall and for cooperating publishers. Another part of publicity is deciding which professional publications we want to advertise in, how much, how often, and, most important, when.

Within a few weeks after mailing the brochures, I start receiving inquiries, usually by phone, so it helps to have a separate phone number with an answering machine. My daily ritual includes listening to phone messages and responding and replying to the mail. This is one of the most time-consuming parts, because I am "on duty" all the time. I try to reply the same day, remembering my own experiences with institutions which lost my calls or letters. As applications and deposits arrive, it is necessary to create data bases, one for fees and general information and one for housing, meals, and miscellany. I also help those who want private housing to find it. Everyone receives a description of all sessions and a session preference sheet to return to us. At the same time, I send university registration cards to credit-seeking participants and, when returned, forward them with tuition fees to the university. In addition to these clerical chores, from time to time I need to attend professional conferences to distribute materials and also to do occasional bulk mailings to cooperating professional organizations or presenters.

One would think that after seven years I could predict the number of enrollees, but each May I have only a fair idea of the number of participants we can expect, because so many teachers register in the two weeks before the official close of registration, and some even up to the day before the start. I am never sure of the final count until the last week. It is like theatre—I don't know how many people I have until the curtain goes up.

The first week of June, Tammy Lantz, my administrative assistant, and I create writing workshop and pedagogy session lists based on participants' preference sheets. We also print course materials and buy supplies for the student folders and for the Writing Fair. For the barbeque, I arrange for a permit for the use of the city beach and contact the college food service for food preparation. Last of all, I have the T-shirts designed and printed for each participant and presenter.

The day before the opening session, I make sure that the building will be open when it is supposed to be, that the reception area has display tables, that the copier has arrived, and that the rooms are set up for the morning and afternoon workshops. Tammy and I purchase food and drink for the reception.

Prior to the reception, Mike, Bob, and I meet with the presenters, then I help participants by checking on any room problems and trying to locate whoever might be missing. At the reception I introduce administrative staff, handle any questions or problems, and pass out room assignments, folders, and T-shirts to presenters and participants. It is particularly enjoyable to match those phone voices with real faces and bodies.

The succeeding four days follow a pattern and are the easiest and most satisfying. I arrive early enough to make coffee and handle any questions or problems until the sessions are underway at 9 A.M. In the afternoon I help out in the Writing Center until 3:30 P.M., especially rewarding because it is my chief opportunity to deal with workshoppers' writing. On Tuesday I put out a sign-up list for the Leelanau tour. On Wednesday I meet the bus, check in participants, pass out box lunches, and depart with the tourists so I can conduct a narration on our travels, pointing out points of interest, giving some historical background, and offering personal anecdotes.

On Thursday I check with the dining room to make sure things are ready for the evening barbeque, make sure the participants are aware of its time and place, and arrive early in the park (about 6:00 P.M.) to help with the setup and wait for participants. After dinner, I introduce the entertainment and help with general clean-up. On Friday, I bring in supplies for the Writing Fair, fetch whatever else is needed to wrap up the workshop, pay presenters and aides, and attend the post-conference meeting of the presenters.

About a month after the workshop I receive final payment from the university. Now I'm able to pay the college rental fees for dorms, conference center, and classrooms. Whatever remains goes to the workshop partners, including a sum set aside to seed the next year's conference.

As a business, the Traverse Bay Teaching Workshop never produces a great profit, and some years we simply break even because of unanticipated expenses or increases in fees. But we continue to "put on the show" because we derive personal and professional satisfaction from the experience, and because, whenever some "alumnus" of the workshop lets us know about the ideas she is still using in her classroom or the writing she is still doing, we can't resist the urge to re-assemble our cast and crew and stage another eager revival.

Timetable

June	Make space reservations. Arrange for credit option. Rent P.O. Box.
July	Create budget. Calculate workshop fees. Contact & contract with presenters. Contact publishers. Arrange for loan (if necessary for seed money).
August	Brochure copy, layout, bid solicitation, proofing, production. Purchase mailing permit and mailing lists.
September	Mail brochures to individuals and supply publishers.
Oct–June	Attend conferences, answer phone calls and letters, register participants.

June	Purchase and prepare materials; verify registrations, reservations, and permits. Workshop Week: Prepare for reception, attend to workshop duties, pay staff. Make space reservations for following year, etc.
July	Pay all outstanding bills.
September	Mail anthologies of teaching ideas.

PHOTO BY CAROLINE ROOT

Robert L. Root, Jr., professor of English at Central Michigan University, teaches courses in composition, the teaching of writing, essay writing, literature, and media; he is a consultant on writing and former co-editor of *Language Arts Journal of Michigan* and former program coordinator (with Michael Steinberg) of the Traverse Bay Summer Teaching Workshops. In addition to articles and convention papers on composition, literacy, writing across the curriculum, and popular culture, he has published four books: *Thomas Southerne* (Twayne, 1981), *The Rhetorics of Popular Culture: Advertising, Advocacy, Entertainment* (Greenwood Press, 1987), *Working at Writing: Columnists and Critics Composing* (Southern Illinois Press, 1991), and *Wordsmithery: A Guide to Working at Writing* (MacMillan, 1994). He has also edited *Critical Essays on E. B. White* (G. K. Hall, 1994). Two books, *The Emergence of an Essayist: E. B. White Composing* (University of Maine Press) and *"Time by Moments Steals Away": The 1848 Journal of Ruth Douglass and Its Backgrounds* (Wayne State University Press), are forthcoming, and he's currently working on a collection of personal essays and *The Fourth Genre: Contemporary Writers of/on Creative Nonfiction* (co-edited with Michael Steinberg).

PHOTO BY CAROLE STEINBERG BERK

Michael Steinberg, professor of American Thought and Language at Michigan State University, teaches courses in composition, creative nonfiction, playwriting, American studies, and English education. From 1988–1993, he co-coordinated the American Thought and Language Overseas Writing Program, and from 1986–1993 was program coordinator (with Robert Root) of the Traverse Bay Summer Teaching Workshops. In addition to his work as a writing consultant, he's presented workshops and convention papers and written articles and essays on teaching and writing, responding to literature, creative writing and composition, and writing across the curriculum. He's also co-author of *The Writer's Way: A Process-to-Product Approach to Writing* (Spring Publishing, 1980) and co-author of a play, *I'm Almost Famous* (Apollo Theater, Chicago, 1984). His essays and memoirs have won several national prizes including a Roberts Writing Award (1991), the Harness Racing Writers of America Feature Writing Award (1993), and the *Missouri Review* Editor's Prize for Essay Writing (1994). His creative nonfiction has also been cited in *The Best American Essays, 1995* and *The Best American Sports Writing, 1995*. Currently, he's writing *Still Pitching: Essays and Memoirs, 1985–1995*, and co-editing *The Fourth Genre: Contemporary Writers of/on Creative Nonfiction* (with Robert Root).

Contributors

Jan Andre teaches seventh grade Language Arts and Social Studies at Forest Hills Central Middle School in Forest Hills, Michigan.

Michael Bacon is a published poet, a secondary English teacher in Kentwood, Michigan, and past charter president of Peninsula Writers, a Michigan-based organization of teacher-writers.

Nancy Bennett teaches English at Hunterdon Central Regional High School in Flemington, New Jersey.

Sharon Chapple is an English and home economics teacher at West Bloomfield (Michigan) High School.

Mary Jo Converse teaches seventh- and eighth-grade Language Arts and Gifted courses at Buchanan (Michigan) Middle School.

Marguerite Cotto, writer and translator, teaches Spanish and History of Latin America at Northwestern Michigan Community College.

Nancy E. Dean teaches second grade at Frederic (Michigan) Elementary School, part of the Crawford-Ausable Schools.

John Dinan, an associate professor of English at Central Michigan University, was co-editor of *The Language Arts Journal of Michigan* and has published articles in *English Journal* and *Arizona English Bulletin.*

Linda Dinan teaches Multi-Age Primary at Mission Creek Early Childhood School in Mt. Pleasant, Michigan.

Suzanne Dodge is a 9–12 English and Special Education teacher at Armada (Michigan) High School.

Veronica Drenovsky teaches Math and American Government Adult Education courses at Durand (Michigan) Area High School.

Phyllis M. Gabler teaches Humanities and English at Romeo (Michigan) High School.

Mary Lou Green teaches American Literature and Advanced Writing at Fairview (Michigan) Area High School.

Jan Hagland is a reading and writing specialist and Reading Recovery teacher at Martell Elementary School, Troy, Michigan.

Mary Beth Handeyside teaches Adult High School Completion at Carrollton (Michigan) Middle School.

Joann Helsley is a sixth-grade teacher at Level Park Elementary School in Battle Creek, Michigan.

Richard Hill teaches English at Romeo (Michigan) High School.

Kathie Johnson is an English teacher at Wayland (Michigan) High School.

Laurie Kavanagh teaches eleventh- and twelfth-grade English at Hunterdon Regional High School in Flemington, New Jersey.

John Kelley, Coordinator of Traverse Bay Teaching Workshops, has retired from teaching English at Northwestern Michigan Community College in Traverse City, Michigan.

Mary Ellen Kinkead teaches ninth-, tenth-, and eleventh-grade English at Marengo (Illinois) High School.

Ann E. Knauer-Bizer teaches first grade at Hickory Woods Elementary School in Walled Lake, Michigan.

Deborah LaGuire teaches fourth grade at Swegles Elementary School in St. Johns, Michigan.

Tamara A. Lantz is a doctoral candidate at Michigan State University, where she teaches a senior seminar in the social/historical foundations of education. Formerly a secondary language arts and social sciences teacher, she is writing her dissertation on the writing development of elementary students.

Mary Beth Looby teaches English at Delta College in University Center, Michigan.

Patrick McGuire teaches English and reading at Providence Catholic High School in New Lenox, Illinois.

Linda Meeuwenberg teaches classes in Dental Hygiene at Ferris State University, Big Rapids, Michigan.

Jan Mekula is a writing teacher at West Bloomfield (Michigan) High School.

Jeanie Mortensen teaches English, French, and Spanish at Ludington (Michigan) High School.

Ruth Nathan, a poet and former elementary teacher, is a public school consultant. She is the editor of *Writers in the Classroom* and co-author of *The Beginnings of Writing* and *Classroom Strategies That Work.*

Melissa (Urban) Newell teaches English, speech, and drama at Deckerville (Michigan) High School.

Gloria Nixon-John, a poet, fiction writer, and public school writing consultant, teaches high school English in Troy, Michigan. Her poetry, fiction, and articles on teaching have appeared in *Writers in the Classroom, Writer's Express, Language Arts Journal of Michigan,* and *Teaching and Change.* She is a Fellow of the Red Cedar Writing Project, a chapter of the National Writing Project.

Anne-Marie Oomen, an award-winning poet, playwright, essayist, and storyteller, has published articles on teaching and writing in *Writers in the Classroom* and regional journals. A former high school teacher, she is a freelance writer and creative writing consultant. Her program, *By Heart*, has received enthusiastic response in schools throughout the Great Lakes area.

Karen Opperman teaches marketing and business education courses at Ludington High School, Ludington, Michigan.

Ann Reasner is Department Chairperson at Tawas City (Michigan) High School and teaches English Literature, Creative Writing, and Advanced Composition.

Barbara Rebbeck teaches at Oakland Intermediate School District in Waterford, Michigan, and served as the 1994–1995 president of the Michigan Council of Teachers of English. Her essay, "Suspenders," was the First Place Essay in the April 1995 Literary Festival issue of *English Journal.*

Wilma Romatz teaches Freshman English and Children's Literature at Mott Community College in Flint, Michigan.

Catherine Short teaches composition and literature at Saginaw Valley State University, University Center, Michigan.

Christa Siegel teaches German, English, and Psychology at Linden (Michigan) High School.

Diana Smith is a Language Arts teacher in the Chesaning (Michigan) Middle School and High School.

John Smolens has taught in the Department of American Thought and Language at Michigan State University and the MFA Program in Creative Writing at Western Michigan University. He is the author of two novels, *Winter By Degrees* and *Angel's Head.*

Patricia Stedman teaches Drama and eighth-grade English at Harbor Springs (Michigan) Middle School.

Kathy Steinbring teaches eleventh-grade English at Lake Park High School in Roselle, Illinois.

Maryalice Stoneback teaches Creative Writing and Language Arts at Ogemaw Heights High School in West Branch, Michigan.

Janet Swenson is Outreach Coordinator for the Writing Center at Michigan State University, where she also teaches graduate English education courses.

Nancy Sypien teaches second grade at Orchard View Elementary School, Forest Hills District, Grand Rapids, Mighigan.

Carol Taylor is a language arts and social studies teacher at Power Middle School in Farmington, Michigan.

Stephen N. Tchudi, Director of Writing at the University of Nevada at Reno, has published young adult fiction (*The Banana-rama Man*) and books and articles on English teaching, including *The ABCs of Literacy, The English Language Arts Teacher's Handbook, The Young Writer's Handbook,* and *Explorations in the Teaching of English.*

Tracey Thompson teaches ninth- and tenth-grade English at Edwardsburg (Michigan) High School.

Nancy Tobey teaches Spanish and English at Manistee (Michigan) High School.

Elizabeth A. Webb teaches English 10, English 12, and AP 12 at Hillsdale (Michigan) High School.

Alan Weber, an essayist, public school writing consultant, and associate professor of Teacher Education at Central Michigan University, has published articles in numerous journals including *Educational Leadership, The Middle School Journal,* and the *Language Arts Journal of Michigan.*

Laura A. Wilson teaches fifth grade at Eastover Elementary School in Bloomfield Hills, Michigan.

Paul Wolbrink is a poet, Spring Lake (Michigan) secondary English teacher, and past president of Peninsula Writers. His poems have appeared in *English Journal* and his articles on teaching in *Inklings.*

Susan M. Wolfe teaches ninth- through twelfth-grade English classes at Line Street Success Express in Chesaning, Michigan.

Acknowledgments

Aworkshop of the kind that ran at Traverse Bay and a book trying to replicate it have been efforts leaving us happily indebted to scores of people. We must acknowledge at the outset Carol Berkenkotter of Michigan Technological University and John Beard of Wayne State University, who were with us at the beginning, as well as John Kelley and Tammy Lantz who have been so important to the daily running of the workshop. The staff at Traverse Bay has been various and, in addition to Mike Bacon, John Dinan, Ruth Nathan, Gloria Nixon-John, Anne-Marie Oomen, John Smolens, Steve Tchudi, Al Weber, and Paul Wolbrink, we need to acknowledge those group leaders whose efforts do not appear in the book: Laurie Cooper, Heather Monkmeyer, Sally Richards, Peter Roop, Leonora Smith, Susan Tchudi, Marybeth Tessmer, and Tom Watson. For expertise in computer magic we have relied on John Dinan and Carole Pasche; for preparation of the manuscript we must thank Sherri Wensley in particular but also Michele Beech, Toni Cheedie, Kim Lutz, Melissa Miller, and Leslie Vickery, all of Central Michigan University. We also thank our editor Dawn Boyer for expert advice in shaping our ideas, as well as our production editor Jamie Hutchinson for guiding the book through publication. Finally, for their infinite patience and support we thank Sue Root and Carole Steinberg Berk.

Bibliography

Reading Logs kept by workshoppers refer to readings drawn from articles on this list.

Blackhawk, Terry. "The Gifts of Story: Using the Oral Tradition in the Classroom." *Language Arts Journal of Michigan* 6.2 (1990): 29–37.

Brinkley, Ellen H. "Secondary Writing Centers: Where There's a Will, There's a Way." *Language Arts Journal of Michigan* 4.2 (1988): 36–45.

Cicotello, David. "The Art of Writing: An Interview with William Stafford." *College Composition and Communication* 34.2 (1983): 173–177.

Colasurdo, Anthony P. "The Literary Magazine as Class Project." *English Journal* 74.2 (1985): 82–84.

Cox, Carole. "Scriptwriting in Small Groups." *Focus on Collaborative Learning*. Ed. Jeff Golub. Urbana, IL: NCTE, 1988. 159–164.

Dahl, Karin, ed. *Teacher as Writer: Entering the Professional Conversation*. Urbana, IL: NCTE, 1992.

Dodd, Anne Westcott. "Publishing Opportunities for Student (and Teacher) Writers." *English Journal* 75.3 (1986): 85–89.

Dorenbusch, Sally J. "Teaching Without Textbooks: Making Creative Writing Real." *Language Arts Journal of Michigan* 6.2 (1990): 8–14.

Fleming, Margaret B. "Getting Out of the Writing Vacuum." *Focus on Collaborative Learning*. Ed. Jeff Golub. Urbana, IL: NCTE, 1988. 77–84.

Fox, Mem. "The Teacher Disguised as a Writer, in Hot Pursuit of Literacy." *Language Arts* 64.1 (1987): 18–32.

Jordan, Janice, Penny Frankel, and Kay Severns. "Staffing A Writing Center Creatively." *Illinois English Bulletin*, 77.3 (1990): 41–46.

Jost, Karen. "Why High-School Writing Teachers Should Not Write." *English Journal* 79.3 (1990): 65–66.

Kail, Harvey. "A Writing Teacher Writes About Writing Teachers Writing (about Writing)." *English Journal* 74.2 (1986): 88–91.

Leland, Bruce H. "Reader Response to Student Writing." *Illinois English Bulletin* 77.3 (1990): 3–9.

Loveless, Jan. "Going Gradeless: Evaluation over Time Helps Students Learn to Write." *Language Arts Journal of Michigan* 5.1 (1989): 42–54.

McAdams, Misti Whitson. "Writing and the First Year Teacher." *Alabama English* 1.1 (1989): 15–18.

Murray, Donald M. "One Writer's Secrets." *College Composition and Communication* 37.2 (1986): 146–153.

Nathan, Ruth, ed. *Writers in the Classroom.* Norwood, MA: Christopher-Gordon, 1991.

Newkirk, Thomas. "The First Five Minutes: Setting the Agenda in a Writing Conference." *Writing and Responses: Theory, Practice, and Research.* Ed. Chris M. Anson. Urbana, IL: NCTE, 1989. 317–331.

Reed, Susan D. "The Write Team: Getting a Foot in the Door." *English Journal* 79.3 (1990): 67–69.

Root, Robert L., Jr. "Writing in the Real World." *Wisconsin English Journal* 32.2 (1990): 22–34.

Rosen, Lois Matz. "Developing Correctness in Student Writing: Alternatives to the Error Hunt." *English Journal* 76.3 (1987): 62–69.

Sanford, Betsey. "Writing Reflectively." *Language Arts* 65.7 (1988): 652–657.

Smith, Frank. "Myths of Writing." *Language Arts* 58.7 (1981): 792–798.

Smith, Gayle L. "Revision and Improvement: Making the Connection." *Revising: New Essays for Teachers of Writing.* Ed. Ronald A. Sudol. Urbana, IL: NCTE, 1982. 132–139.

Smith, Leonora H. "Revising the Real Way: Metaphors for Selecting Detail." *English Journal* 77.8 (1988): 38–41.

Sommers, Jeffrey. "The Writer's Memo: Collaboration, Responses, and Development." *Writing and Responses: Theory, Practice, and Research.* Ed. Chris M. Anson. Urbana, IL: NCTE, 1989. 174–186.

Steinberg, Michael. "Personal Narratives: Teaching and Learning from the Inside Out." *Writers in the Classroom.* Ed. Ruth Nathan. Norwood, MA: Christopher-Gordon, 1991. 1–13.

Swoger, Peggy. "Navigating English Waters: The Value of the Learning Log." *Alabama English* 1.1 (1989): 31–36.

Tchudi, Stephen N. "Reading and Writing as Liberal Arts." *Convergences: Transactions in Reading and Writing.* Ed. Bruce T. Petersen. Urbana, IL: NCTE, 1986. 246–259.

Thomas, Sharon, and Michael Steinberg. "The Alligator in the Fishbowl: A Modeling Strategy for Student-led Writing Response Groups." *Language Arts Journal of Michigan* 4.2 (1988): 24–35.

Thompson, Edgar H. "Ensuring the Success of Peer Revision Groups." *Focus on Collaborative Learning.* Ed. Jeff Golub. Urbana, IL: NCTE, 1988. 109–116.

Trimmer, Joseph F. "Story Time: All About Writing Centers." *Focuses* 1.2 (1988): 27–35.

Voss, Margaret M. "The Light at the End of the Journal: A Teacher Learns About Learning." *Language Arts* 65.7 (1988): 669–674.

Weber, Alan. "Linking ITIP and the Writing Process." *Educational Leadership* 47.5 (1990): 35–39.